The Question of Language in
African Literature Today
17

AFRICAN LITERATURE TODAY
Editor: *Eldred Durosimi Jones*
* 1, 2, 3 and 4 Omnibus Edition
   5 The Novel in Africa
   6 Poetry in Africa
   7 Focus on Criticism
   8 Drama in Africa
* 9 Africa, America & the Caribbean
*10 Retrospect & Prospect
  11 Myth & History

Editor: *Eldred Durosimi Jones*
Associate Editor: *Eustace Palmer*
Editorial Assistant: *Marjorie Jones*
  12 New Writing, New Approaches
*13 Recent Trends in the Novel
*14 Insiders and Outsiders
Issues 1–14 were published from London by
Heinemann Educational Books and from
New York by Africana Publishing Company

The new series is published by
James Currey Publishers and Africa World Press
*ALT 15 Women in African Literature Today
*ALT 16 Oral & Written Poetry in African Literature Today
*ALT 17 Language in African Literature Today
ALT 18 The Oral Tradition in African Literature Today
The deadline has passed
ALT 19 Critical Theories & African Literature Today
Deadline for articles is 30 June 1991
ALT 20 New Writers in African Literature Today
Deadline for articles is 30 June 1992

*Copies of back issues marked with an asterisk
may be purchased from your bookseller or direct from
James Currey Ltd
for £7.95 plus £1 postage sterling cheque with order
Place a standing order with your supplier

*Before embarking on articles contributors are advised to submit proposals
to the Editor, Professor Eldred Durosimi Jones; Fourah Bay College,
University of Sierra Leone, PO Box 87, Freetown, Sierra Leone. Unsolicited
articles are welcome, but will not be returned unless adequate postage
arrangements are made by the author.*
*All articles should be well typed preferably on A4 paper and double
spaced. References to books should include the author or editor, place,
publisher, date and the relevant pages.*
Contributors are advised to keep a spare copy in case of loss in transit.

The Question of Language in African Literature Today

Borrowing & Carrying

A review
Editor: ELDRED DUROSIMI JONES
Associate Editor: EUSTACE PALMER
Editorial Assistant: MARJORIE JONES

JAMES CURREY
LONDON

AFRICA WORLD PRESS
TRENTON N.J.

James Currey
www.jamescurrey.com
is an imprint of Boydell & Brewer Ltd
PO Box 9, Woodbridge, Suffolk IP12 3DF, UK
and of Boydell & Brewer Inc.
668 Mt Hope Avenue, Rochester, NY 14620, USA
www.boydellandbrewer.com

Africa World Press
P.O. Box 1892
Trenton, New Jersey 08607

Transferred to digital printing

A catalogue record is available from the British Library

ISBN 978-0-85255-517-0

Typeset in 9/10pt Melior by Colset Pte. Ltd., Singapore

Contents

EDITORIAL   vii

ARTICLES

Style and Purpose in Armah's *Two Thousand Seasons*
A.N. Mensah, University of Botswana   1

Things Fall Apart Revisited: A Semantic and Stylistic
Study of Character in Achebe
A. Lekan Oyeleye, Oyo State College of Education,
Nigeria   15

Language and Characterization in Cyprian Ekwensi's
People of the City and *Jagua Nana*
N.F. Inyama, University of Nigeria, Nsukka   24

Technique and Language in Uchenna Ubesie's Fiction
Ernest Emenyonu, University of Calabar   31

Language, Literature and the Struggle for Liberation in
South Africa
Daniel P. Kunene, University of Wisconsin   37

Linguistic Characteristics of the African Short Story
F. Odun Balogun, University of Benin   51

Language, Ideology, Desire: Rereading Soyinka's *The Road*
Simon Gikandi, University of Massachusetts   61

Theme and Language in Soyinka's *Madmen and Specialists*
Obi Maduakor, *University of Nigeria*   71

Truth from Contraries: A Study of Form in the Work of Femi Osofisan
Chris Dunton, *National University of Lesotho*   81

Language Pluralism in Sierra Leonean Drama in Krio
Julius Spencer, *Fourah Bay College, University of Sierra Leone*   91

Guillaume Oyono-Mbia: A Bilingual Playwright
Unionmwan Edebiri, *University of Lagos*   98

Graphology and Meaning in the Poetry of Christopher Okigbo
Modupe Olaogun, *York University, Toronto*   108

From Rhetoric to Occultism: The Word as Music and Drama in Okigbo's *Labyrinths*
Catherine O. Acholonu, *Alvan Ikoku College, Nigeria*   131

The Rhetoric of J.P. Clark's *Ivbie*
Isaac I. Elimimian, *University of Calabar, Nigeria*   141

Dimensions of Language in New Nigerian Poetry
Ezenwa-Ohaeto, *Anambra State College of Education, Nigeria*   155

The Language of Post-war Nigerian Poetry of English Expression
J.O.J. Nwachukwu-Agbada, *Imo State University, Nigeria*   165

Index   177

Editorial

In spite of very plausible arguments in support of the view that genuine African literature should only be written in indigenous African languages, most mainstream African authors outside the Arabic-speaking areas continue to use one or other of their adopted European languages in preference to their mother tongues. Those who write in their indigenous languages risk obscurity in a worthy cause. Ngugi insures against this by issuing English translations of his own works now written originally in Gikuyu. Wole Soyinka did the memory of Chief D.O. Fagunwa, and African literature, a service by translating his novel, *Ogboju Ode Ninu Igbo Irunmale*, into *The Forest of a Thousand Daemons* and revealing to a wider audience the mysterious Yoruba world of myth and popular belief from which his own work and that of Amos Tutuola derive so much.

The great majority of first-language users of indigenous languages use those languages only orally and are not literate in them. Written literature even in African languages is therefore still inaccessible to its potential audience unless directly through drama and readings.

The 'dilemma' of the African author who, by accident of history, uses English (or any other foreign language) is dramatized by the plight of the black South African who, though conscious of the limitations of his English, still burns the midnight oil to acquire competence in that language because in his opinion he has to address the 'oppressor' in the latter's own language. Yet the vast majority of his own compatriots who should be his primary audience do not speak or understand the oppressor's language and when he greets them in that foreign language he receives a contemptuous snub. This is worsened by the fact that his black audience is split into many language groups so that in his own native tongue he can only address one particular group.

The use of a European language has problems of its own. Developed for centuries to express and reflect a particular culture, the language has to be naturalized into a completely different environment and made to convey messages in conflict with its native traditions. It is probably in the area of dialogue that the difficulties are most apparent. Characters have to be represented as speaking English when in their environment they will be speaking an African language with images and idioms arising from a completely different geographical and social situation. In the hands of the

vii

most accomplished writers a new complexion is given to the borrowed language. Leaving aside the 'old' masters in the novel – the Achebes, Ngugis, Soyinkas – the prose of Chenjerai Hove, the 1989 Noma Prize winner, for example, is English with a distinctive Shona resonance.

For some time it was thought that the French language resisted this kind of localization but it is inevitable that any language must change if it is removed from its natural environment, and certainly in the hands of the creative writer no language is safe. Modern writers come to English no longer embarrassed by their mother tongue as their predecessors may have been made to feel when they first confronted the aggressive imperialism of what was to become their adopted language; on the contrary, they now come confident in the resources of their own linguistic culture and impose the imprint of their background on their adopted language. At the basic level they do this by introducing vocabulary items, particularly cultural terms, into the ordinary syntax of English but at later stages they strain its very structures to bear their new message. All this is while English remains recognizably English. But the process is taken further; the adopted language becomes pidginized and creolized, thus providing the writer with additional varieties.

Writers are making increasing use of pidgin and creolized languages, which reach the majority of urban populations irrespective of their original mother tongues, bypassing the standard language. The playwrights of Freetown, Lagos and Ibadan employ the whole range of English from its most standardized forms through a cline into pidgins and creoles in order to distinguish character, situation and atmosphere. Femi Osofisan in his plays, Cyprian Ekwensi in *People of the City*, Chinua Achebe in *Things Fall Apart* and *No Longer At Ease* and the various Sierra Leonean playwrights examined in this issue all employ these expressive deviations from received English. Ayi Kwei Armah in *Two Thousand Seasons* selects for his epic mode the high style of the griot or traditional oral narrator. His aim is to elevate the language above the register of ordinary speech to bear an oracular message. By contrast, in *Madmen and Specialists*, Wole Soyinka seeks to reduce language to its basic components to dramatize the plight of the wretched and the damned of the earth at the hands of their glib cynical kinsmen oppressors. Christopher Okigbo's verbal artistry employs, with daring assurance, even the unintelligible nonsense syllables of Igbo infants grappling with English nursery rhymes to suggest his own and his people's spiritual pilgrimage. African writers have indeed made a borrowed language their own.

Future Issues

ALT 18, *The Oral Tradition in African Literature Today*, already in preparation, will focus on oral literature.

ALT 19, *Critical Theories & African Literature Today*, will be on the theme of critical theories and their application to African literature. Articles can examine the relevance of structuralism, deconstruction, Marxism, feminism, post-modernism, black aesthetics and traditional criticism to

African literature in general, individual authors or particular works. Deadline for articles is 30 June 1991.

ALT 20, *New Writers in African Literature Today*, will examine the works of new writers who have appeared (or have developed significantly) in the last two decades in any of the genres. Deadline for articles is 30 June 1992.

Style & Purpose in Armah's *Two Thousand Seasons*

A.N. Mensah

A central problem in discussing Ayi Kwei Armah's *Two Thousand Seasons* is to decide what kind of work it is. It appears to be a highly skilful work on a subject which should appeal to African readers, but which seems not to have gained the attention and acclaim granted to *The Beautyful Ones are Not Yet Born* or *Fragments*. It is my suspicion that this book's 'strangeness' is responsible for its rather lukewarm reception and my concern in this essay is to offer some suggestions on what kind of literary composition this is and to point out some consequences of Armah's choice of fictional mode.

Several critics have pointed to the rather different quality of this 'novel'. Robert Fraser in a very good discussion of this work remarks that 'the term *novel*, though it appears clearly on the title page, sits oddly on a book so apparently remote from existing novelistic models'.[1] Fraser correctly points to the kinship between this work and the oral traditions of Africa but decides to place it in the same lineage as Ouologuem's *Bound to Violence* and Andre Schwartz Bart's *Le Dernier de justes*. Admittedly, Armah's 'novel' shares with these others the coverage of a broad his-torical period, but there most of the similarity ends. Ouologuem's novel is a totally ironic work which invokes Africa's history and traditions in order to mock them. In its cynical iconoclasm the work - at least in attitude - is very modern and Western. Armah's work is of a very dif-ferent kind; its intention is the very opposite of Ouologuem's, namely, to give dignified expression to Africa's ancestral values. Generically, as I intend to demonstrate fully in the course of this essay, *Bound to Violence* and *Two Thousand Seasons* do not belong together, despite the obvious similarities.

Again, remarking the unusual quality of this 'novel' Emmanuel Ngara comments on it as follows: 'Can we therefore describe it as an epic novel, a novel which is much more than an ordinary novel?'[2] This takes us close to the truth about this 'novel', although, as often happens in discourse about literature, one is not able to give total agreement. Ngara assumes without debate that Armah's work is a novel, but a novel which has characteristics that properly belong to the epic, and he does an admirable job of cataloguing and discussing those elements in this novel which relate it to the epic. A similar and independent discussion of the epic elements in *Two Thousand Seasons* has been performed by another writer in a remarkably good unpublished dissertation.[3] My disagreement with this approach is in the assumption that Armah's work is in fact a novel – properly so called. The objection is fundamental, for *epic* and *novel* as literary artefacts spring from very different historical and, more importantly, philosophical outlooks – and it is the fundamental outlook informing the work which determines whether it is an epic or a novel rather than the presence of any number of an indeterminate set of characteristics. Thus it is possible to argue that several of the qualities which are considered epic – lengthy narration of skilful workmanship, the amalgamation of history and fiction, the strong national significance – can be found in such other and different works as Ngugi's *Petals of Blood* and Sembene Ousmane's *God's Bits of Wood*. Are we to say that these also are novels which are 'much more than ordinary novels'? And at what point does a novel become more than ordinary?

Other commentators have been content to go along with the author's suggestion that this is a historical novel and have discussed the novel as belonging to that order of literary composition[4] and not surprisingly some have run into consequent difficulties. Thus it has been argued that, compared with Achebe's historical novels, *Two Thousand Seasons* has no complex human beings,[5] whereas it may well be the case that Armah's work does not employ the same technique of characterization as *Arrow of God* or *Things Fall Apart*, and that to compare these with *Two Thousand Seasons* may well be like comparing Joyce's *Ulysses* with Dickens': *A Tale of Two Cities* and faulting the former for not possessing an exciting story-line.

What precisely is Armah trying to do in *Two Thousand Seasons*? What literary experiment is he trying to pull off? I shall now put forward a rather simple and tentative answer – but merely as a way of getting started: *Two Thousand Seasons* represents Armah's first thoroughgoing effort to 'Africanize' his style as a novelist, and perhaps I should add that I believe that what results from that experiment is not properly a novel but something else. Certainly the idea of an African style or an Africanized English style is not new and was not new even in 1973 when Armah's novel was first published. Achebe, Okara, Ama Ata Aidoo and, perhaps inadvertently, Tutuola have all been pioneers in the project. But Armah's is a more thorough effort. Where others had concentrated on dialogue in their effort to give an African quality to their work, Armah attacks the problem from the very basic element, namely the narrator himself. For it is the nature, the tone of the narrator that determines the design of the story as well as our view of the people who inhabit its landscape.

Let us begin our exploration with a brief consideration of the opening paragraphs of the first chapter.

We are not a people of yesterday. Do they ask how many single seasons have flowed from our beginnings till now? We shall point them to the proper beginning of their counting. On a clear night when the light of the moon has blighted the ancient woman and her seven children, on such a night tell them to go alone into the world. There, have them count first the one, then the seven, and after the seven all the other stars visible to their eyes alone.

After that beginning they will be ready for the sand. Let them seek the sealine. They will not have to ponder where to start. Have them count the sand. Let them count it grain from single grain.

And after they have reached the end of that counting we shall not ask them to number the raindrops in the ocean. But with the wisdom of the aftermath have them ask us again how many seasons have flowed by since our people were unborn.[6]

There are many interesting features in this passage but I should like to concentrate for the moment on the kind of narrator we find here and on the tone of the narration. The telling of the story begins with the word 'We' and, throughout, the narrator speaks in the first person plural. Ngara has described the narrator as 'a collective voice in the true tradition of African Communalism',[7] and this is true. Armah's narrator, speaking for the group, exemplifies one of the book's important messages – the truism that strength, survival and even beauty are to be found in togetherness. But the really important thing for the purpose of a stylistic discussion of this work is not the use of the plural (that is important for theme) but the use of the first person. It immediately creates the illusion of a speaker actually addressing a listener – in this case, the reader.

There are several additional features in the passage quoted above which help to project the narrator towards the reader, giving him a more than usual degree of immediacy. One such device is the use of the rhetorical question in the second sentence: 'Do they ask how many single seasons have flowed from our beginnings till now?' The effect obviously is that of the direct address, of a living voice addressing an audience. And again this effect is enhanced by what I will describe as the rhetorical (or public address) use of repetition in the fourth sentence: '*On a clear night* when the light of the moon has blighted the ancient woman and her seven children, *on such a night* tell them . . .' It is an emphatic structure to be sure, but it is how people talk in a formal address when they think a long parenthetical clause or phrase may have distracted the audience from the flow of the sentence. Then in the final sentence of the first paragraph, there is the dramatic use of the deictic 'there', followed by an emphatic pause typical of a speaker halting for effect, and then followed by a piling up of phrases all of which are objects of the verb 'count' but with each phrase dramatically extending the magnitude of the counting to be done and therefore suggesting futility: 'There, have them count first the one, then the seven, and after the seven all the other stars . . .'

What is happening here is quite clear: Armah is trying to re-create in writing the effect of the speaking voice – an effect which is sustained throughout the work, making this one of the most 'oral' works ever written. Each single sentence seems to have been consciously crafted to serve this end. But what we hear here is not just any speaking voice; it is formal and dignified and above all it is invested with authority. But what is this authority and how is it expressed? It is there in the tone, in the contemptuous tone in which the narrator dismisses questions about the antiquity of Africans. Just as only a fool would endeavour to count the stars or the grains of sand on the shore or the raindrops in the ocean, so only a fool would wish to count the years in order to arrive at the immemorial epoch when the African people originated. It is a tone which suggests wisdom as well as impatience with the folly of Europe's ways. But, in addition to tone, the passage exemplifies another of Armah's devices for investing the narrator with authority – and this is the deep knowledge of African things. 'The ancient woman and her children' mentioned in the fourth sentence is the translation of the Akan name for one of the constellations in the heavens at night. Throughout the novel, the reader is overwhelmed by the narrator's encyclopaedic knowledge of Africa's rivers, trees, peoples, names and supposedly its history. Armah is obviously re-creating the voice of the court historian, the griot, or, at the very least, the wise grandparent who on an evening would tell the young ones, of the village or household, tales of long ago. Robert Fraser is probably right when he observes that 'where before we searched in vain for an instance of recognizable authorial intervention, here we find the writer taking upon himself a role of obtrusive commentator from the very first sentence'.[8] There is an unusually authoritative narrator/commentator recounting the events of this story and Fraser assumes this is the author speaking as himself, but I believe that the relationship of narrator to author needs to be stated with greater circumspection. And I believe that, to state this relationship satisfactorily with regard to *Two Thousand Seasons*, a contrast ought to be made with the situation of the European novel.

The novel in Europe has developed in the direction of an increasing reduction of the author's presence within the work. In the past the occasional moralizing statement or the supercilious irony would give away a George Eliot or a Jane Austen, whereas in a Joseph Conrad irony tends to disperse truth and make it almost impossible to identify the author with any viewpoint. 'The artist, like the God of creation,' wrote Joyce, 'remains within or behind or beyond or above his handiwork, invisible, refined out of existence, indifferent, paring his fingernails.'[9] And yet, despite this movement towards impersonality, the novel is always in one sense a personal document offering a personal vision in a situation where a collective vision and commonly held values are no longer available. For the novel, as Lukacs has so persuasively argued, is the chronicle of a fragmented world – of a time when existence and essence are divorced, when available social relations no longer provide ultimate satisfaction and when the *hero* (the word is really a misnomer when applied to the novel) and by implication the author feel the need to search for private satisfaction or indeed justification or consolation.[10]

Interestingly, this homesickness, this feeling that life is without satisfaction is also a central idea in the African novel. It is there in *Things Fall Apart*, which like Laye's *The African Child* is about a process of disintegration that will lead to the homesickness and isolation of the hero and therefore raise the issue of life as a deep puzzle. In *No Longer At Ease* the disintegration is complete and the unfortunate hero is caught in a life without any given significance. By the time we arrive at a more recent work like *Petals of Blood*, what we find is a novel in which the fragmentation (or alienation) is seen to have reached an acutely vicious form and in which the author tries to restore meaning through a subjectively imposed ideology – Marxism. So that both in Africa and the West the novel is always one author's effort to find meaning or harmony in a fragmented life. His effort to refine himself out of his work can be taken as an indication of his bewilderment in the face of the complexities or fragmentation of his society.

Two Thousand Seasons attempts to be different and seeks to offer a communal vision, affirming values which all Africans can supposedly accept and share. The invaders may have destroyed a great deal of Africa's heritage; things may appear to have fallen apart, driving Okwonkwo to suicide, Samba Diallo into a state of mental paralysis and the hero of *Fragments* to insanity, but according to this work that lost collective *ethos*, that wholeness, is reclaimable. Africa has seers and utterers who not only still know the lost 'way', but have the eloquence to tell of it. The narrator of *Two Thousand Seasons* is such a special one. He is Armah in so far as he articulates views which all Africans of good sense (including the author) should presumably find acceptable, but his authority, his language, his sententiousness make him something other than any modern African (including the writer) and he confidently claims to speak not for any one person or author, but for the entire black race. Thus, first and foremost, it is its denial or attempt to deny itself as a personal document which makes this a problematic novel and pushes it toward the epic. The 'epic' characteristics are merely a consequence of this initial impulse.

Let us dramatize the situation a little and imagine the author declaring as follows: 'I have a story of great importance to tell Africa. Not one of those stories of Africa's disintegration or of an individual African's inability to belong. No, this is something larger and more wholesome, telling of the tribulations of the tribe and ending with a glorious vision of Africa's reawakening and unification. Indeed, a grand public theme. But how do I tell such a story, this Pan-African saga? Of course! In the manner of the griots of old! In the manner of Niane's *Sundiata!*'

The decision to use the tradition of the court historian as model – a consequence of the impulse to tell a story affirming public values – is almost inevitably a commitment to what Northrop Frye has described as the 'high mimetic' mode: 'The high mimetic poet is essentially . . . a counsellor or preacher, a public orator or a master of decorum.'[11] Frye emphasizes two features of the high mimetic work – a category that comprises most epics and tragedies but *not* novels – the nature of the hero and the tone and purpose of the work. In the high mimetic mode the hero is superior in degree to other men, but not to his environment. He has authority, passion and powers of expression far greater than ours, but what he does is subject to social criticism and to the order of nature. He is always an exceptional man. Whereas in the 'low mimetic' mode – where the novel belongs – the hero is one of us and we demand from the poet the same canons of probability that we find in our own experience. The hero's speech need not be more exalted than our own and his passions need not be greater than ours. Thus *Othello* is a work in the high mimetic mode, whereas *David Copperfield* and *No Longer At Ease* are in the low mimetic.

It is easy to see how an awareness of this distinction would prevent the kind of unfair comparison mentioned earlier between *Two Thousand Seasons* and Achebe's historical novels. Achebe's works are decidedly low mimetic and we expect his characters to have the complexity or inconsistencies of ordinary men. But characters in *Two Thousand Seasons* tend to be superlatives and this too is typical. The author, it would seem, tries to avoid making any one of his characters the hero of the tale. Abena, Tawia, Juma, Kakra, Soyinka, Dedan and the others are each supposed to have qualities which contribute to the survival of the group. That too is part of 'the way'. And yet even in this tale extolling communal values there is an exemplary character, indeed a hero in the strictest meaning of the word, and that is Isanusi, who in typical high mimetic fashion is exceptionally gifted: a great orator, a profound seer and an intrepid man of action, altogether a shining embodiment of the virtues of 'the way'.

But it is the tone of this work and the style which gives rise to it that I would wish to dwell on. Frye points out that the high mimetic writer is essentially a master of decorum, selecting words to fit his grand purpose.[12] Certainly, every kind of writer selects and arranges appropriate linguistic items, but the high mimetic writer, engaged on an epic or a tragedy, is always especially concerned with achieving what is traditionally called a 'high style' – a style which sets itself apart from ordinary language through a conscious use of formal elaborations. The writer feels that the weight and dignity of the subject-matter itself demand a special and ceremonial kind of language. And he or she will tend to speak not as him/herself but as one inspired by God or the Muses or as one who has been trained by masters and belongs to a sacred guild of orators. The epic writer/narrator as he begins his story is always self-conscious – whether he is writing the *Odyssey* or *Paradise Lost* or *Sundiata* – as one who has assumed an immense task demanding a more than human degree of eloquence. And *Two Thousand Seasons* fits right in this tradition. Here is Armah announcing his purpose:

> The linking of those gone, ourselves here, those coming; our continuation, our flowing not along any meretricious channel, but our living way, the way: it is that remembrance that calls us. The eyes of seers should range far into purposes. The ears of hearers should listen far towards origins. The utterer's voice should make knowledge of the way, of heard sounds and visions seen, the voice of the utterer should make this knowledge inevitable, impossible to lose. (p. xiv)

His task as an 'utterer' – and it is important to be aware of the oral import of that term – is to express knowledge about Africa's history and ethos in such a way that it is accepted and cherished for ever, never again to be lost. It is a grave mission whose accomplishment is necessary, it is claimed, for Africa's health. Above all here is an utterance that cannot be made casually; hence the ceremonial quality of the prose:

Our way is reciprocity. The way is wholeness. Our way knows no oppression. The way destroys oppression. Our way is hospitable to guests. The way repels destroyers. Our way produces before it consumes. The way produces far more than it consumes. Our way creates. The way destroys only destruction. (p. 39)

Here in this litany to 'the way', Africa's ancestral way of life, we have the most pronounced instance of the style that characterizes this work. The most salient device is repetition – repetition with variation, balance, antithesis. The repetition and balance are not simply a matter of certain words or phrases being repeated, such as in 'Our way . . . The way . . . Our way . . . The way', but also whole syntactic structures which are repeated and held in balance or antithesis, such as 'Our way is reciprocity. The way is wholeness' or 'Our way is hospitable to guests. The way repels destroyers.' The effect is like that of a ritual incantation owing to the regular rhythm created by the repetition of words and structures. Indeed the style and effect are not unlike those of certain parts of the King James Bible – another book on a grand epic theme – in which the same devices of repetition, variation, balance and antithesis are used. The more general effect in *Two Thousand Seasons* is to lend the narration the aspect of inspired oration, a vatic utterance.

Where these devices are employed in the description of some action or event in the story, the effect is to elevate the event – which may be as unsavoury in itself as a shooting – to the level of a ritual, almost sacred, happening. This for instance is the narrator's account of one of the story's many 'exciting' moments:

'Shoot into the light,' Juma said. Ashale fired, Abena fired, Kwesi fired, Kgosana fired, Sobo fired, Kamara fired and Juma fired, so fast and close together the sound was like one long rent in the night. (p. 195)

The style does not emphasize excitement because the effect of the roll-call of names, itself a characteristic device of oral narratives, is to slow down the narration so that the almost simultaneous action of all those people shooting at once is recounted rather as a repetition of the same event. In this way, attention is directed not at the speed and excitement of the moment, but its *significance*. The event is revealed through the style as an instance of many people acting in concert and a further illustration of one of the principles of 'the way' – co-operation, harmonized action.

Perhaps one reason why Armah's rather lurid account of the sexual excesses of Africa's Arab invaders and the correspondingly ruthless way in which these Arabs are destroyed has attracted adverse comment is because the style in those episodes seems to depart so radically from the dignified and ceremonial tone of so much of the work.[13] Kole Omotoso has revealed in a recent article that Armah's depiction of the Arabs has caused concern in some Arab circles.[14] In fact, however, the same stylistic methods largely apply in these episodes as are to be found elsewhere in the work. Let us consider the fate of the homosexual Faisal:

Faisal sang that night. Laughing he sang. The words, what were they but a demented Arab praise song to black bodies? The lyrics were a confession Faisal wished to make, having lost control of the last remnants of his will, a confession that all his religion's stories of odalisks and little white virgins were fantasies for weak, crippled minds with little of the power of imagination, and no knowledge at all of real truth. Faisal beckoned to the black woman of his dreams. Beautiful as a walking dream Azania went to the Arab Faisal and he screamed his incredulous delight at her being real. Azania welcomed the predator Faisal, welcomed him with exquisitely knowing caresses, prepared him for love and then took him in spite of all his fumbling, took him into herself and moved under him with a smooth grace that gave him his first ecstasy with a female. But Faisal, it had not been his intention to orgate into Azania all by himself. He wanted his young askari in him – from behind – while Azania welcomed him inside herself, so that he would himself be firmly clasped between his lower and his higher joys. So the scream that forced its way out of Faisal's throat during his first ecstasy was not Azania's name but the young askari's. This was not the first, not the thirtieth, not the thousandth time that the zombie had heard his name shouted with such loud desire. He strode forward at the urgent call and in a moment was naked upon his master's back, ploughing the predator's open arsehole while the master tried to keep his forgetful penis in Azania. Then the joy of having his askari mount him overwhelmed all Faisal's senses. For long moments he lay insensate, hardly breathing. By degrees he lost all semblance of his former grip on Azania's body. And Azania herself, she slowly, lovingly helped him slide off her, so gently she did not disturb him or the askari pumping manseed into his Arab master. Azania did not have to use the dagger she had hidden in the cushions to which the predator Faisal was now clinging. The young askari had brought a sharp war spear with him even to this feast – great is the force of habit. Azania took the spear and pushed it with the energy of seasons and seasons of hatred shown only as love, pushed it through the askari's right side, so hard it went through him into the Arab panting beneath, threading him also in his right. The two, the predator and his askari were thus fused together when agony of death usurped their sweeter pain. (pp. 22–3)

Obviously, the overall effect here is gross mockery of the Arab. As always in the book not the excitement but the significance is what is emphasized and mockery is part of the significance. Thus the Arab is ridiculous, even contemptible, in his over-zealous and fumbling approach to the African woman. And the fact that he is a homosexual is (at least as far as this narrator, though not necessarily the author, is concerned) an added reason for contempt. The African woman in obvious and stark contrast – and the hyperbole of that contrast is again a feature of oral narration – is not only superlatively beautiful, but is in absolute control and plays the dominant role in this travesty of the act of love. Now, even in the presentation of this undignified scene, there is an attempt to maintain the measured ceremonial language characteristic of the entire work. The repetitions are still here: 'Faisal sang that night. Laughing he sang' or 'Azania welcomed the predator Faisal, welcomed him with . . .' or again '. . . then took him in spite of all his fumbling, took him into herself'. And of course there is the rather unusual and poetic syntactical structure of 'Laughing he sang.' Through his self-conscious style, the narrator interposes himself between the reader and the event, thereby slowing it down and underlining its import. Thus the repetitions emphasize Faisal's foolishness by dwelling on his sottish histrionics, while, in contrast, the effect of the repetition when it is applied to Azania's actions is to emphasize their deliberate gracefulness – which, as we discover, is calculated to conceal a deadly purpose.

However, the calm wise flow of the episode is interrupted with the entrance of the askari and is replaced by a headlong rush in the narration in which spectacle seems more important than significance. And it appears for a moment as if the narrator/writer is so engrossed in the sensational quality of the picture he is painting that, like Faisal, he becomes 'forgetful' and neglects to maintain the dignified tone: He [the askari] strode forward at the urgent call and in a moment was naked upon his master's back, ploughing the predator's open arsehole while the master tried to keep his forgetful penis in Azania.'

Wole Soyinka has remarked that this novel sometimes reads like an adventure story and this, he argues, is because 'Armah's prose style appears unequal to the task of capturing action and rendering it totally convincing'.[15] Soyinka does not support this criticism with examples, but it strikes me as grossly unfair. For in fact the whole point of Armah's style is to prevent the presentation of action from sounding like mere adventure. The style seeks always to bring out the wisdom or the moral in the event. Isanusi's fight to the death with the would-be assassin sent by the king is a case in point. The single combat – another recurrent feature of epic narrations – is told in great and exciting detail, but at no point in the narration is the reader allowed to forget that this is a combat not only between good and evil, but also between mere unthinking hulk on the one hand and disciplined skill on the other. The prose, while conveying the 'adventure' of the occasion also enacts the nimbleness, the coolheadedness of Isanusi:

His [the killer's] body, already much fuller in its growth than his mind, was gorged with the blood of anger and the fear of danger. A heavy body it was, far more massive than Isanusi's slender frame. In the fighting the killer's aim was plain: he would fling his weight relentlessly against his prey, force him down with the sheer weight of his mass, then choke him dead. The first time he leapt at Isanusi it was with a cry part way between fear and defiance. Isanusi, he fought like a dancer, calmly, always waiting till another moment's waiting would have been disastrous, then stepping aside and letting the killer's impetus take him past in frustrated violence. The killer turned, leaped, missed, turned again and leaped again. He missed a third, a fourth and a sixth time, but did not change his aim. (p. 188)

Surely this, considering the subject-matter, is very fine writing indeed and it is fine precisely because there is an idea shaping the account.

What then is the purpose behind or, better still, the effect of the sudden change in style in the account of Faisal's death? Gone all at once are the repetitions, the carefully balanced syntactic structures, the ceremonious diction, and in their place a starkness of vocabulary and phrase. The effect of this deliberate lapse in decorum is to reduce the Arab to a one-dimensional monster – a depraved, subhuman thing totally undeserving of a ceremonial style. When such monsters are destroyed by the women of Africa, the reader is supposed to be more amused than revolted by the cruelty, for the prose has tended to deny the Arabs any humanity, and their deaths are laughable because they are so eminently fitting.

It is now time to discuss some of the consequences of Armah's style and the social/moral vision it upholds. Despite the tremendous power of the prose, indeed because of it, the work seems to run into some difficulties. One important consequence of the style is the reductive and stereotyped way in which Armah presents those he conceives as the enemies of Africa, namely, the Arabs, the Europeans and Africa's own kings. My objection to the presentation is not simply based on realism: the point is not that real Arabs or Europeans or African kings were and are not like that. Very few people could ever be as idiotic as the old king is at the opening of *King Lear* but no one denies the significance of what he represents. The real objection to this presentation is that it over-simplifies the problems. The view that chieftaincy in Africa is a parasitic and corrupt institution is persuasive, and yet there are Africans who to this day see the king as a unifying figure and the living embodiment of the people's 'way'. Soyinka for instance seems to advocate such a view of the king in many of his works. Certainly part of Armah's argument is that the admirable qualities that make a good king cannot be inherited and therefore chieftaincy should not be handed down in one family; but, on the other side, there is the argument that there are ways of assisting a potentially incompetent king as well as of nullifying his capacity for damage and that selecting him from one lineage is a way of containing protracted strife. It can even be argued that the weakening of chieftaincy is the reason for political instability in Africa. The matter is complex and is grossly misrepresented in this work, in which every king is a bloated and depraved idiot out to deflower any virgin in sight. The complexity would have been maintained by simply balancing things up wth a good chief ready to defend the rights of his people, as indeed some kings were willing to do. The absence of such a character indicates Armah's bias. It tells us that, much as this work pretends to speak for all Africa, it cannot help but remain a personal viewpoint.

Again, on the same subject, let us consider this hilarious reversal of the European's 'civilizing mission'. The speaker of course is Isanusi:

Hear now the last wish of the white men. They have a road they follow, and something called a god they worship – not the living spirit there is in everything but a creature separate, raised above all surrounding things, to hear them speak of it rather like a bloated king. It is the white men's wish to take us from our way – ah, we ourselves are so far already from our way – to move us on to their road; to void us of our soul and put their spirit, the worship of their creature god, in us. For this they do not think it will be necessary to reward the king and his courtiers. They say it will be reward enough when we have lost our way completely, lost even our names; when you will call your brother not Olu but John, not Kofi but Paul; and our sisters will no longer be Ama, Naita, Idawa and Ningome but creatures called Cecilia, Esther, Mary, Elizabeth and Christina. (p. 83)

This is truly fine writing, in which the familiar concept of a supreme God is 'defamiliarised', to borrow Shklovsky's concept, by being seen from the point of view of a 'pantheistic' traditional African.[16] But the intriguing element is the way Armah succeeds in emptying the Christian names, making them appear unexciting and dull. How is this done? Partly, it is the result of the fact that these names become linked with the European's impudent self-imposition on Africa – an imposition which assumed that Africa's ancestral culture was valueless, whereas, as Armah argues, it was supremely beautiful. Partly also, this mockery of Christian names is the result of their being placed alongside African names which are decidedly more sonorous on account of their more open vowels and especially on account of their tonal (and therefore melodious) quality – a quality which contrasts with the accented and harsher quality of the Christian names. Here again we are reminded of the oral character of this work.

However, a question arises. In our time, there are Africans who are profoundly Christian and for whom names like John, Paul, Mary and Cecilia have deep significance. For such Africans Armah's mockery may be skilful but ultimately impertinent. In our time both Islam and Christianity are an entrenched part of African reality and a work which does not take account of this is in danger of merely remaining an elaborate irrelevance.

Ultimately the question is this: Is it possible to write an epic in these times? Armah, to express his grand theme, has had to refashion and adapt the style of the griot – a style appropriate to the authority of the narrator and the seriousness of the work. The style alone has proved difficult for some: it is too slow, too long-winded, too self-conscious. The ordinary reader in our time – and Armah's message is intended for the general reader – wants a plainer language, i.e. wants the low mimetic mode.

But style is not the major problem – indeed, this is brilliant writing as any persevering reader finds out. It is the authority itself of the narrator which, as we have begun to see, is questionable. For who in our time can speak for all Africa given the multiplicity of ideologies and passionately held viewpoints? Who can in such a situation claim the authority to propound a 'way' acceptable to all, without seriously engaging those ways which are at present so passionately held? In this situation, any viewpoint or values advocated in a literary composition, no matter how elaborately disguised or persuasively urged, are bound to be personal and subjective. One has to admit, of course, that Armah is aware of this problem; he knows that modern Africa is split into various political and ideological camps. He has attempted to argue the irrelevance of Marxist thought and practice in the African situation.[17] One can expect a strong reply from those Africans who are also Marxist. But, in any case, it is because of such profound differences that a Pan-African choric voice is impossible: someone is bound to disagree, whereas the griot or the story-teller of old entranced us all with his or her sweet wisdom. So that, despite its elaborate style which attempts to suggest the opposite, the message of *Two Thousand Seasons* is not a piece of wisdom which is immediately accept-able to all Africa; the message remains just one more ideal which is subjectively imposed on the chaos of Africa's actuality, just as it is in Ngugi's *Petals of Blood*.

We conclude then by returning to our initial question. Is *Two Thousand Seasons* a novel or an epic? Moving beyond that casual usage in which any long story in prose is a novel, I have examined the work from the point of view of two literary theories. Borrowing from Frye, I have tried to show that its style and to some extent its characterization, being in the high mimetic mode, are not typical of the novel. Its style and tone are those of the epic. The more interesting revelations arise from the application of some of Lukacs's ideas from *The Theory of the Novel*. The epic, Lukacs says, speaks for simple integrated societies whereas the novel usually expresses an individual ideal in a fragmented world.[18] *Two Thousand Seasons* has the curious duplicity of coming out of a fragmented Africa and yet seeking to express an integrated vision. It tries to be an epic in the time of the novel. In a stylistic *tour de force* it presents its reader with a very powerful 'history' of the black people and makes an eloquent statement of their ancestral ethos – a communal, egalitarian, industrious, thrifty and life-respecting way of life. But even for an African there is something meretricious about the power of this work. Some Africans now are royalist, others republican; some believe in the multi-party 'democracy', some in the one-party state, and yet others in workers' congresses; some are Christian, many syncretic in their religious beliefs and practices, and some Muslim; some are committed capitalists, others various kinds of socialist; and indeed not all in our time are black, even though for the neo-negritude narrator of this work Africa is the land of the black people. *Two Thousand Seasons* does not sufficiently challenge all those Africans who, abandoning 'the way', have adopted newfangled ways. Thus, when the majestic resonance of the elegant prose recedes, the reader is likely to find that most of his modern prejudices are untouched by this simplifying voice from the past.

NOTES

1. Robert Fraser, *The Novels of Ayi Kwei Armah*, London, Heinemann, 1980, p. 64.
2. Emmanuel Ngara, *Stylistic Criticism and the African Novel*, London, Heinemann, 1982, p. 123.
3. See Appiah Sackey, 'Two Thousand Seasons and Petals of Blood as modern epics', unpublished BA dissertation, Legon, University of Ghana, 1981.
4. See Hugh Webb, 'The African historical novel and the way forward', and Bernth Lindfors, 'Armah's histories' in *African Literature Today*, no. 11, 1980.
5. Lindfors, op. cit., p. 90.
6. Ayi Kwei Armah, *Two Thousand Seasons*, Nairobi, East African Publishing House, 1973 and London, Heinemann, African Writers Series, 1979, p. 1. All references are to the Heinemann edition.

7. Ngara, op. cit., p. 119.
8. Fraser, op. cit.
9. James Joyce, *A Portrait of the Artist as a Young Man*, London, Jonathan Cape, 1916, reprinted by Panther Books, 1984, p. 194.
10. Georg Lukacs, *The Theory of the Novel*, Berlin, P. Cassiner, 1920, reprinted by M.I.T. Press, 1975, chapter 4, pp. 70–71.
11. Northrop Frye, *Anatomy of Criticism*, Princeton, Princeton University Press, 1957, paperback edn 1971, p. 58.
12. Ibid., p. 34.
13. Lindfors, op. cit., speaks of 'the scenes of sexual perversion and the almost Homeric descriptions of bloodshed, gore and corporeal mutilation told in gleeful, gloating detail' (p. 95). And Wole Soyinka in *Myth, Literature and the African World*, Cambridge, Cambridge University Press, 1976, says, 'There is a gleefulness, a reckless ascendancy of the vengeance motif', and 'the human sensibility tends to recoil a little' (p. 110).
14. Kole Omotoso, 'Trans-Saharan views: mutually negative portraits', in *African Literature Today*, no. 14, 1984, pp. 113–17.
15. Soyinka, op. cit., p. 114.
16. See Victor Shklovsky, 'Art as technique' in *Russian Formalist Criticism: Four Essays* ed. L. Lemon and M. Reis, Lincoln, University of Nebraska Press, 1965, pp. 2–23.
17. Ayi Kwei Armah, 'Masks and Marx: the Marxist ethos vis-a-vis African revolutionary theory and praxis', *Présence Africaine*, 131, 1984.
18. Lukacs, op. cit., chapter 3, 'The epic and the novel', pp. 56–69.

Things *Fall Apart* Revisited: A Semantic & Stylistic Study of Character in Achebe

A. Lekan Oyeleye

So much has been said by critics over the years about the subject-matter of Achebe's *Things Fall Apart*. Over and over again critics have identified and analysed the epic dimensions of this novel; but the vital issue of Achebe's use of the English language as an aid to character presentation, especially his ability to externalize the resonances of the human mind, and the compassion with which human faults are depicted – all these seem to have received very scanty treatment. However, our attempt in this essay is not in any sense an exhaustive treatment of all the characters in the novel, but two principal instances have been selected for a fairly thorough discussion with a view to demonstrating a good linguistic reading and understanding of aspects of character presentation in Achebe's *Things Fall Apart*.

In the traditional African society, a man's individuality is often summed up in the proper or personal name he bears. Each person's name is essentially inseparable from him. Since Achebe deals with aspects of African culture in the novel under study, Igbo culture precisely, it is not surprising that he has taken pains to make use of this ontological fact of the naming system in the presentation and treatment of many of his characters. For example, this traditional belief appears well dramatized in an actual situation by Achebe in his later novel, *No Longer At Ease*, to show the reader the place of names in Igbo cosmology. Obi's sister, Agnes, has been asked to carry the little children, sleeping on the floor, to their beds; instead of calling them by their names before waking them up, she just 'grabbed the first child by the wrist and pulled him up.'

> 'Agnes! Agnes!' screamed their mother, who was sitting on a low stool beside the sleeping children. 'I have always said that your head is not correct. How often must I tell you to call a child by name before waking him up?' (*NLAE*, p. 56)

Obi's reaction to their mother's outburst is a good summary of the belief system:

> Don't you know ... that if you pull him up suddenly his soul may not be able to get back to his body before he wakes? (ibid).

In an ontological sense, therefore, the essence (or soul) of a person resides in his name. Thus names in many African cultures are invariably

15

carefully constructed (in a semantico-syntactic sense) to manifest specific meanings which in a way are meant to portray the personality of their bearers and their anticipated roles in the society. Achebe has made much use of this feature in *Things Fall Apart* since many of the Igbo names in it can well be regarded as linguistic stretches of familiar expressions in the Igbo language. We shall attempt to demonstrate in this essay this stylistic trait by using the two principal characters in the novel, Okonkwo and Obierika.

The first page of *Things Fall Apart* offers the reader an account of Okonkwo's character in Achebe's own authorial voice:

> Okonkwo was well known throughout the nine villages and even beyond. His fame rested on solid personal achievements. As a young man of eighteen he had brought honour to his village by throwing Amalinze the Cat . . . Okonkwo's fame had grown like a bush fire in the harmattan. He was tall and huge, and his bushy eyebrows and wide nose gave him a very severe look. He breathed heavily, and it was said that, when he slept, his wives and children in their out-houses could hear him breathe. When he walked his heels hardly touched the ground and he seemed to walk on springs, as if he was going to pounce on somebody. And he did pounce on people quite often. He had a slight stammer and whenever he was angry and could not get his words out quickly enough, he would use his fists. He had no patience with unsuccessful men. He had no patience with his father. (*TFA*, pp. 3–4)

This vivid account is almost biographical in its details. It appears to share a close affinity with the semantico-syntactic make-up of the name itself; in Igbo 'Oko' means 'man' while 'Nkwo' is one of the four market-days of the week:

> Oko + Nkwo   → Okonkwo
> (Man) + (born on 'Nkwo' day) → (A man born on 'Nkwo' day)

The morphological agglutination seen in Okonkwo above can yield some semantic possibilities (in an interpretative sense) in a further analysis. A market-day in Igbo culture is a very important day indeed. There are four market-days in a week: *Eke, Orie, Afo, Nkwo*. We can then conclude from the semantic manifestation of the name above that Okonkwo was probably born on the great Nkwo (market) day, one of the most important days of the eight-day week. In the belief system of the Igbo people, a man of such description would be expected to behave accordingly. Achebe must have considered all these connotations of the lexical item 'Okonkwo' before giving it as a name to his hero of *Things Fall Apart*, a character with remarkable physical prowess and uncommon fame in the whole of the Umuofia community. However, Okonkwo's character is delineated mainly through his actions rather than his words because he is 'a man of action and not of words'. He rules his household 'with a heavy hand':

> His wives, especially the youngest, lived in perpetual fear of his fiery temper and so did his little children. (*TFA*, p. 12)

The authorial comment continues to give us the man's psychological make-up:

> his whole life was dominated by fear, the fear of failure and of weakness ...
> it was not external but lay deep within himself. It was the fear of himself, lest
> he should be found to resemble his father. (pp. 12–13)

The repetition of the word 'fear' in the quotation is probably to underscore the neurotic tendency of the protagonist. The alliteration of the fricative sound 'f' is particularly appropriate to the image of a hyperactive neurotic – or the 'Roaring Flame' as he is popularly called.

Okonkwo's private and public life is highly remarkable. We are told that he has 'a large compound' where all his wives and children live. He has brought fame to Umuofia by throwing 'Amalinze the Cat'. But his tempestuous nature often gets the better of him; he beats his wife during the week of peace, thus violating the sacredness of the week, and he nearly kills one of his wives by firing his rusty 'dane' gun at her.

In the majority of the authorial comments on Okonkwo we see words and expressions that can be examined under two major lexical set memberships: violence and physical prowess cum hard work. First, some of the authorial comments:

1. Okonkwo's fame had grown like a bush-fire in the harmattan. (p. 3)
2. He was tall and huge, and his bushy eyebrows and wide nose gave him a very severe look. (p. 3)
3. Okonkwo ruled his household with a heavy hand. (p. 12)
4. His wives, especially the youngest, lived in perpetual fear of his fiery temper. (p. 12)
5. Okonkwo never showed any emotion openly, unless it be the emotion of anger. (p. 26)
6. The only thing worth demonstrating was strength. (p. 26)
7. Okonkwo bit his lips as anger welled up within him. (p. 27)
8. He would be very much happier working on his farm. (p. 34)
9. He told his children only 'masculine stories of violence and bloodshed'. (p. 48)
10. Dazed with fear, Okonkwo drew his matchet, and cut him [Ikemefuna] down. (p. 55)
11. A sudden fury rose within him and he felt a strong desire to take up his matchet, go to the church and wipe out the entire vile and miscreant gang. (p. 139)
12. Okonkwo was popularly called the 'Roaring Flame'. (p. 139)

We may now examine the lexical organization of the above comments taken from different pages of the book, *Things Fall Apart*. The formal concept of collocation – the company lexical items keep (Catford 1965), their preference for some lexical neigbours and environments – will be of relevance here. But allowance will be made for considerable overlap, since items may belong to more than one set – bivalent/multivalent items. A look at the comments abstracted from the different pages will reveal

that they are dominated by a string of items that either belong to the set
membership of 'violence' or to that of 'physical prowess cum hard work',
as follows:

A Violence	B Physical prowess cum hard work
grown (1)	fame (1)
like a bush-fire (1)	grown (1)
harmattan (1)	
tall and huge (2)	tall and huge (2)
bushy eyebrows and wide nose (2)	
a very severe look (2)	
with a heavy hand (3)	ruled (3)
in perpetual fear (4)	
fiery temper (4)	
emotion of anger (5)	
strength (6)	strength (6)
bit his lips (7)	working (8)
anger (7)	on his farm (8)
masculine stories (9)	masculine stories (9)
violence and bloodshed (9)	
dazed with fear (10)	
drew (10)	drew (10)
matchet (10 & 11)	matchet (10 & 11)
cut (10)	cut (10)
sudden fury (11)	
strong desire (11)	strong desire (11)
wipe out (11)	
vile and miscreant (11)	
Roaring Flame (12)	

The first set – 'A' set – has items of violence or items capable of being
attracted into 'violence' through collocation, while the second set – 'B'
set – has items that can easily verbalize the commendable qualities of
physical prowess and hard work. It will be further observed from the
above analysis that there is a preponderance of violence items in the
authorial comments on the character of Okonkwo from those portions of
the novel quoted. However, in spite of our apparent dichotomization of the
lexical items, the two sets are interrelated within the context of the
personality of Okonkwo and his role in the novel. The violence set
verbalizes his tempestuous and neurotic nature: he rules his family with
a heavy hand; he beats his wife during the week of peace; he nearly kills
one of his wives by firing his 'rusty gun' at her; he deals the blow that
kills Ikemefuna; his gun explodes and kills Ezeulu's son; he kills the white
man's messenger and finally hangs himself. The physical prowess and
hard work set appears to express the commendable aspects of his
personality: his overwhelming triumphs in wrestling matches; his leadership in times of war (bringing home to Umuofia many human heads as

symbols of manhood and strength); finally his meteoric rise to a position of eminence in the Umuofia community. The fact of his suicide unequivocally proves the dominance of the violence set over the physical prowess cum hard work set.

Apart from the authorial comments examined above, let us see Okonkwo at a closer range through his own mind and speech. The author has of course told the reader that 'Okonkwo was not a man of thought but of action' (*TFA*, p. 62). However, when there was nothing requiring physical action talking was the next best thing, and perhaps thinking aloud. After the killing of Ikemefuna, we find Okonkwo in his *obi* (hut) thinking aloud:

> 'When did you become a shivering old woman, Okonkwo asked himself, you, who are known in all the nine villages for your valour in war? How can a man who has killed five men in battle fall to pieces because he has added a boy to their number? Okonkwo, you have become a woman indeed'. (*TFA*, p. 59)

Here Achebe uses the psycho-stylistic technique of thinking aloud to reveal that neurotic streak in Okonkwo through his thought processes. The speech reveals a slight but perceptible rise in the dramatic urgency of the emotional situation in which we find Okonkwo. The rhetorical questions in the 'thought speech' help to further underline his confused state of mind. A passage of brilliant craftsmanship, the logic of Okonkwo's stream of consciousness argument above can be further illuminated using Searle's (1965) concept of the propositional act. Searle has suggested that 'a propositional act includes the subsidiary acts of referring to someone or something and of predicating some property or act of that to which one has referred'. He further suggests that an utterance has two (though not necessarily separate) parts: a proposition and a function-indicating device which marks the illocutionary force. The so-called function-indicating devices in English may include 'word-order, stress, intonation contours, punctuation, the mood of the verb and the set of so-called performative verbs'. In each of the utterances in the quoted passage, we are suggesting that the thinker/speaker expresses the proposition that he (Okonkwo) has become a woman – a rather anomalous proposition if considered literally – that is, he predicates the act of becoming a woman of himself, though only in the last utterance does he finally perform the illocutionary act of 'asserting' with his use of the intensifier 'indeed' as a tag at the end of the sentence: 'Okonkwo, you have become a woman indeed.'

The emotional crisis implied by this assertion will be properly understood if the anomaly in it is resolved. The co-referentiality of 'Okonkwo' and 'you' in the utterance is significant here for the sake of emphasis – the stress on 'you' is naturally greater than on 'Okonkwo' in actual speech. We shall gloss the verb 'become' as having a transformative thrust in its context above. The anomaly that is being foregrounded now becomes meaningful when we take the putative properties of the noun 'woman' into consideration in a typically male-dominated society like Umuofia; thus we have in addition to its componential features:

+ frail
+ prone to tears
+ cowardly
+ emotional
+ irrational etc.

When we merge these putative properties of 'woman' with the expression 'shivering old woman' (first utterance of the above quotation) it becomes clearer why his rebirth/transformation is not regenerative. Notice, too, that this degeneration process is feared to have been completed:

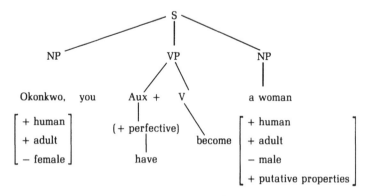

We are further reminded by the connotative meaning of the word 'woman' of Okonkwo's constant fear – that 'he should be found to resemble his father', the latter having been considered 'a woman' by the community in his life.

This style of writing has allowed Achebe to merge speech with narrative and to reinforce the neurotic individuality of Okonkwo since the reader is now able to see the controlling passion of the hero more intimately through his own mind. Later Okonkwo goes to Obierika for a chat and possibly to salve his racked conscience. During their discussion Okonkwo tells Obierika:

I am worried about Nwoye . . . But I can tell you, Obierika, that my children do not resemble me. (*TFA*, p. 59)

Obierika's reply is a pertinent one:

You worry yourself for nothing . . . The children are still very young. (*TFA*, p. 60)

Okonkwo must have worried himself also for nothing at the end of the story because, in spite of his murder of the District Commissioner's messenger and his eventual suicide, Umuofia people will continue to go to the new church in greater numbers, for the reality of the tragic situation is that the white man has brought a new culture which 'has put a knife on the things that held us together and we have fallen apart'. (*TFA*, p. 160).

So much for Okonkwo's portrait. We may turn now to Obierika, whom Achebe has characterized by a rather Western method. Quite apart from his epigrammatic name, it is his utterances that actually individualize him. As a complete antithesis to Okonkwo, Obierika's name will yield the following semantico-syntactic analysis:

Igbo morphemes		English partial translation
obi	:	heart/mind
ē	:	it
rika	:	many (great numbers)

By morphological agglutination:

Obi + ē + rika $\longrightarrow$ Obierika
(Heart/mind + it (is) + many)

The semantic manifestation of the English rendering will then be equivalent to, 'There are many human hearts/minds in this world.' By implication within the context of the story, Obierika's name seems to suggest that Okonkwo's mind is one out of the many there are in this world; thus Okonkwo's kind is rare. Only a few can do what Okonkwo does in the novel.

Unlike Okonkwo, 'Obierika was a man who thought about things'. (*TFA*, p. 113). Quite often he has remonstrated with his friend, Okonkwo, over the latter's unusually excessive zeal and intemperate behaviour. After the murder of Ikemefuna, Okonkwo is seen in Obierika's house enquiring why he did not join the murder squad that killed the boy. Let us hear the two men out:

'I cannot understand why you refused to come with us to kill that boy,' he asked Obierika.
'Because I did not want to,' Obierika replied sharply. 'I had something better to do.'
'You sound as if you question the authority and the decision of the Oracle, who said he should die.'
'I do not. Why should I? But the Oracle did not ask me to carry out its decision.'
'But someone had to do it. If we were all afraid of blood, it would not be done. And what do you think the Oracle would do then?'
'You know very very well, Okonkwo, that I am not afraid of blood; and if anyone tells you that I am, he is telling a lie. And let me tell you one thing, my friend. If I were you I would have stayed at home. What you have done will not please the Earth. It is the kind of action for which the goddess wipes out whole families.'
'The Earth cannot punish me for obeying her messenger,' Okonkwo said. 'A child's fingers are not scalded by a piece of hot yam which its mother puts into its palm.'
'That is true,' Obierika agreed. 'But if the Oracle said that my son should be killed I would neither dispute it nor be the one to do it.' (*TFA*, pp. 60–1)

This dialogue shows Obierika as a more thoughtful man than Okonkwo. The expression of his own passionate feelings is made in coherent and carefully structured sentences which indicate his considerable self-control, while Okonkwo's fearless but crude declarations, with an obsessive quality to his tone, reflect an abnormal emotional state of mind. For example, Obierika's 'You know very very well, Okonkwo, *that I am not afraid of blood* . . . And let me tell you one thing, my friend. *If I were you*, I would have stayed at home' has been carefully constructed, with the two subordinate clauses (italics) thrown in to give his speech a measured dignity; he also uses markers of involvement – 'you know', the use of the first name 'Okonkwo' and 'my friend' – which are linguistic devices meant to maintain some informal or intimate relationship with his interlocutor and also to convey to Okonkwo in a rather informal tone that what he had done was ill-advised. In contrast to this, we find Okonkwo's utterances containing lexical items of violence such as 'kill', 'authority', 'die', 'blood' and their substitutes (it, do it), which further lend credence to his impetuous character. Obierika's last sentence in the quotation shows him as a man who really accepts compromises, though not in a slavishly obsessive manner. He recognizes the merit in Okonkwo's proverb, 'A child's fingers . . . its palm', which the latter has used to justify his action, but counters that argument in a mature and thoughtful manner by saying: 'if the Oracle said that my son should be killed I would neither dispute it nor be the one to do it'. The use of 'neither . . . nor' is very significant here. It shows that Obierika's loyalty to the community gods is not as overzealous and thoughtless as Okonkwo's brand of loyalty. Achebe has made Obierika, a highly principled man, use two negatives to achieve a positive policy assertion in this utterance.

As a man of thought and foresight, Obierika has hinted to Okonkwo during one of their conversations that to fight the white man would amount to committing suicide because

> our own men and our own sons have joined his religion and they help to uphold his government. If we should try to drive out the white men in Umuofia we should find it easy. There are only two of them. But what of our own people who are following their way and have been given power? They would go to Umuru and bring the soldiers, and we would be like Abame. (*TFA*, p. 159)

Obierika has adopted this stylized and formal speech because it is the only style that befits the grave situation in which the people now find themselves. Note the hypothetical conditional use of 'if' in the quotation which Obierika employs to raise a positive proposition, and the adversative 'but' inserted immediately after to counter the proposition. These two conjunctives, apart from giving a logical cohesion to his utterances, help make his argument more convincing. In the same cycle, further in his delivery, the whole tragedy of the clan is summarized thus:

> How do you think we can fight when our own brothers have turned against us? The white man is very clever. He came quietly and peaceably with his religion. We were amused at his foolishness and allowed him to stay. Now he has won our brothers and our clan can no longer act like one. He has put a knife on the things that held us together and we have fallen apart. (*TFA*, p. 160)

Obierika has chosen to co-ordinate his ideas in this last quotation, using sentences whose clauses are paratactically arranged with the employment of the 'and' co-ordinator. Through parataxis – the placing of clauses one after another with or without explicit connecting co-ordinators – Achebe has achieved for Obierika a certain degree of economy of expression and spontaneous emphasis which helps to reinforce our impression of the tragedy of the situation being portrayed.

After Okonkwo has gone to hang himself, we find Obierika ('There are many hearts/minds in this world') on the scene as if to symbolically remind us again that only a rare mind can afford ever to contemplate suicide. Mingling narrative with actual speech, Achebe writes:

> Obierika, who had been gazing steadily at his friend's dangling body, turned suddenly to the District Commissioner and said furiously: 'That man was one of the greatest men in Umuofia. You drove him to kill himself; and now he will be buried like a dog . . .' (TFA, p. 187)

This is the only time Obierika can afford to be justifiably furious, having been moved by righteous indignation.

In conclusion, it will be clear from the foregoing analysis that Achebe can sustain the reader's interest not only through the nexus of his very fine stories but also (and probably more importantly) through the animating linguistic manipulation of his characters. We have seen the spontaneous dramatic effects which are created through the polarization of two contrasting characters, the immediacy and tragic consequences resulting from personality defects and the artist's masterly use of language as a primary function of his narrative – all making *Things Fall Apart* a classic of African writing.

BIBLIOGRAPHY

Achebe, C., *Things Fall Apart* (TFA), London, Heinemann, 1958.
———, *No Longer At Ease* (NLAE), London, Heinemann, 1963; repr. 1978.
Catford, J.C., *A Linguistic Theory of Translation*, London, Oxford University Press, 1965; repr. 1974.
Iwundu, M., 'Igbo anthroponyms: A linguistic evidence for reviewing the Igbo culture', *Names: Journal of American Name Society*, vol. 21, no. 1, March 1973.
Leech, G.N., *Semantics*, Harmondsworth, Penguin, 1974.
Searle, J.R., 'What is a speech act?', in *Philosophy in America*, ed. M. Black, Ithaca, Cornell University Press, 1965, pp. 221–39.

Language & Characterization in Cyprian Ekwensi's *People of the City* & *Jagua Nana*

N.F. Inyama

Cyprian Ekwensi is one of the most famous of all Nigerian novelists. His creative enthusiasm has yielded results in the areas of adult novels, teenage thrillers and tales for children. As one of the pioneer Nigerian novelists, Ekwensi was given early critical attention. Generally, he was enthusiastically received. However, serious and detailed studies of his novels have sometimes yielded sharp criticisms of his craft as a novelist, especially in the area of language and characterization.

In an article entitled 'Cyprian Ekwensi: An African Popular Novelist',[1] Bernth Lindfors declared that 'Cyprian Ekwensi . . . best illustrates the dictum that practice does not make a writer perfect' and that his novels 'can serve as excellent examples of how not to write fiction'. In another essay, B.I. Chukwukere drew attention to Ekwensi's inadequacies in the art of novel-writing. He wrote that 'Weakness of characterization as a result of inadequate grasp and control of relevant levels of language is most pronounced in Cyprian Ekwensi's writings.'[2] Both critics cite instances from Ekwensi's novels to support their assessments of the author's skill. There is some truth in both these judgements, but Ekwensi's real position as a manipulator of language and characterization seems to lie somewhere between those critics' assessments and Ernest Emenyonu's largely sympathetic appraisal of this writer's skill.[3] This article is not conceived as a rescue plan for Ekwensi's artistic reputation; it rather aims to highlight his positive achievements in the areas of language and character portraiture, especially in his two best-known novels, *People of the City*[4] and *Jagua Nana*.[5] Essentially, I will attempt to show that in these two novels Ekwensi demonstrates a credible and purposeful consistency in his use of language levels as indicators of social class, as marks of strength or weakness in his characters, especially in interpersonal relationships, and as indicators of the moral standing of his characters in public issues and actions.

Jagua Nana, which contains his best-realized fictional characters and has the sharpest narrative focus of all his novels, provides a good starting-point. When the story opens, the heroine, Jagua Nana, a prostitute, has already spent a number of years in Lagos, where she had settled after running away from a boring marriage. She has done some trading in cloth, has become well known as a fashion pace-setter, and ultimately has become the most glamorous and desired of the prostitutes that visit the Tropicana night-club. But more significantly, she is 45 years old and is worried by this fact, mainly because she is in love with a much younger man, Freddie Namme. Although she has him under her sexual control, she is still disturbed by the possibility of losing him because of the gap between their ages. The novel is therefore an account of Jagua's career in Lagos, and especially about her explosive relationship with Freddie.

One of the most remarkable aspects of Ekwensi's presentation of his heroine is in her use of language; he confines her to pidgin English, the common language of Nigerian city-dwellers, especially the illiterate and semi-literate. There is a consistency in Jagua's use of pidgin English which identifies the heroine as a tough-minded woman of the streets, fluent in the language of her environment. Right at the beginning of the story, Jagua is seen looking at herself in the mirror lamenting the visible crow's-feet: ' "I done old," she sighed. "Sometimes I think say Freddie he run from me because I done old. God have mercy" ' (p. 5).

The early introduction of Jagua in this mode of speech is not accidental. It is a deliberate authorial device to acquaint the reader with the speech style or level which the heroine will use for the rest of the story. Indeed, Jagua's mode of expression sets the tone for the subsequent dialogues in the novel, primarily because the majority of the characters encountered thereafter are within Jagua's bracket of the illiterate or semi-literate.

Jagua, veteran of the streets and the Tropicana night-club, is totally at home in this language level which she has acquired during her years in Lagos. It is her business language with her clients and the language of her daily conversations, even in her house. In all her discussions with Freddie, a teacher by profession and an aspiring lawyer, the medium of expression never rises above the pidgin level. For example, when she is discussing an issue as academic as Freddie's future education in England, trying to get him out of his despondent mood, she makes no attempt to rise above her normal level of language use:

> Nothing is impossible, Freddie! I know how you wan' to go study in England. By de help of God, you mus' go. You better pass many who done go and come. You young too. You know what you doin'. You serious with your work. Yes! Government kin give you scholarship. If dem don' give you we must try pull togedder to sen' you. (p. 7)

In the above passage, Jagua sounds as serious and convincing as though she spoke in the most polished and formal English. Indeed, it is doubtful whether she would sound so convincing and hopeful in a different language level.

In lighter situations, too, she is equally authentic in her pidgin English. For instance, when Freddie complains about her outrageously short dress, she answers him in vibrant, teasing pidgin English:

> 'I know das what you going to say. But speak true, dis be naked?'
>> She pouted, holding the flimsy edge of her skirt and twirling round and round.
> 'Dis be naked?' She reached for a powder-puff and began to powder her face.
> 'You don' know de fashion, Freddie!' (p. 6)

Everything the reader knows about the character rhymes with her manner of speaking, and there is no feeling of discomfort or awkwardness as he listens to Jagua in this level of language. Similarly, one finds that Ekwensi often groups his characters on the basis of linguistic level, not only in *Jagua Nana* but also in other novels, with the result that it is possible to identify a character's environment or quality by his level of language. Nancy Oll, Jagua's rival for Freddie's love, speaks fluent pidgin. Though she is not in Jagua's profession, she has grown up in that world, her mother being, like Jagua, a prostitute, and she uses pidgin naturally when, for instance, Freddie wants to 'sweet-talk' her into yielding herself to him:

> At firs' I fear, Freddie. All de young men in Lagos dem talk sweet – like you doin' now, Freddie. But when dem get a gal on de bed, you never see dem again. And if dem give de gal belly she mus' carry de belly alone and dem will run and lef' her . . . So I use to fear. (p. 5)

Appropriately, then, when Jagua and Nancy quarrel and fight in Freddie's room, their altercations are in eloquent and inflamed pidgin. There is no need to quote the scene, but the common level of language usage establishes the affinity of environment of the two characters and fixes them in a credible language level.

Furthermore, because most people Jagua comes into contact with are often on the same limited educational level or function in the lower-class environment of her habitation they, too, are placed on an identical language level. Thus Mama Oll (Nancy's mother), Rosa (the young prostitute who comes to live with Jagua), Dennis Odoma (the robber who dwells in the slums of Obanla), Uncle Taiwo (the crude and vicious politician who later becomes Jagua's lover) and other minor characters all speak pidgin English in a manner that authenticates and vivifies their individual characters.

Likewise, when Ekwensi introduces characters that are removed from Jagua's world, either by education or by social position, their levels of language usage are clearly different from the pidgin usage of Jagua and similar characters. In such cases Ekwensi shows a consciousness of the subtle distinctions which language can give to different characters. Thus the British Council lecturer in *Jagua Nana* speaks with an easy cocktail urbanity; Wilson Iyari's language in *Beautiful Feathers* has the sloganeering quality of the political activist; in *Iska*, Raimi's father laments his son's riotous ways in the distinguishable rhythms of rural folk speech.

In society it is not criminals and negative elements alone who use pidgin English; but in Ekwensi's novels, particularly in *People of the City* and *Jagua Nana*, this level of language seems to be predominantly assigned to the less likeable or 'low' characters. And this is where the two novels have their key link. The characters one encounters in *People of the City* appear to have their counterparts in *Jagua Nana*. The indecisive and unstable Beatrice the First of *People of the City* seems to have metamorphosed later into the tough Jagua; Amusa Sango of *People of the City* is recognizably reproduced in Freddie of *Jagua Nana*; Uncle Taiwo of *Jagua Nana* has his opposite number in the unnamed politician–landlord in *People of the City* to whom Amusa Sango is taken in his search for accommodation. He also has his crude equivalent in Lajide, another landlord in *People of the City*. Indeed, Ekwensi seems to have used *People of the City* as a testing ground for the leading characters in *Jagua Nana*.

To a certain extent Ekwensi's attitude to some of the characters mentioned can be discerned from the kind of language he makes them speak. A character like Uncle Taiwo, for instance, is not a favourite of the author and he is not presented with any degree of amelioration in his crudeness. The reader is expected to share this authorial dislike, and one way of ensuring that he does so is by making the character condemn himself through what he says, but more especially by how he says it. In his most impassioned moment Uncle Taiwo is made to speak the crudest of pidgin, such as when he instructs Jagua on campaign speech-making:

> 'Tell them to vote for O.P.2 What? You tellin' me you don' know what you will say?' He began to laugh and slap his knees, the stool shaking till the beer glasses bounced off the stool. 'You don' know what you will tell dem? Oh, you just too funny. Tell dem to vote O.P.2! Tell dem our Party is de bes' one. We will give dem free market-stall, plenty trade, and commission, so dem kin educate de children. Tell dem all de lie. When Uncle Taiwo win, dem will never remember anything about all dis promise. Tell dem ah'm against women payin' tax. Is wrong, is wicked. Tell dem ah'm fightin' for equality of women. Women mus' be equal to all men . . . (p. 107)

Evidently, Uncle Taiwo is not a likeable or honourable person, quite unlike the unnamed politician we meet in *People of the City* whose perception of politics is at total variance with Uncle Taiwo's. He is altruistic and patriotic, and shows a confidence in his capabilities and prospects not born of the habit of corrupting and lying to the electorate, as Uncle Taiwo does. But, apart from giving him all these admirable qualities, Ekwensi gives him an educated level of English; pidgin has no place in his discourse.

The other area in which language use is an indication of authorial attitude to his characters is in the way the language level used by characters seems to indicate their strengths and weaknesses in interpersonal relations. That is, the stronger person in a friendship or association appears to influence the weaker in the use of language. One finds this to be so in Jagua's relationship with Freddie, and in Amusa Sango's relationship with other characters in *People of the City*. *Jagua Nana* is essentially a tale about Jagua, and her personality dominates the whole story, just as Amusa Sango's personality dominates in *People of the City*. Jagua's involvement with Freddie is an example of the strong–weak relationship in which the stronger partner's manner of speaking dominates the weaker partner's, becoming the primary indicator of their inner qualities. Although authorial commentary informs us that Freddie and Jagua converse in pidgin English in order not to be reminded of clan and custom (which would be the case if they spoke in Ibo language), this commentary can only be acceptable to a very limited extent, especially when one realizes that Freddie's life, until the final explosive quarrel with Jagua, is ruled by the latter. Apart from Freddie's obvious helplessness

in the face of Jagua's powerful eroticism, the author's only other tool for
highlighting the dominance of Jagua over Freddie is in the way she has
totally acculturated him into her style of speaking. As long as Freddie is
under Jagua's sexual power his language is constantly pidgin English.
Even on occasions that are visibly academic or highbrow, Freddie, the
aspiring lawyer, is unable to rise above this level of usage. Thus, at the
British Council where he goes with Jagua for a lecture, his remark about
the lecturer is couched in pidgin: 'Dis man he kin lecture wonderful' (p. 8).
It is difficult to imagine that a statement like 'This man is a wonderful
lecturer' would be too much for Jagua to understand. At any rate, it is the
Jagua presence or aura that the author emphasizes and that dominates
from the moment when the two enter the lecture hall:

> As soon as they entered the public lecture room a mild sensation swept through
> the audience. The speaker had already begun his lecture, but it seemed to Jagua
> that all eyes turned in their direction and this was what she always liked . . .
> With satisfaction she saw the whispering lips, shielded, the heads lowered
> behind the programmes. (p. 8)

Admittedly, there are other indications of Freddie's weakness in the
relationship with Jagua. The ease with which she reclaims him after their
quarrels over her love adventures is one example; again, Jagua has affairs
with other men, while Freddie is so frightened of her that he keeps his
association with Nancy Oll furtive until the last explosive moment when
Jagua discovers Nancy in his room. However, when Freddie finally breaks
from the Jagua habit we notice a dramatic change in the quality of his
language. When he and his friend catch Jagua soliciting for men on the
streets, his disgust and anger are expressed thus to his friends. 'You were
quite right, oh God you were! Now I should chop her head off with an axe'
(p. 40). The next morning Freddie moves away from the common yard
where he has been living with Jagua and the relationship comes to a close.
It is significant that at the moment when Freddie finds the strength
to reject Jagua the first indication of this new strength is a linguistic
liberation from pidgin English.

Now, if we compare Freddie with Amusa Sango of *People of the City*,
the point being made on the relationship between language level and
character quality might become clearer. Both characters are conceived
approximately on the same lines: they are both young, handsome and
single. Both have frequent contacts with Lagos night-clubs, the haunts of
tempting free women. However, Amusa Sango is much more exposed
to these temptations than Freddie, for, in addition to being a regular
journalist by profession, he also plays the trumpet for a night-club band.
Unlike Freddie, however, Amusa seems to be in greater control of his
relationships with people – especially the women. Although his style
appears callous at times, he is capable of breaking with women when he
thinks they are becoming an embarrassment. He is strong in a way that
Freddie is not; otherwise, he would have fallen under the spell of Beatrice
the First, just as Freddie did with Jagua. Beatrice is conceived in the same
mould as Jagua. She is beautiful, restless and dissatisfied with her

marriage. She escapes, like Jagua, into the world of night-clubs. She meets Amusa frequently, and is in love with him, as many other girls are. But Amusa is able to resist her with the same strength with which he fights the blackmailing tactics of Aina, another female character.

As earlier stated, Amusa Sango dominates the story of *People of the City* in the same manner that Jagua dominates the story of *Jagua Nana*. In *Jagua Nana* the dominant form of dialogue is pidgin English – Jagua's dominant medium of expression – and even an educated but weak Freddie finds himself overtaken by it because he is the weaker partner in their friendship. In *People of the City* the strong Amusa is assigned a polished or educated level of language. The characters who come within his sphere of life speak in the same manner. We can only attribute this development to an authorial equation of toughness of character with a linguistic dominance. Otherwise there would be no other plausible explanation for the fact that Aina and Beatrice the First, characters who are not much better than Jagua or Nancy Oll, should speak polished or educated English while the latter cannot.

In *People of the City* and *Jagua Nana* the levels of language used by the characters reflect their social levels, their moral positions and their aspirations. Such a perception of the nature of language is an authorial one, and Ekwensi transmits this perception primarily through the language levels he assigns to the hero and heroine of the respective novels. In *People of the City* Amusa Sango retains an ultimate moral view of life and his own future, in spite of the various temptations and distractions that bedevil him. The novel seems to have a more pronounced moral tone than *Jagua Nana*; but at the same time it is a less finished and much more tentative novel than the latter in terms of setting and characterization. The city in *People of the City* is fast and dangerous, but it is not described in a manner that emphasizes its allure, as in *Jagua Nana*, where characters and environment are more settled and, ultimately, more corrupt. The impression one gets of characters in *People of the City* is of a collection of individuals engaged in a struggle to escape morally or physically from the city and its ways. The hero, Amusa Sango, eventually succeeds in this struggle. He does not acquire one of the tools that ultimately distinguish the truly committed Nigerian city-dweller – the pidgin language – which is a symbol of 'city-wisdom' as well as the city's bastardization of linguistic and other values.

In *Jagua Nana*, on the other hand, Jagua's pidgin usage is a mark of her total commitment to the city life. She can hardly endure a separation of any appreciable length from the city, but must hurry back to it. The city is her life, with all its corruptions and deceits. All who must share her life in the city must also share this commitment to its dominant mode of linguistic expression and communication – the pidgin language. It is this commitment that makes her not want to speak Ibo with Freddie. Pidgin English shows her power over the city, and Freddie speaking it with her reassures her of her power over him. Pidgin English, for Ekwensi, also expresses the corruptions and evils that exist in the city, especially the absence of a moral vision on the part of individual characters. In spite of Freddie's legal education, his moral vision is no different from Uncle

Taiwo's. His reason for going into politics is disgraceful – quick money – and he tells this to Jagua in pidgin English. It is no surprise that, like Uncle Taiwo, he dies in the pursuit of this mean goal. Cyprian Ekwensi may indeed not be the most artistically sophisticated of Nigerian and African novelists. He may have more enthusiasm than craft. But at the same time he seems to me to have a greater grasp of the raw materials of his creativity than he has been given credit for. It is probably in the same area of novel-writing that he has been faulted most – the harmonization of language with character – that he also shows his own peculiar sophistication and perception of the form and function of language usage in fiction writing and character portraiture.

NOTES

1. In *African Literature Today*, no. 3, 1969, pp. 2–14.
2. B.I. Chukwukere, 'The problem of language in West African creative writing', *African Literature Today*, no. 3, 1969, pp. 15–26.
3. Professor Emenyonu has written a full-length book on Ekwensi titled *Cyprian Ekwensi*, London, Evans Brothers, 1974; in his *The Rise of the Igbo Novel*, Ibadan, Oxford University Press, Ekwensi's writings also receive substantial coverage.
4. Cyprian Ekwensi, *People of the City*, London, Heinemann Educational Books, 1964. All page references are to this edition.
5. Cyprian Ekwensi, *Jagua Nana*, London, Panther Books, 1964. All page references are to this edition.

Technique and Language in Uchenna Ubesie's Fiction

Ernest Emenyonu

Tony Ubesie may be an unfamiliar name to many readers of contemporary African fiction whose reading comprehension excludes materials written in the Igbo language. Yet he is a very important contemporary Nigerian writer and probably the most gifted of the second generation of Igbo writers in the second half of the twentieth century. Author of several successful novels including *Ukwa Ruo Oge Ya O Das* (1973),[1] *Isi Akwu Dara N'ala* (1973),[2] *Mmiri Oku Eji Egbu Mbe* (1974),[3] *Ukpana Okpoko Buru* (1975)[4] and *Juo Obinna* (1977),[5] Ubesie's distinction as a writer lies in his stylistic innovations and thematic realism. He brings a fresh awareness to familiar themes and discusses contemporary social and cultural issues in ways that show an intriguing understanding and perception of the varying alternatives. Ubesie's art is characterized by a mastery of language usage which makes his writing not only inviting but easy to read, an inimitable sense of humour which totally traps the reader, sophisticated irony which leaves the reader wondering about meanings and motives in every human action and authentic characterization which fixes the human beings in the environment of the novel indelibly in the mind of the reader. His patterns of resolution of the human conflicts in his works are neither forced nor melodramatic. The total effect of each scene is one of wonderment, suspense and curiosity which produces the desire not just to go on reading but to want to grab another of the author's novels.

Ubesie has an abundance of anecdotes in his novels. The humour in them is effusive and contagious, creating in the reader an internal feeling of delight. For example, in the course of a narration of serious events set in the Nigerian civil war, Ubesie interjects this:

> Obinna had by now become very annoyed with God. He recalled the song of the man who said that his reason for going to church and at the same time sticking to his ancestors is that any day God does not answer his prayer; his ancestors will come to his aid. Obinna reasoned in his mind that, maybe, the gun shots heard these days everywhere in Igboland have led God to abandon the Igboland in favour of a more peaceful place. (*Juo Obinna*, pp. 104-5)[6]

No one can afford to laugh while witnessing intense suffering and the tortuous frustrations of the masses caught in a tragic war situation. The

31

Igbo must indeed have felt abandoned by God. That is a very serious situation for a people. Yet we are charmed, as R.N. Egudu observes, by 'the jocular manner in which it is described'.[7]

Egudu has explained that, 'when in Igbo tradition someone wants to express admiration for a story, he or she says that it is "sweet" ', that is, it triggers off hearty laughter. One primary element that makes for this effect in a story is the narrator's 'putting salt here and there in his story'. 'Salt' stands for verisimilitude or historical detail and for fabulous or folkloric anecdotes. These are the salt with which stories are seasoned, just as, according to Chinua Achebe, 'proverbs are the palm-oil with which words are eaten'.[8] Ubesie adds just the right amount of salt to make each dish that he sets before his readers a most delicious one. Two of his novels, *Juo Obinna* and *Isi Akwu Dara N'ala*, based on the Nigerian civil war will provide detailed illustrations.

Juo Obinna is an ironic commentary on the Biafran 'straggler', the loud-mouthed 'we must fight to the last man advocate' who shows his dexterity in dodging military conscription at the hour of need. He is an adept in military tactics without reaching any war front. Ubesie makes him, at the same time, a simple yet a complex and pathetic character. He has a fantastic imagination and can weave endless stories about his gallantry so effortlessly, fitting in every minute detail of military manoeuvre, that his audience cannot help but believe and acknowledge him as a distinguished war hero. His audience is always the womenfolk who adore him for his heroic deeds, his daredevil adventures and his indefatigable commitment to win the war. Biafrans would recognize him as an alarming ironic symbol of their delusion created by Ubesie to show them 'where the rain began to beat them'.

In the following passage, Obinna, the protagonist after whom the novel takes its title, reports a supposedly major chivalrous action to two gullible ladies to whom he explains the origin of the scars on his body:

> We slid through an unguarded part of the military camp until we reached where their soldiers were sleeping and released two grenades . . . But as we were making our escape I was hit by a bullet on the arm while another bullet hit my batman on the thigh. He collapsed, I vowed to perish rather than abandon him there. Ignoring my own bullet wound, I carried him single-handedly until I was able to get help . . . I have two other bullet wounds which I shall ever carry with me as a testimony of when a man was indeed a man.

This episode, which comes on the second to last page of the novel is typical of Ubesie's technique of delaying the downfall of the villain till the very last moment. In this case, Obinna is allowed to have his laugh until nearly the very end when his foil, Mazi Onyido, exposes him for what he is. He is not punished in the all too familiar manner of instant retributive justice; his punishment is, instead, slow and painful because it costs him all his public image. Mazi Onyido, who has arrived unnoticed in the course of Obinna's egotistic narration, does not confront him through a direct repudiation. Instead, he entertains Obinna's audience with a story whose design is too obvious to miss:

I can also tell you the story of a friend of mine who fought in the war. His name is Obinwanne. One difference between him and Obinna is that each was a hero in his own way. Obinna has the scars of two bullet wounds. So does Obinwanne. Another difference is that my friend never fired a shot in the war despite his bullet wounds. He evaded the war till the end. It was while stealing petrol that he was hit in an air raid. That accounts for his first wound. He got the second one as he was trying to steal a bale of stockfish at the end of the war . . . About the only thing he 'captured' in the war was a bale of stockfish . . . But he could disguise himself and pass in turns as a critically injured soldier and a military officer in a Captain's full outfit which he managed to steal somewhere . . .

Ogbenyeanu could not restrain herself anymore. 'Mazi,' she asked, 'who do you say this Obinwanne is?' 'Obinna knows him. Ask Obinna' [hence the title, *Juo Obinna*, Ask Obinna].

The two episodes achieve several things. They establish Obinna as a fraud and a pathological liar. They show him as a liability to Biafra and not the gallant hero that he consistently advertised himself as. They provide the moment of truth and self-knowledge for the audience and, by coming at the conclusion of the story, reinforce with dramatic impact the truism that appearance must not be mistaken for reality. But the novelist achieves these without robbing the reader of the charming delight which a narrative well told evokes. Obinna's audience has the last laugh. His integrity is on trial in the 'people's court' and he is found wanting. It is a gradual process of revelation made more effective by the rhetorical question with which the novel ends. This is Ubesie's favourite style of ending his novels. The title of the book and its ironic significance come at the very last line of the narrative in the form of a witticism or an aphorism which is a terse summation of the theme or moral purpose of the novel. This technique is employed in *Juo Obino*, *Isi Akwu Dara N'ala*, *Ukwa Ruo Oge Ya O Das* and *Ukpana Okpoko Buru*. Each ends as it starts on a high philosophical note. The beginning introduces a psychological probe into an aspect of human behaviour which constitutes a serious social problem. The ending shows Ubesie's resolution of the problem with an insight into the rationale for the ultimate choice.

In the Igbo version of the passage under discussion, Ubesie does not translate words from the English language which have become common vocabulary among the Igbo; instead, they are retained and rendered in the local versions: hence *greneedi* for grenade, *awa* for hour, *komando* for commando, *soja* for soldier, *kaptin* for captain, *mejo* for major, *galon* for gallon – illustrating the capacity of the Igbo language in particular and the culture in general to absorb new ideas.

Although irony is a highly developed and powerful tool in Ubesie's art, it is not his only literary device. The subtle humour in his anecdotes is usually satirical in effect. *Juo Obinna* is replete with these and a few examples will suffice.

Obinna is visited by Captain Emeka, a close friend in whom he can confide and to whom he narrates his vicissitudes during the war:

He told Emeka how he joined a new Spiritual Church so that they could pray for him not to be conscripted into the army. Well, he quit the church after military officers came right into the church and conscripted people. He also told Emeka how Mazi Onyido, a renowned medicine man, made for him charms to render him invisible to conscriptors. But then, Mazi Onyido himself got conscripted. (*Juo Obinna*, p. 22)

Myths of the invulnerability of certain segments of the Igbo society were rife during the war. Recourse to famous medicine men was well known even if spoken about only in hushed tones. What could be more ironic than the conscription of the very man who makes charms to render people unconscriptable? The first part of the episode clearly portrays Obinna's cowardice but Ubesie must add the second segment to reinforce and complete the portrait of Obinna as a half-hearted unpatriotic element in the emerging republic.

In another anecdote, Obinna, who is at a loss to understand how the whole world is turning against him, recalls the story of the rat and the pot of soup:

A rat fell into a pot of soup and quickly scampered out and fled. People pursued him with shouts of 'catch him! catch him!' The bewildered rat turned round and asked his aggressors: 'What is the idea of four men pursuing a rat . . .?' (*Juo Obinna*, pp. 120–1)

In yet another anecdote, Obinna is being led through thick bushes by Ndubuisi, an accomplice in crime. They are looking for a safe place to share their booty. The bush path seemed interminable but Obinna dared not ask a question or protest:

They waded through the bush. Obinna never asked where they were going to. For, if you are praying with a Reverend Father in the church and suddenly he asks you to close your eyes, don't argue: simply obey him. He must have seen something. The Reverend Father is no small child in the business of praying. (*Juo Obinna*, p. 143)

One is struck by the unusual imagery in the story – criminals looking for a safe place to help themselves to stolen bags of money, and the divine priest and supplicants in the course of an elevated religious ritual-prayer. But Ubesie shows the depravity in the profane by its relative contrast with the sacrosanct.

In *Isi Akwu Dara N'ala*, the focus is on another perspective of the war. Chike, the protagonist, is what every woman would want in a husband. He is what every mother longs to have in a son. He is every child's hope of a father. He is handsome, educated, fabulously rich and famous for his kind-heartedness and broad-mindedness. While the going is good, his family life is intact and harmonious. When the times change and money and food are hard to come by (even palm-kernels and lizard meat become luxurious delicacies), his family life disintegrates. His wife Ada goes after the men in uniform for her individual survival, abandoning her children. She even betrays her husband to army officials because he appears to stand in the way of full amorous gratification. She further complicates the situation by having a child by one of her numerous military 'bedfellows' and, when she runs to him at the end of the war, finds out that he is a happily married man with children. As a last resort she goes to Chike, who feels no qualms in throwing her back to the road.

This is a familiar theme in Nigerian post-war fiction but Ubesie's handling of the theme is at once new and refreshing, different and enlightening. The uniquely humorous proverbs and sayings are there. The creaking suspense is evident. The subtlety and philosophical under-currents abound as we are treated to incongruities in human values and behaviour. Ubesie unveils another 'war front' as ravishing and devas-tating as the tanks and armoured cars. Elegant wives and young ladies are high targets of the men in uniform. They could be snatched or lured away or could voluntarily offer themselves in exchange for security and personal survival. Ubesie probes the feminine mind caught in each of these situations and highlights the social consequences.

Ada's action is a crime against her children, her people and the land. Ubesie uses various situations to depict her wilful and remorseless behaviour as in the following passages:

> Every day Ada would kill a fowl and cook soup with it . . . Although the Igbo custom demands that a man should kill the fowl, Ada never asked any man. Chike would be given some food by her, but without any meat whatsoever. (pp. 133-4)

> In the Igbo custom, a woman cannot eat a fowl's gizzard when her husband is around. But the war has led people to trample on sacred customs. (p. 126)

> Ada fed fat and desecrated the land, daring anyone to challenge her. (p. 129)

> When old people poured libations and made incantations they prayed God to save their sons from such a wife as Ada . . . When you mentioned her name to anyone, he would tell you to change the subject. (p. 144)

His economical style of characterization makes the desired point much better than pages of descriptions. Ada is clearly portrayed through her action as a wilful, inconsiderate and callous person. Her wilful killing of the fowl fully underscores this, and Ubesie intensifies the image of monstrosity by depicting Ada's orphan-like mode of feeding her husband. The wonder is that he does not react violently to her absurd conduct. This may be Ubesie's pointer to the kind of domestication of men which was fostered in the Igbo society during the war, by women with new-found power – an unholy alliance with home-wrecking military officials. Thus the bravado which Ada manifests in these passages only serves to reflect her diminishing integrity and degenerating personality.

In sharp contrast to his wife's false appearance of security and courage, Chike's fortitude and resilience are apparent. These passages reveal the kind of society in the novel and the author's ability effectively to reflect its changing moods. At the beginning of the novel, Ubesie emphasizes Ada's beauty (as well as Chike's wealth) through charac-terization. At the end, Ada's depravity (like Chike's maturity and spiritual purification) is again emphasized through characterization and we see the society (peaceful and warlike) in its changing but not necessarily conflicting roles.

A reader of Ubesie must at all times be alert to his pace of narration and the ingredients of his art. The continuous flow of proverbs, striking in their sound and message, challenges the intellect all the time. At the height of the disintegration in the family, the totally disoriented Chike is described in this disconcerting manner:

> Chike was shaking all over ... like a boiling kettle. He felt dizzy and people looked like rats to him ... hunger had sapped him of all strength. If he hit any person with all his strength, he would himself collapse. (p. 112)

There is a tinge of irony in the image of a man who hits an opponent with all his strength, and then collapses. Ubesie is drawing attention to the devastating impact of hunger, for, in the hectic days of the war, starvation was used as a deliberate weapon.

Whether he is writing about the tragedies of war, courtship and marriage, the fantasies of youth, chieftaincy and power struggles or armed robbery, Tony Ubesie is consistent in his sensitivity to language and an almost geometric control of his subject-matter. He has become, in the true Igbo narrative tradition, the 'story vendor' and 'owner of words'.

After nearly half a century of struggling, loss and near-extinction, the Igbo novel has been rediscovered. Tony Uchenna Ubesie has restored to it its vital missing links of authentic form and a pleasing voice with which it was endowed at birth in 1933 by that treasured founding father, Pita Nwana, in his classic, *Omenuko*.[9]

NOTES

1. T. Ubesie, *Ukwa Ruo Oge Ya O Das*, Ibadan, Oxford University Press, 1973.
2. T. Ubesie, *Isi Akwu Dara N'ala*, Ibadan, Oxford University Press, 1973. Page references are to this edition and are indicated within the text.
3. Tony Ubesie, *Mmiri Oku Eji Egbu Mbe* Lagos, Longman Nigeria, 1974.
4. Tony Uchenna Ubesie, *Ukpana Okpoko Buru*, Ibadan, Oxford University Press, 1975.
5. Tony Ubesi, *Juo Obinna*, Ibadan University Press Limited, 1977. Page references are to this edition and are indicated within the text.
6. All English translations used in this paper are mine. It must be acknowledged that to translate Ubesie in this near-literal way is to destroy his art.
7. R.N. Egudu, 'Achebe and the Igbo narrative tradition', *Research in African Literatures*, vol. 12, no. 1, spring 1981, p. 51.
8. Ibid. p. 42.
9. Pita Nwana, *Omenuko*, London, Longman, 1933; repr. 1963. Pita Nwana was the first Igbo to publish fiction in Igbo. His only novel *Omenuko* was published in 1933 after it had won an all-Africa literary contest in indigenous African languages, organized by the International Institute of African Languages and Culture in London. *Omenuko* was a bestseller among Igbo readers for over three decades.

Language, Literature & the Struggle for Liberation in South Africa

Daniel P. Kunene

The Problem Defined

The contemporary South African scene makes exacting demands on the writer who chooses to accept the challenges of the current political realities of that beleaguered country. 'Chooses' is almost certainly an inept word in this context. Nadine Gordimer, the noted South African novelist and critic, has observed that 'Black writers choose their plots, characters and literary styles; their themes choose *them*.'[1] In other words, the themes arising out of the contemporary milieu in that country stare the writer in the face daring him to ignore them. If he does, he will be irrelevant to the human drama daily enacted there. If he accepts the challenge, he inevitably situates his characters within the daily trials that surround the black person's life. 'In this sense,' says Gordimer, 'the writer is the voice of the people beyond any glib political connotations of the phrase.'[2]

The writer is the synthesizer and conduit of the concerns of the society for which he claims to speak. As such, he may be regarded as not only having a stronger-than-ordinary sensitivity to the human problems of his milieu, but also a strong sense of empathy with his audience. Since, however, language, in the sense of speech, is his only means of reaching that audience, his task becomes complicated and more difficult if any of his readers employ languages different from his own. In his effort to reach them, therefore, it is incumbent on him to be linguistically versatile and temperamentally attuned to their emotional needs. This is a challenge that faces every committed writer in South Africa. The message is one. It is the message of liberation and the creation of a new society. The linguistic environments in which the audiences have been nurtured differ to varying degrees.

The widest gap, both linguistically and culturally, is that between white and black South Africans. This is mentioned here because the need arises every so often for the black writer to address his message to his white neighbour. This division between white and black is how all discussions of the South African socio-political situation begin, or should begin. After all the problem in that country is the problem of colour politics. White racist supremacists have, over the years, unleashed a relentless propaganda, both direct and by insinuation, that has defined hard lines that divide the people by colour, *not by class*. We are despised people for the simple reason that we are black. Steve Biko has said that

> in South Africa, after generations of exploitation, white people on the whole have come to believe in the inferiority of the black man, so much so that while the race problem started as an offshoot of the economic greed exhibited by white people, it has now become a serious problem of its own. White people now despise black people, not because they need to reinforce their attitude and so justify their position of privilege but simply because they actually believe that black is inferior and bad.[3]

This message is conveyed also by Walter Rodney in his *How Europe Underdeveloped Africa*. And, needless to say, it is a lesson that has, unfortunately, had to be learnt by blacks in the process of trying to cope with their social environment. The writer addressing himself to the white oppressor has to control his anger at the same time as he finds ways of making the English language do his bidding.

The writer's first duty is, of course, to maintain a dialogue with his black brothers and sisters, whom he must constantly inspire with the message of hope. In doing so, he must come to terms with the fact that these brothers and sisters speak either Zulu or Sesotho or Setswana or Xhosa or Sepedi or Ndebele and so on. So the linguistic challenges multiply. The immediately contemporary South African situation highlights these problems in a most singular manner. This is because one of the demands on the author today is that he, like the oral narrator, must stand face to face with his audience and harangue them with his own voice. Again, as in a typical oral narrative situation, the audience feedback is immediate and not always concurring. But that is another problem, to which we shall return. For now, we wish to draw attention to the challenge posed by the fact that the audience receiving the writer's or poet's or dramatist's message is in most cases a multilingual one. What must the committed artist do in order to overcome this problem, or perhaps even turn it to his advantage?

When the struggle has progressed to a certain point, the demon of fear is conquered. The politics of fear are replaced by the politics of confrontation, for the oppressed can now speak to his oppressor from a position of equality. This stage was reached quite decisively in the late sixties and early seventies. For the writer, the problem of choosing a suitable linguistic medium then becomes more complex. For let it be stated, almost superfluously, that white people as a group do not know the African languages, and any black wishing to talk to them has to defer to this white man's deficiency. One example of this is the English-language poetry that gushed out of the students of Soweto and other black townships following the bloody massacre of schoolchildren by police beginning 16 June 1976 and continuing with varying degrees of savagery to this day. The students struggled with the English language, they struggled with form, but their message was strong and unequivocal, and, while also serving to galvanize the struggling masses, its most prominent feature was that it spat in the face of white authority.

This, then, is the broad context within which the writer has to choose the language or languages he will use to address his respective audiences.

The Traditional Oral Praise Poet

Creating a militant poetry in the African languages is a challenge that faced the oral poet in the nineteenth century as the Boers encroached more and more on the African's land during the so-called Great Trek and beyond. The contemporary young activist poet of the seventies and eighties can take courage from, and also feel humbled by, the fact that his activity is nothing new. He has a tradition to fall back on. He has poetry of high calibre that used powerful imagery and direct exhortation, that was created in the heat of the wars of dispossession. His courageous forefathers resisted the invaders, and his artistic predecessor immortalized them in his poetry of praise. He is therefore able to measure his own efforts against his glorious past. One must emphasize here first the necessity to become aware of this poetry, for I have no doubt that many of the younger poets have, unfortunately, never availed themselves of it. The pride and humility which will, of necessity, follow such an exercise will be to their advantage.

Here is an example. During the War of Disarmament (also known among the Basotho as *Ntoa ea Lithunya* or the Gun War) in the latter part of the nineteenth century resulting from the British Administration's decision to deprive the blacks of their guns, the Basotho found themselves split into the 'Loyalists' (Mateketa) and the 'Rebels' (Marebele). One of the most outstanding rebels who fought personally in many of the battles was Chief Maama. In his glorious career, he performed many outstanding feats including his killing of Erasmus, the savage Boer soldier who played havoc among Basotho warriors as he skilfully drove his equally fearsome grey horse into their midst. Maama therefore deserved the highest praise for his deed. Being himself a poet of no mean order, he composed a long poem based on the episode, creating numerous eulogies for himself in the process. Often Maama assumes a dramatic posture as he chooses to address himself to this or that audience, defined in the poem. To his peers and comrades-in-arms he says:

Le se mpate bahlankana beso!
Ha le ke le re ke nna ka mo thula!
Ha le re ke nna ka bolaya pele?

Do not hide my actions, young men of my country!
Will you not say it was I who struck him?
Will you not say it was I who killed first?[4]

To the white people, the enemy, whom he refers to as the white men 'by the sea', he speaks through the surviving Boer soldiers.

He refers to Erasmus as the 'child' of the white people for whom the message is intended:

Ba re: 'Re le tjee re tloha re tswa ntweng,
Re tswa kgabong ka ha Ramabilikoe.
Ka mona ka ha Mafa le Ramabilikoe,
Ka mona ha Suhlane le Rampoi,
Kgalong la Boleka le la Mathebe,
Eitse ha re bapala motho a wa.
Ngwan'a lona o jelwe ke Koeyoko,
O jelwe ke Koeyoko ya Letsie,
Koeyoko, Seja-bana-ba-makgowa?'

They said: 'As you see us here, we have just returned from battle,
We've just come from the flames at the place of Ramabilikoe.
Not-far-from-here, at Mafa's and Ramabilikoe's,
Not far from here, at Suhlane's and Rampoi's,
At the mountain passes of Boleka and Mathebe,
It happened, while we were playing, a man fell.
Your child has been devoured by the Koeyoko,
He has been devoured by the Koeyoko of Letsie,
The Koeyoko, Devourer-of-the-children-of-the-white-man!'

Of course 'the white men by the sea' did not hear him. Neither were they
intended to in a physical way, firstly because they were not present when
the poem was recited, and secondly because the words spoken were in
Sesotho. Why then does the poet engage in all the game-playing? The fact
is that these words were all intended for the Basotho audience, who
derived pride, courage and a boost of their morale from the knowledge
that their warrior was capable of doing such a deed to their enemy. The
poet was sharing with the home side, the Basotho, the sense of confidence,
of daring the enemy. He was telling them there was no room for fear and
diffidence in their ranks.

Language Diversity and the Felt Need for Unity

The Boers, in their northward wanderings, first met the Xhosa, then the
Zulu, then the Basotho, and so on. (This is, of course, after they had
virtually wiped out the San as 'vermin'.) The poets in these language
groups all composed poems similar to the one quoted above. There was
a growing realization, however, that, despite language differences and
sometimes even conflicting interests at the local level, the new threat
called for a united voice and united action. Politically this was to happen
in a decisive way in 1912 when the first organization to unite all blacks
under one banner was formed, namely, the South African Native National
Congress, which was later to become the present African National
Congress of South Africa. This was a direct response to the formation of
the Union of South Africa in 1910 under a constitution that excluded all
blacks from participation in the political life of South Africa. The composition of the leadership strongly reflected this sentiment. It included John
L. Dube (Zulu, President), Walter Rubusana (Xhosa, Co-Vice-President)
and Sol T. Plaatje (Tswana, Secretary-General). It was a recognition of
the fact that the Union united Boer and Briton, and brought the erstwhile

independent provinces under one central government, in order to facilitate a more thorough exploitation of the blacks.

At about the same time as the war between the whites and the blacks was passing completely from the battlefield to the political arena, around the turn of the century, the blacks were consolidating their newly acquired skill of writing. The verbal artist was henceforth going to be able to write down his compositions on paper. Such well-known writers as Thomas Mofolo, John L. Dube, S.E.K. Mqhayi and Henry Masila Ndawo were producing the beginnings of a written literature. This period may be characterized as one in which written African literature was in its infancy. For reasons of survival, this literature largely steered clear of political themes. It also gave a wide berth to themes and concepts that might be considered offensive to the missionaries, who, after all, owned and controlled the printing works and publishing houses.

Poetry, however, was another matter, for it was here more than anywhere else where war imagery could be, and was, easily adapted to the new phase of the struggle, or the new war whose warriors were the educated man, the political or civil leader, and so on. Heroic poetic techniques are found in abundance in poems of this nature, in which persons of worth are praised while they live and lamented when they die. An excellent example of this is provided by S.E.K. Mqhayi in his anthology of poems, Inzuzo.[5]

Since this presentation is intended largely to examine the contemporary scene, we must, rather abruptly, take a giant leap into the sixties, the seventies and the eighties and see what happened there.

The Contemporary Scene

This period is one characterized by a new political awareness referred to as the Black Consciousness Movement. What makes this period unique is that, beginning in the late sixties and continuing throughout the seventies and into the present day, the young black students in the 'bush' colleges turned the tables on the authorities. The colleges had been established by the government with the intention of controlling the minds of the students; yet, by a strange irony, it was precisely out of these colleges that a new and revolutionary definition of the struggle and the role of the black person therein was born. This was the political coming-of-age of the blacks. Steve Biko, the 'father' of Black Consciousness, stressed that the first prerequisite was self-liberation. He said that 'the most potent weapon in the hands of the oppressor is the mind of the oppressed. If one is free at heart, no man-made chains can bind one to servitude.'[6] This underscores the need to conquer fear before one can stand up and declare one's own views with conviction.

The spirit of daring manifested itself in the political sphere through acts of defiance such as the workers' strikes in Durban and Port Elizabeth in the early to mid-seventies. The workers knew that it was illegal for blacks to engage in strike action, and that they were risking heavy fines and sentences. Organizations such as the South African Students Organization

(SASO) and the Black People's Convention (BPC) came into existence. The word 'black' took on a new significance, symbolizing both the new sense of liberation and the unity of all oppressed under one, positive defining concept. Thus the intellectual process and political action reinforced and constantly redefined each other.

For purposes of this discussion, the importance of this new sense of confidence, self-identity and lack of fear is that the white man suddenly became willy-nilly part of the black writer's target audience. We must therefore examine the question of communication, through literature, with white authority by blacks whose mother tongue is not English. Mongane Serote, one of the contemporary young black poets, interviewed by Michael Chapman in 1980, made the following significant statement: 'I am not English-speaking. I have worked hard at the English language. I didn't complete high school, and of course the English press made me very conscious of the fact that English isn't my home language. There was no way that could stop me from writing. I worked hard. I spent nights at the typewriter writing and re-writing.'[7] The most obvious follow-up question Michael Chapman might have asked, but did not, is: 'Why then do you write in English?' To which Serote might conceivably have responded: 'If I wrote in my own language, this interview would not be taking place!' Or perhaps Serote might have said: 'If I wrote in my own language I could not convey to my oppressor and tormentor this important message: "I do not fear you any more!"'

It seems to me it is just as well that the question of why the contemporary black South African writers write in English should be asked, not by the white South Africans, English-speaking or otherwise, but by the black critics and ultimately by the black writers themselves. It is not a futile academic exercise, but a practical approach to a problem of communication. Surely there must be a strong reason why Serote would 'work hard at the English language'. It is one thing to spend 'nights at the typewriter, writing and re-writing'. It is quite another to decide what language this process is to take place in. Serote chose English. He could have 'spent nights at the typewriter writing and re-writing' in Sesotho. The question then is relevant and important: Why in English?

This question quite clearly sometimes bothers some of these writers, and they feel the need to confront it head-on. Sipho Sepamla wrote in 1976 that he had sometimes questioned the correctness of the English used by black writers, including himself. As regards the question whether English should be abandoned as a medium his answer is an emphatic 'No, never.' Later he declares his belief that 'writing in English is going to be strengthened' because of its common use on social occasions, the clamour for its use as a medium of instruction in schools, its use in industry, the influence of the English-language newspapers among blacks, and its use in the neighbouring black independent states.[8]

I have no doubt the question, if seriously posed, would evoke a miscellany of responses, some flippant, some arrogant, some confused. Some people might even wonder why they hadn't thought about it before. A few might take it seriously. Perhaps some might even see some absurdity in performing poetry in English in the black townships.

Some might have had experiences similar to those reported by Sepamla, who says:

> I owe nobody an apology for writing in English. Yet inside me is this regret that at the moment there is a handicap that mars complete communication between me and my audience, particularly the black audience.

He believes there have been ominous rumblings of discontent in the black audiences, and that the artists may, in fact, be alienating the people:

> When people talk of izifundiswa (the educated) or when they say khuluma isiZulu (speak Zulu) ha re utlwe bua seSotho (we do not hear, speak Sotho) then the divisions begin. Those who speak in English will tend to avoid such hecklers. And what will happen to the effort of uplifting ourselves and those down there? I think we have a serious problem here. I have watched the same problem rear its head when such stage productions as *Sizwe Bansi is Dead* and *How long?* are presented. Either people have gone to sleep or they have shouted khulumani isiZulu.[9]

One wonders what questions arise in the minds of writers and performers faced with this hostile reaction from their audiences. Does this not make them doubt the wisdom of oral performances of this nature being carried out in English? One would hope that such performers would not be tempted, as Sepamla fears they might, to avoid black audiences who indulge in such interjections. If that were to happen, then the alienation would be complete.

When we go back to the interview of Serote by Chapman, then we see how the ironies multiply. Michael Chapman's next question to Serote is: 'Whereas your first two collections seem directed at both a black and a white audience, *No Baby Must Weep* (1975) indicates a distinct shift in perspective, and seems directed primarily at fellow blacks. Would you comment on this?' Serote:

> It's directed at Africans in particular. Look, I don't simply want to write for the colours of skins. I want to try to understand the complex issue of the scale of privileged positions in South African society, which includes the white, the Indian and the coloured – I have been called a 'kaffir' by all of them. This is complex, but I have become increasingly aware that it is the Africans who hold the tools of liberation in South Africa. And it is to them *No Baby Must Weep* is addressed.[10]

The claim that a book written in English is addressed to blacks makes no sense unless one specifies that it is for those blacks who have acquired enough English to be able to read and understand it. Then we would understand that it is not intended for the masses, counted in millions, who do not have that skill.

Ezekiel Mphahlele, interviewed in 1979 by Noel Chabani Manganyi, makes a similarly surprising statement. Referring to the mid-fifties, he claims that the then budding, elitist group of writers, who were mostly journalists working for *Drum* magazine, wrote a '*proletarian literature*':

People were really writing furiously in a lively, vibrant style. It was quite a style of its own, an English of its own ... There was, as I say, a new kind of English being written. Significantly, *it was the black man writing for the black man.* Not addressing himself to the whites. *Talking a language that would be understood by his own people ... Ours was really a proletarian literature.* [My emphasis] [11]

Even restricting one's comments to Johannesburg, one cannot see stories written in English reaching any significant number of workers, let alone the millions of rural Africans and migrant workers for whom *Drum,* an urban magazine, was so totally irrelevant.

The problem with the *Drum* generation of writers is that they failed to place their writing within the context of the long tradition of verbal art, both oral and written, especially that devoted to the struggle. A knowledge of the tradition and an acknowledgement of its contribution to the long, continuous fight against the forces of oppression would have broken this self-imposed isolation and instilled a salutary sense of humility, if not of pride. It might also have opened the eyes of the *Drum* group to the fact that a proletarian literature can only be written in a language that is understood by the masses.

Mphahlele himself, commenting on the *Staffrider* generation of writers, strongly advocates this sense of tradition:

What I see in *Staffrider* is a real, vibrant literature. But it lacks a myth. By myth meaning this, what you are saying, that there is a tomorrow. That literature captures the agony of the moment. It has no resonance because it has no past either. It has no past to work on. We were just saying earlier that our present day writers have been cut off from the fifties. They don't even know that it existed. They think literature begins with them. So there is no resonance going to the past and no resonance going to the future. This is what we must move beyond. [12]

Sound advice which, however, fails to come to terms with the fact that the fifties were not the beginning of African literature either. Mphahlele's dismissal, elsewhere, of African-language literature as 'Anaemic writing that is meant for juveniles' [13] is too facile a way out. There is a bit more to African-language literature than that. What needs to be done is to break down these walls of isolation and let tradition flow.

The problem of language choice and what motivates the black writer to choose one language as against another is therefore also a problem of attitude. The fifties, no less than the seventies, failed to look at the literatures written in the African languages for guidance and inspiration. For, even though there was no 'school' as such, there is an unmistakable periodicity noted. There is no question in my mind but that the era of the oral heroic bard ought to be regarded as a literary period whose major instigating force was the immediate danger of the loss of land, property and liberty, a compelling motif and a unifying force.

Since writing meant that publication was the passport to reaching an audience, and the means of publication and dissemination were in the hands of someone other than the composer of the verbal art, the introduction of writing brought in a 'middleman' between the artist and his audience. The ideological and commercial interests of this 'middleman' became a powerful instrument which he used to control the artist. That is why written prose fiction showed so little of the daring and outspokenness of the oral poetry and prose. It is curious, however, that written poetry and song were less inhibited in their criticism. Reuben Caluza composed the words and music of the song 'i-Land Act', which was a bitter attack on the notorious Land Act of 1913.[14] Many similar songs were written by other composers whose intention was to keep up the African's awareness of his plundered rights. Needless to say that, in order for the fifties and the seventies to have had the greatest possible impact, they should not have forgotten or ignored these earlier artists of the struggle.

English and African-language Writing

Not all African writers in English are motivated by a sense of commitment to social change. I would suggest that, for some, the promise of wide exposure and possible recognition in the white-dominated field of literary criticism is a strong factor. This ensures that even a mediocre piece of writing will at least be talked about, if not given a prominence way out of proportion to its merit. It is therefore relevant to ask what makes a mediocre poem written in English a better poem than an excellent one written in Sesotho? Mrs N.M. Khaketla, one of the best poets I know, wrote many a poem in her native language Sesotho, in which she indicted the British Colonial Administration in Lesotho before independence. Her husband, also a poet in addition to his other literary activites, had just been expelled from his teaching job at the Basutoland (now Lesotho) High School for political reasons. Their daughter, born shortly after this event, was named *Molelekeng* ('Chase-him away/Chase-her-away). Mrs Khaketla wrote a poem[15] in which she wove the name of her daughter into her husband's (and of course her own) harassment at this time. The poem is written in dramatic form in which the persona assumes different roles and creates a lively contrapuntal dialogue among the several 'voices' or 'characters'.

From the third line of Stanza 4 and for the whole of Stanza 5, the persona's voice is interrupted by a white man's voice, a government official in Maseru. The voice speaks through a letter the white man is writing. This could also be considered to be the persona-as-poet's-husband suspending his own words in order to quote the white man, who says, inter alia:

[Stanza 4, partial]

Moshemane ha a ikentse kheleke,
A bile a khanya ka ho bua haholo,
O tla ruta bana ho rola litlhong.
Le 'metsetse kamose, Forei Setata
Etlere ha a bua polesa le thunye

When a boy brags of being so eloquent,
And makes a habit of speaking too much,
He will teach the little ones to put aside their modesty.
You must throw him across the river, into the Free State
Where, the moment he opens his mouth, a policeman will shoot him.

[Stanza 5, partial]

Moshemanehali enoa oa khantsa
E ka hoki, o ja a ntse a rora,
O halala sengoatho le phophi ea lebese,
O batla polokoe le khamelo e lolobetse.

This overgrown boy is too proud,
He is like a pig that grumbles as it eats,
He is not satisfied with a piece of bread and a drop of milk
But demands the entire loaf plus a milk-pail full to the brim.

A wealth of imagery. Sesotho proverbs rearranged and woven into the fabric of the poem. A name, a child's name, undergirding the major poetic image, the 'chase him-away' image. And then the inevitable return, the epic hero come back to oust the usurper. The richness of the imagery, the easy flight into metaphor, symbol and allegory, are all facilitated by the fact that N.M. Khaketla draws her inspiration and her testimony from the constantly bubbling spring, the *Ntswanatsatsi*, of Sesotho culture. Words are released from their daily meanings to re-emerge with cultural codings that engage the reader in the fascinating game of 'do-you-recognize-me?': 'My mother had not even the smallest piece of cloth to cover her naked shoulders'; 'My father rejects me though I have come from his loins'; 'My little mother is not telling the truth'; 'The beast I earned'; 'I am fit to be given a wife'. 'Mother', 'father', 'little mother', 'beast', (cow), 'wife', these are surrogates for meanings much deeper than their surface denotations. Yet Mrs Khaketla never got to be interviewed by any of the numerous white self-styled experts of African literature. But that is not the real tragedy. The tragedy is that African-language writers of Mrs Khaketla's calibre were never taken as a source of inspiration by either the fifties or the seventies, for the fifties and the seventies considered themselves sufficient unto themselves. So they never learnt humility.

One can mention many other cases of militant writing. Jac Moco-ancoeng's poem 'Exoda'[16] uses the metaphor of the movement of the Israelites out of the house of bondage, to preach the message of freedom. No white man read it, for it was written in Sesotho. S.M. Mofokeng wrote the play *Senkatana*[17] based on an old Sesotho legend in which the young man, Senkatana, left alone with his mother after an enormous monster has swallowed all living things, goes and slays the monster with his single spear and releases its captives. The message of liberation again is quite clear. No white critic read it. But again the tragedy is that no black man seems to have read it either. It is a safe bet that, one day when an African writer receives the Nobel prize, it will not necessarily be for the most meritorious work, for no other reason than the linguistic inaccessibility of many excellent works to those entrusted with the frightful task of selecting the winner.

Conclusions and Some Practical Suggestions

Once the black writers confront the question squarely and honestly: Should we or should we not write in English? it is predictable that the answer, by an overwhelming majority, would endorse the continued use of English. However, the affirmative answer would result from reasons as complex as the South African situation itself. Having come to that conclusion, they would have to devise a *modus vivendi* whereby they can retain the respect of their black audiences at the same time.

I would suggest, as the first prerequisite, that, in reading to black audiences, the readers *must* read in one or other of the black languages of South Africa. It doesn't really matter whether one reads a Zulu poem to a predominantly Sesotho audience. There might be no way of determining this predominance, anyway. A Mosotho in such an audience will appreciate your Zulu or Xhosa or Ndebele, etc, even if he may not understand much of what you are saying, just as readily as he will feel offended by your English, which to him is a measure of your alienation from your own people.

Given the government's ethnic zoning of the townships, an assessment of the linguistically dominant group in any given township audience might not be too difficult a task, thus turning this divide-and-rule trick into advantage. One is constantly inspired by the fact that the South African Students Organization (SASO) and the Black Consciousness Movement arose out of a ghetto college which was subverted by the students to a beneficial use quite in opposition to its original purpose.

When the poets read in the situations described above, they must never miss the opportunity to explain that they also *have to* write and read in English because they have a message for the white oppressor, who would otherwise not understand what they are saying. They might even go to the extent of translating some of their more militant poems into an African language, just so that their audience might partake of the joy of this new-found emancipation. For it is an act of self-emancipation to be able to confront your oppressor face to face and tell him in uncensored language what you think of him. The poetry suddenly becomes alive with the I (black man) – you (white man) confrontation, in which the accusatory 'you' is hurled like a barbed spear at the white oppressor. The language explodes with swear-words like 'shit' and 'fuck', and images of violence such as 'throw up', 'vomit', 'throttle', 'retch', which are scattered all over the poetry. Yet these are neither swear-words nor words of violence. They are an expression of freedom as legitimate as the shout 'I'm free!' They constitute an explosion of the bottled-up feelings of forced restraint over these many centuries. Sharing this feeling will make any oral performance session much more consciously an educational event aimed at consciousness-raising.

Composing originally in an African language and later translating into

English may be another way of boosting the morale of one's black audience. Let the poem be born in the black language. Such poets would be in good company. Ngugi wa Thiong'o, after all, reached the hearts of the Kikuyu people much more readily and deeply when he reverted to writing in Kikuyu; Mazisi Kunene composes in Zulu and translates into English. They would also be in the company, of course, of the old oral poets and creators of myths, whose tradition continues in some contemporary poets writing in praise of modern heroes.

As regards the so-called 'coloureds', the Indians and the Malay, the principle would be the same as for the Africans – continue writing in their languages, i.e. the naturalized forms of English and Afrikaans, which are found, to varying degrees, in writers like Alex la Guma, Adam Small, Achmat Dangor, and so on. Of course these groups will have to make an effort to acquire some knowledge of an African language. After all the black man has been, and continues to be, the one called upon to meet all the other groups in their territory, linguistically speaking. Such efforts should be serious,, and not mere tokens.

In summary, we may state some of the writer's problems as follows:

Firstly, even as the story gets born in his head (hopefully in his heart as well) the writer must seriously ask himself: For whom is my story intended? Bearing his audience constantly in mind will help him focus his plot and motivate his characters with a great deal more purpose and conviction. He will, hopefully, realize, even as he picks up his pen, that a story intended for the proletariat, for the millions and millions of labourers, ought to be written, not in English, but in the languages of the people.

If the story is intended for a readership that includes English-speaking people, both in South Africa and elsewhere, then of course it will be inevitable to write it in English. This will facilitate communication among all shades of blacks in South Africa. One way to achieve this is, of course, to engage in extensive translation projects with a clear purpose in selecting the works to be translated. This means translating both into and out of English.

Secondly, the writer might take his cue from the many African-language writers who have stated their intended didactic messages quite openly in prefaces and introductions to their stories. Not that writers need to use prefaces and introductions. One does not want to summarize a story for one's readers. The message is to be carried in the mind of the writer as he begins to write, and constantly thereafter. This will determine whether the work is intended to be a contribution to the struggle, or is purely for entertainment, or to satisfy the writer's ego, or as a commercial venture, and so on. Many of these are, in any case, not mutually exclusive. We are talking more about emphases than mutual preclusions.

Thirdly, assuming a given work has a didactic purpose, and given further the necessity for oral communication with audiences in the townships throughout South Africa as the writers and poets perform their works, the question arises whether such sessions are used optimally to raise the political consciousness of the audiences involved. As stated earlier, the artist here has the opportunity to engage his audience, and be engaged by them, in a direct dialogue in which ideas are shared, something possible only in oral performances. When the audience interrupts and shouts 'Theth' isiXhosa, asiva!' of 'Bolela Sepedi, ha re kwe!' and so on, the performer must immediately engage the interrupter, whom I refuse to call a heckler, in a dialogue describing the problem of language choices, of audiences targeted, and so on as already described above. It is important, and it bears repeating, that a member of the audience who is suddenly moved to say something, whether the comment is approving or critical, is not heckling, but is asking for a dialogue.

Fourthly, the oral performer or performing group must in one way or another always include the message of unity to their audiences. The question of the high degree of mutual intelligibility among their languages, and of their cultural homogeneity must be underscored. It must be emphasized that ethnic separation in the locations is intended to divide the people, and it must not be permitted to succeed. The students in the ethnic colleges have not allowed this physical separation either to divide them or to stifle their minds. There is an even greater danger on the horizon, and we must prepare for it now. After we have attained our independence, there will be numerous neo-colonialist interests waiting to sow dissension among us. If we as artists constantly speak to our people with wisdom and clarity, we will strengthen them against such onslaughts when they do happen.

My final statement is this: The theoreticians, the leadership, the strategists, and the enunciators of the ideology on which political action is based will probably find English a useful tool. At the grass-roots level, however, there is a compelling need to talk to the people in their own languages, thus reinforcing their pride and their sense of identity.

NOTES

This article first appeared in *Staffrider*, Johannesburg, vol. 6, no. 3, 1986.
1. Nadine Gordimer, *The Black Interpreters*, Johannesburg, SPRO-CAS/Ravan, 1973, p. 11.
2. Ibid.
3. Steve Biko, *I Write What I Like* (a selection of his writings edited with a personal memoir by Aelred Stubbs, C.R), San Francisco, Harper and Row, 1978, p. 88.
4. Daniel P. Kunene, *Heroic Poetry of the Basotho*, Oxford, Clarendon Press, 1971, p. 60.
5. S.E.K. Mqhayi, *Inzuzo*, Johannesburg, Witwaterstrand University Press (Bantu Treasury Series), 1957; first published 1953.
6. Biko, op. cit., p. 92.
7. Michael Chapman (ed.), *Soweto Poetry*, Johannesburg, McGraw-Hill, p. 114.
8. Ibid., p. 117.
9. Ibid., p. 116.
10. Ibid., p. 42.

11. Noel Chabani Manganyi, *Looking Through the Keyhole*, Johannesburg, Ravan Press, 1981, pp. 36–7.
12. Ezekiel Mphahlele, *The African Image*, New York, Praeger, 1974, p. 205.
13. The Natives Land Act of 1913, one of the early pieces of legislation passed by the government of the Union of South Africa founded in 1910. The aim of the Act was to remove Africans occupying land on white-owned farms (which meant virtually every single farm in South Africa). It created hundreds of thousands of homeless people taking to the roads with their cattle and meagre personal belongings, not knowing where they were going.
14. N.M. Khaketla, 'Molelekeng', in her collection of poetry *Mantsopa*, Cape Town, Oxford University Press, 1963, pp. 10–13.
15. Mr B.M. Khaketla's middle name, which means 'Surprise', 'Amazement', etc. It is translated in the poem as 'Surprised-One' since it is used as the proper name of a person.
16. Jac G. Mocoancoeng, *Tseleng ea Bophelo le Lithothokiso tse Ncha*, Johannesburg, Witwatersrand University Press (Bantu Treasury Series), 1955.
17. S.M. Mofokeng, *Senkatana*, Johannesburg, Witwatersrand University Press (Bantu Treasury Series), 1952; 1961 reprint in the revised South African orthography.

Linguistic Characteristics of the African Short Story

F. Odun Balogun

Next to poetry, the short story is the most exacting of verbal art forms.[1] The genre demands from its practitioners the most scrupulous discipline in the use of words. It is not, according to Anatole Broyard, that the artist must use 'uncommon words' but that he must use 'common words uncommonly well'.[2] To achieve this goal, the writer, in the words of Hallie Burnett, must 'give thought to each word and weigh each one spoken or written for its true sense, its effectiveness, and its color'[3] because 'each word a fiction writer uses must have meaning, weight, feeling, and particularity'.[4] In fact, from Edgar Allan Poe onwards every master in the genre has known that a single inappropriate or superfluous word can spoil a good short story.

When African short stories are measured against these very tough standards, it is evident that many of our writers have diligently obeyed the laws of this demanding literary form. From the angle of language usage, not too many African short stories in English can be faulted. In fact, a lot of stories that might otherwise have failed due to the shallowness of their themes or the poor handling of plot are redeemed by the high competence in language usage. For example, even though Ekwensi's stories tend to be thematically thin and melodramatic in resolution, the level at which language is handled is generally high in spite of a critic's just claim that his language tends to be cliché-ridden.[5] In his best stories, this fault is compensated for by Ekwensi's 'sophisticated sense of detail',[6] his adroit use of pidgin[7] and the appropriateness of his diction and faultless syntax. Similarly, the only redeeming quality in Bereng Setuke's journalistic story, 'Dumani' (AS, pp. 58–68), is its language, which manifests an authentic knowledge of the speech of its characters and a competent use of verbal irony, metaphor and rhythmic repetition. Although Mtutuzeli Matshoba's 'To Kill A Man's Pride' is like a journalist's sociological report, its high points are when language is used poetically (as on AS, p. 116). There are other stories which fall into this category, but I should stress that I am certainly not claiming linguistic competence for all African short stories since there are failures in this regard. What I am claiming is that African stories are generally well written from the standpoint of language usage, which, all said and done, is the most crucial aspect of the short story as a genre.

51

One of the factors responsible for the success of the language of African short stories is their scrupulous terseness and compactness. Few writers indeed produce the long short story that shares a common boundary with the novella; most write the short story and the majority of the highly successful stories often fall under ten pages; a large body of stories qualify as the short short story, spreading between two and five pages. The writers achieve this terseness through a variety of means. They employ accurate imaginative diction and condensed syntax. Most writers go straight into the action of their stories without wasting words on preliminary introduction. Contracted forms and elliptical syntax are often used and the writers sometimes employ poetic licence and disregard certain rules of grammar. Thus, it is common to have incomplete sentences, one-word sentences, and even paragraphs that are shorter than a line. The result is that with a few deft strokes the best writers succeed in introducing their themes and characters, accurately establishing the particular setting and subtly evoking the proper mood. The best stories of Achebe, Ngugi, la Guma, Paton, lo Liyong, Easmon, Aidoo, Owoyele, Kibera, Tshabangu, Nicol, Musi and Heyns, some of which qualify as masterpieces, are written in this manner.

Sometimes the writer departs deliberately from the demand of conciseness to cultivate the deliberate grandeur of epic narratives. Such is the case with Easmon's 'The Feud' (pp. 1–39) and Kunene's 'The Spring of Life' (AC, pp. 87–103). Other times, the tedious length might be intended to achieve a set artistic objective as in the case of Paul Zeleza's 'The Journey Home' (ND, pp. 94–108), whose humorous ramblings, digressions and circumlocutions are meant to comically reflect the character's confused mind. It is for this reason that it might paradoxically be true that on occasions a short story that is actually short in length might be too long. An example is Zeleza's 'At the Crossroads' (ND, pp. 126–32), which is overwritten – a point that becomes clearer if compared with his other story 'The Wrath of Fate' (ND, pp. 170–7) and with Alan Paton's 'The Waste Land' (DGH, pp. 79–84), two stories that end at the appropriate moment. Moreover, 'At the Crossroads' shares a common theme with 'The Waste Land'. Similarly, the nature of the syntax may be dictated by the tempo of the action. Although 'The Feud' is a long story, the tempo of narration is fast because Easmon wants the fast dramatic action of his epic plot to be matched by a fast tempo of narration. Consequently, he predominantly uses short sentences. Ngugi's sentences in 'A Mercedes Funeral', on the other hand, are long and winding in order to make the consequent slow tempo of narration reflect the leisurely atmosphere of the setting, which is a beer parlour.

In some respects, the short story resembles drama with its emphasis on action and dialogue, concentrating as it does on the minimum of actions and making them permanently memorable by dramatizing them. Even though African short-story writers also compose introspective stories, the vast majority of their stories are dramatic and some strikingly so. Alan Paton seems to be the most outstanding in this respect and his 'Debbie, Go Home' and 'The Waste Land' are hardly distinguishable from radio dramas. Other masters, such as Achebe in 'Civil Peace' (GAW, pp. 82–9), are no less successful in their skilful dramatization, nor can we ignore the artful balancing of description, action and dialogue in writers like Saidi ('Haruba', *VOZ*, pp. 66–74), Mphahlele ('The Coffee-cart Girl', *ASS*, pp. 137–44), Essop ('The Betrayal', *ASS*, pp. 124–9) and Gurnah ('Bossy', *ASS*, pp. 49–60). Some writers, particularly Ama Ata Aidoo, experiment with the language of dialogue. Aidoo, for instance, in at least four of the stories in her collection, *No Sweetness Here*, records only one side of a conversation but in such a way that the responses from the second speaker are known to the reader even though they are not orchestrated. This seems an attempt, and it is quite a successful one, to combine the solemnity and seriousness of introspection (since her themes are usually weighty and tragic) with the demand for memorable dramatic action.

Another factor responsible for the linguistic success of African short stories is the writers' imaginative approach to the use of language. Since these writers aimed at capturing African reality, and English, the medium of expression in our case, is overburdened with the reality of a different culture, they had of necessity to do violence to standard English – to quote Komey and Mphahlele[8] – in order to create an authentic image of Africa. Consequently, the English of the African short story is certainly not the same as that in British or American short stories. Not all the writers succeed in accurately capturing in their stories the nuances of English used in Africa, but all the great masters do, and this more than thematic preoccupations is what defines the Africanness of the African short story in English. Furthermore, this rather than the competence in the handling of the stylistic and technical devices of the short story is what constitutes the essence of the African short-story writer. When this language yard-stick is applied, we will sadly discover that we do have many competent short-story writers in Africa but not many competent African short-story writers. This is what makes a collection like *No Sweetness Here* a much more interesting work than the equally competently written collection, *The Feud*;[9] the narrators and characters in the former unlike the latter speak precisely the way Africans (in this case Ghanaians) speak – the words they use, the pattern and tone of their speech, the figures of speech they employ, the nature of their conversations and their mannerisms. In this respect Ama Ata Aidoo's use of gossip as a narrative technique in 'Something to Talk About on the Way to the Funeral' is most effective.

The various attempts to make language authentically reflect African reality are evident in the increasing use of translated and untranslated words and phrases from indigenous African languages, urban colloquialism and slang, especially in Southern African short stories. While Gwala, for instance, would not translate items of the African language he uses in 'Reflections in a Cell' (*ASS*, pp. 150–159), Mzamane translates incorporated Africanisms in 'The Soweto Bride' (*SCSA*, pp. 117–32) even though he does not in 'A Present For My Wife' (*AS*, pp. 22–34). Serote's 'Let's Wander Together' (*EW*, pp. 160–3) and Melamu's 'Bad Times, Sad Times' (*AS*, pp. 41–53) demonstrate a good use of colloquialism. Musi ('Cops Ain't What They Used To Be', *AS*, pp. 180–2), Heyns ('Our Last Fling', *AS*, pp. 183–6) and Motjuwadi ('What Is Not White Is Darkie', *AS*, pp. 187–9) are deft users of slang. Pidgin and proverbs are frequently used in West African short stories, and the stories of Achebe, Aniebo and Ekwensi are typical in this respect. East African short-story writers are not as aggressive in this matter as their counterparts from Southern and West Africa though Ngugi and Ogot occasionally use translated and untranslated Africanisms. For instance, Ogot's use of indigenous exclamatory words in 'The Green Leaves' (ASS, pp. 40–8) is artistic and Ngugi accurately captures the speech mannerisms of his narrator in 'A Mercedes Funeral' (SL, pp. 113–37).

Generally, the language of African short stories is consciously rhythmic; indeed the language of some stories is so carefully arranged that the resultant stories are regular prose poems. Two spectacular examples of short-story prose poems are Achebe's 'The Madman' (GAW, pp. 1–10) and Tshabangu's 'Thoughts in a Train' (AS, pp. 156–8). To a lesser extent, the stories of Mubitana (VOZ, pp. 1–6, 89–94, 122–30) are poetic. What makes these stories and those similar to them rhythmically poetic is the extreme terseness of their language and the use of the devices of repetition, song, sound devices, figures of speech, imagery and symbolism. Only a few examples of stories which exhibit these poetic devices can be given here.

The terse nature of the language of African short stories has already been discussed; it remains only to add that in short-story prose poems terseness closely approaches the level in poetry. Repetition, often with variation, of the same or similar single words, phrases and sentences is evident in the following among other stories: Kibera's 'The Spider's Web' (ASS), Gurnah's 'Bossy' (ASS), Ngugi's 'Minutes of Glory' (SL), Gordimer's 'The Bridegroom' (SMFS), Mzamane's 'A Present For My Wife' (AS), Matthews's 'Azikwelwa' (AS), Khumalo's 'I Did Not Know' (VOZ), and Mubitana's 'Song of the Rain', 'The Day of the Ghosts' and 'The Spearmen of Malama' (VOZ).

Songs and refrains are frequently employed in Mubitana's stories mentioned above and in Rukuni's 'Who Started the War?' (AS). Ogot uses dirge and sound devices such as onomatopoeia and alliteration in 'The Green Leaves' (ASS). Figures of speech such as simile, metaphor, hyperbole and metonymy occur in Kibera's 'The Spider's Web' (ASS), Gordimer's 'Bridegroom' (SMFS), Head's 'Snapshots of a Wedding' (CT), Heyn's 'Our Last Fling' (AS) and Owoyele's 'The Will of Allah' (ASS). Ogot's images, often drawn from nature, are visual and strikingly beautiful even out of context: 'And bending across the path, as if saying prayers to welcome the dawn, were long grasses which were completely overpowered by the thick dew' ('The Green Leaves', ASS, p. 45); 'The red rays of the setting sun embraced Oganda and she looked like a burning candle in the wilderness' ('The Rain Came', PASS, p. 22). The equally nature-based images of la Guma are similarly visual and captivating: 'The sun hung well towards the west now so that the thin clouds above the ragged horizon were rimmed with bright yellow like the spilt yolk of an egg' (WN, p. 125); 'The sun was almost down and the clouds hung like bloodstained rags along the horizon' (WN, p. 128).

Often the images are symbolic. For instance, the picture of the young girl, Oganda, who looks like a burning candle in Ogot's story, is a symbolic reminder of her role as a sacrificial lamb. Kibera's story, 'The Spider's

Web', is among the best written of African symbolic stories. The story has a systematic, well-constructed, symbolic structure anchored on objects such as a young tree, a spider's web, a queen bee, a cap, a knife, a coffin, books and a bow and arrow. The spider's web, for instance, goes beyond its physical reality on the roof to encompass other metaphoric webs. The latter include the imperceptible growth of the exploitation of blacks by blacks to the extent that colonial exploitation becomes even preferable. It also stands for the gradual erosion of the expectations and promises of independence which in its turn weaves a web of discontent, revenge, murder and suicide in the minds of the exploited, represented here by Ngotho. The emasculation of the new elites like Mr Njogu, Ngotho's master, is symbolized by the replacement of bow and arrow by books and medicine tablets in the master's bedroom. There is a web of blood in the knife which stabs the base of the tree, which stands for both the queen bee, Mrs Njogu, and her husband, the bee. Ngotho often vents his anger on this tree planted by Mr Njogu since at first he could not directly confront either Mr Njogu or his wife. The elite's refusal to confront reality is symbolized in the image of the man who prefers blurred vision: 'Mr Njogu didn't like what he saw. He threw his glasses away and preferred to see things blurred' (ASS, p. 70). The hopelessness of the situation is suggested to Mr Ngotho by the fact that even the future elite will be like the present in their refusal to face reality. This is symbolized by the cap that obscures vision, 'But as he looked at their pregnant wives he could foresee nothing but a new generation of innocent snobs, who would be chauffeured off to school in neat caps hooded over their eyes so as to obstruct vision; (ASS, p. 68).

The use of complex symbols necessarily makes some African stories difficult for the unsophisticated reader. The difficulty is further compounded by the use of ambiguity and literary and other allusions. The ending of Kibera's symbolic story, 'The Spider's Web', is left hanging but the details are suggestive of suicide. Similarly, only the well-read reader who is familiar with Eliot's wasteland symbolism will fully grasp the meaning of Paton's story 'The Waste Land' (DGH, pp. 79–84).

The African writer is more inclined than his European counterpart to employ the rhythms of poetry in his prose.[10] This is because the modern African short story is a continuation of the traditional tale, which employs the devices of oral poetry such as repetition, song, refrain, alliteration and onomatopoeia. The recent claims that the short story is not an outgrowth of oral literature, that the two 'represent closed artistic systems',[11] that they are 'mutually exclusive forms that cannot shade or develop into each other',[12] must, of course, be ignored. This is not simply because many critics have affirmed the contrary[13] but because the evidence is overwhelmingly in favour of the existence of a past and still growing link between the oral tale and the short story.[14] In any case, the most significant trend in all the genres of African literature in recent times is the attempt of our writers to enrich written literature with forms and techniques borrowed from oral literature.

In the area of the short story, the attempt began with not just an anthropological but a creative gathering and retelling of oral tales. Two good examples are lo Liyong's 'Eating Chiefs' and Martha Mvungi's 'Three Solid Stones'. Writers like Leshoai ('Tselane and the Giant', *SCSA*, pp. 58–67) and Curtis ('About a Girl Who Met a Dimo', (*SCSA*, pp. 40–1) have also translated Setswana and Sesotho tales into English. The homecoming attempt is now at its sophisticated level of creating modern tales as well as deftly incorporating the stylistic elements of folk-tale into the short story. These attempts have already produced results, the most significant being the short stories and modern tales by lo Liyong (*Fixions*),[15] Marechera ('Protista', *ASS*, pp. 130–6) and Kenyatta ('The Gentlemen of the Jungle', *ASS*, pp. 36–9). There are many short stories which require that the reader suspend disbelief since their plots are partly or wholly fantastic, in the manner of traditional folk-tales. Of course, the folk-tale may not be the exclusive source of the fantastic plot since our writers are familiar with European Gothic stories, science fiction and Western surrealistic prose, among other possible sources. Nonetheless, it is improbable that the African folk-tale has no influence on works soaked in mystery, witchcraft, dream and superstition such as Ekwensi's 'The Great Beyond' (*RC*, pp. 34–9), Saidi's 'The Nightmare' (*VOZ*, pp. 14–21) and Nicol's 'The Judge's Son' (*MASF*, pp. 162–71). There are short stories which use folk-tale narrative formulas unchanged or slightly altered. The formula for beginning a tale is echoed in Gurnah's 'Bossy', which begins: 'A long time ago that was, sitting on the barnacled pier, swinging our legs through the air (*ASS*, p. 49). This beginning formula is similarly retained by Leshoai in the folk-tale he inserted into his story, 'The Moon Shall Be My Witness': 'There were once two friends who lived in Mahlomola, by the names of Ou Breench and Skeelie' (*AS*, p. 129).

Except for a few linguistically dense short stories like lo Liyong's 'Sages and Wages' (*F*, pp. 11–20), Deressa's 'Opaque Shadows' (*MMAS*, pp. 132–43) and Marechera's 'Protista' (*ASS*, pp. 130–6), the language of African short stories takes after the simplicity of the folk-tale. Also, following the tradition of the folk-tale, the modern African short story is seldom merely for entertainment but generally has a didactic intention.

Both in language[16] and in plot (except for a few stories with fabulous plots), the objective of the authors of African short stories is to create the illusion of reality. Similarly, language is employed to present character, setting and other details in the story realistically. Indeed, the tendency to create realistic stories has led some writers into producing naturalistic fiction and sociological, journalistic documentations that do not seriously qualify as short stories. This tendency is noticeable in many stories by Gordimer and Head. It is also prominent in individual stories by other writers. Some examples are Omotoso's 'Isaac' (*M*, pp. 35–42), Katema's 'The Baby' (*VOZ*, pp. 134–41), Liswaniso's 'The Mystery of the Metal' (*VOZ*, pp. 51–6), Setuke's 'Dumani' (*AS*, pp. 58–68), Matshoba's 'To Kill a Man's Pride' (*AS*, pp. 103–27) and Sepamla's 'King Taylor' (*AS*, pp. 80–91).

What has not been adequately discussed, however, is the attempt by some African writers to transcend realism through modernist linguistic experimentation. The tendency to adopt the fabulous plot of folklore, already discussed, is one obvious example of transcending realism.

Aidoo's experiments with narration, also discussed above, should similarly be seen as an attempt to improve upon the methods of realism. The capturing of two concurrent realities – the official interrogation and thoughts of the hero – which leads to an unusual textual arrangement at the beginning and end of Kunene's 'The Spring of Life' (AC, pp. 54–86) is also an obvious improvement on the traditional mode of registering reality in realistic stories. Marechera's 'Protista' (ASS, pp. 130–6) very strongly resembles existentialist and surrealist fiction of the West. In 'The Journey Home' (ND, pp. 94–108), Zeleza is obviously trying to make his form reflect his content. He is presenting a confused, forgetful character and so he makes his style a verbose, digressive, comic rigmarole. The cynically ironic tone of narration in Gurnah's 'Bossy' (ASS, pp. 49–60) goes beyond the propriety of realism. So does the dense symbolic language of Kibera's 'The Spider's Web'. Also the studied casualness of the style of Serote's 'Let's Wander Together' (EW, pp. 160–3) and this story's plotlessness and narration sustained almost wholly by colloquialism and slang are signs of its modernism. And Deressa's 'Opaque Shadows' (MMAS, pp. 132–43) with its existentialist characters and dense language certainly has gone a step beyond realism.

However, the most consistently modernist of our short-story writers is Taban lo Liyong, who is in fact a post-modernist artist. I have analysed elsewhere his absurdist language and stylistic techniques; it remains only to restate here without again going into details that his collection, The Uniformed Man, will make a lot more sense if read as a parody of modernist techniques. For instance, he uses the story, 'Project X' (UM, pp. 36–46), to parody the modernist minimal story. His excessive use of digressions and allusions are a parody of these techniques as used by modernist writers. His over-familiarity with, and almost insulting attitude to, the reader, the almost pornographic breaking of taboos with regard to sex, and the over-assertion of his over-confident ego in the stories must be seen in the same parodic light.[17]

Undoubtedly, the single most prominent aspect of the language of African short stories is irony, which is verbal (rhetorical), situational or structural in character. Irony in African stories is not merely a device to elicit humour for a good laugh but also an instrument to ensure aesthetic balance in stories whose emotional content is otherwise too tragic. The shocking revelation, for instance, that peacetime in post-civil-war Nigeria was far more dangerous to life and property than the period of the civil war itself is emotionally cushioned by a generous use of verbal and situational ironies to produce laughter in Achebe's story 'Civil Peace' (ASS, pp. 29–34). The stories about the inhumanities of apartheid would have been too emotionally sapping to read because of their tragic realities but for the generous sprinkling of the various types of irony in those stories. In fact, not only does irony help to restore emotional balance in stories like Jacky Heyns's 'Our Last Fling', Obed Musi's 'Cops Ain't What They Used to Be' (AS, pp. 180–6) and Casey Motsisi's 'Sketches of South African Life' (MASF, pp. 124–8), it is doubtful if these works would have qualified to graduate from the category of mere sociological jottings to the status of the short story but for their use of irony. Thus, irony constitutes the 'art' in these stories. To fully appreciate how irony transforms a mere gathering of sociological details into a narration which yields positive aesthetic pleasure, one has to read Moteane Melamu's ironically humorous presentation of the tragedy of an unhappy marriage in 'Bad Times, Sad Times' (AS, pp. 41–53).

In the best of African stories, irony goes beyond ensuring aesthetic satisfaction to becoming the medium for making fundamental philosophical statements about life. Achebe uses a subtle play of ironies in his story 'The Madman' to cast doubts on our ability to accurately perceive reality and also to suggest thereby a more humane treatment of the madman and the other unfortunate members of the society since, often, society is itself the root-cause of their misfortunes.[18] Similarly, it is the deft application of irony which enables Alex la Guma to indirectly suggest in 'A Matter of Taste' (WN, pp. 125–30) that the only solution to apartheid is the restoration in South Africa of the principle of the good neighbour as advanced in Christ's parable of the Good Samaritan whereby human beings are urged to treat one another, irrespective of race and colour, as each other's keepers.

To conclude, the African short story in English is linguistically competent. And this is because its authors have meticulously obeyed the demands of the genre for economy and scrupulous, almost poetic, discipline over diction and syntax. The English language of the best stories is authentically African in tone; and narration, which is often informed by folklore, rises at times to the level of poetry through imaginative adaptation of the devices of poetry. The art of narration, which is also enhanced by dialogue, is generally simple and realistic, though it is frequently heightened by irony and modernist experiments in the hands of the best writers.

NOTES AND REFERENCES

1. The texts used for this study are the following short stories in English from Africa South of the Sahara. For the purposes of convenience, title abbreviations in parentheses will be used in the body of the essay and the notes.
   A: Multiple-author anthologies
      – E.N. Obiechina, ed., *African Creations*, Enugu, Fourth Dimension Publishing Co., 1982, 1985 – (AC).
      – Mothobi Mutloatse, ed., *Africa South: Contemporary Writings*, London, Heinemann, 1980, 1981 – (AS).
      – Chinua Achebe and C.L. Innes, eds., *African Short Stories*, London, Heinemann, 1985 – (ASS).
      – Stephen Gray, ed., *On the Edge of the World*, Johannesburg, Ad. Donker/Publisher, 1974 – (EW).
      – Charles R. Larson, ed., *Modern African Stories*, Glasgow, Fontana/Collins, 1970, 1976 – (MAS).

- Ellis Ayitey Komey and Ezekiel Mphahlele, eds., *Modern African Stories*, London, Faber and Faber, 1964, 1977 – (*MASF*).
- Charles R. Larson, ed., *More Modern African Stories*, Glasgow, Fontana/Collins, 1975 – (*MMAS*).
- Barbara Nolen, ed., *More Voices of Africa*, Glasgow, Fontana/Collins, 1972, 1975 – (*MVA*).
- Neville Denny, ed., *Pan African Short Stories*, London, Nelson, 1965, 1967 – (*PASS*).
- Richard Rive, ed., *Quartet: New Voices from South Africa*, London, Heinemann, 1963, 1977 – (*Q*).
- Paul A. Scanlon, ed., *Stories from Central and Southern Africa*, London, Heinemann, 1983 – (*SCSA*).
- Mufalo Liswaniso, ed., *Voices of Zambia*, Lusaka, National Educational Company of Zambia Limited, 1971 – (*VOZ*).
B: Single-author collections
- Bessie Head, *The Collector of Treasures*, London, Heinemann, 1977 – (*CT*).
- Alan Paton, *Debbie Go Home*, Harmondsworth, Penguin, 1961, 1979 – (*DGH*).
- Taban lo Liyong, *Fixions*, London, Heinemann, 1969, 1978 – (*F*).
- Chinua Achebe, *Girls At War and Other Stories*, London, Heinemann, 1972, 1978 – (*GAW*).
- Cyprian Ekwensi, *Lokotown and Other Stories*, London, Heinemann, 1966, 1975 – (*LT*).
- Kole Omotoso, *Miracles and Other Stories*, Ibadan, Onibonoje Publishers (Nigeria), 1973, 1978 – (*M*).
- Paul Zeleza, *Night of Darkness and Other Stories*, Limbe, Malawi, Popular Publications, 1976 – (*ND*).
- Ama Ata Aidoo, *No Sweetness Here*, London, Longman, 1970, 1972 – (*NSH*).
- Cyprian Ekwensi, *Restless City and Christmas Gold*, London, Heinemann, 1975 – (*RC*).
- Kofi Aidoo, *Saworbeng*, Tema, Ghana Publishing Corporation, 1977 – (*S*).
- Ngugi wa Thiong'o, *Secret Lives*, London, Heinemann, 1975 – (*SL*).
- Nadine Gordimer, *Some Monday For Sure*, London, Heinemann, 1976 – (*SMFS*).
- Sembene Ousmane, *Tribal Scars*, London, Heinemann, 1962, 1974 – (*TS*).
- Taban lo Liyong, *The Uniformed Man*, Nairobi, East African Literature Bureau, 1971 – (*UM*).
- Can Themba, *The Will To Die*, London, Heinemann, 1972, 1978 – (*WD*).
- Alex la Guma, *A Walk in the Night*, London, Heinemann, 1962, 1977 – (*WN*).
- I.N.C. Aniebo, *Of Wives, Talismans and the Dead*, London, Heinemann, 1983 – (*WTD*).
2. Hallie Burnett quoting Anatole Broyard in *On Writing the Short Story*, New York, Harper & Row, 1983, p. 46.
3. Ibid, pp. 46–7.
4. Ibid, p. 72.
5. Anna Rutherford, 'Cyprian Ekwensi', in *Cowries and Kobos*, ed. K.H. Petersen and A. Rutherford, Mundelstrup, Denmark, Dangaroo Press, 1981, p. 65.
6. Komey and Mphahlele, 'Introduction', *MASF*, p. 11.
7. Helen Chukwuma, 'The Prose of Neglect', paper presented at the Third Ibadan Annual African Literature Conference, 10–14 July 1978, p. 23.
8. Komey and Mphahlele, 'Introduction', *MASF*, p. 12.

9. This is one of the more serious faults Jack B. Moore's review finds in Easmon's collection, The Feud (African Literature Today, no. 14, 1984, pp. 152-4).

10. The novelist, Manuel Komroff, is quoted as having said that he always took care to prevent his prose from resembling poetry (Burnett, op. cit., p. 46).

11. Editorial comments in Cowries and Kobos, op. cit., p. 10.

12. Kirsten Holst Petersen, 'The short story', in Cowries and Kobos, op. cit., p. 62.

13. The following critics among many have affirmed the common heritage of the oral tale and the short story: Chinua Achebe, 'Introduction', ASS, p. ix; Eileen Julien, 'Of traditional tales and short stories', in Toward Defining the African Aesthetic, ed. L.A. Johnson, B. Cailler et al., Washington, DC, Three Continents Press, 1982, pp. 83-93; Carolyn Parker, 'A Swahili proverb story', in Artist and Audience: African Literature as a Shared Experience, ed. Richard O. Priebe and Thomas A. Hale, Washington, DC, Three Continents Press, 1979, pp. 55, 57; Helen Chukwuma, 'The Prose of Neglect', op. cit., p. 20; Charles R. Larson, 'Introduction', MAS, p. 7; Philip A. Noss, 'Creation and the Ghaya tale', in Artist and Audience, op. cit., pp. 3, 13, 15, 17-18.

14. It would be equally incorrect not to distinguish between the folk-tale and the short story as different genres; but, certainly, what they share in common far outweighs what separates them. All the articles cited in note 13 show an awareness of the futility of either totally divorcing or totally merging the two related genres.

15. For Elizabeth Knight 's excellent discussion of lo Liyong's modernist-folklorist style see: 'Taban lo Liyong's narrative art', African Literature Today, no. 12, 1982, pp. 104-17. It must be pointed out, however, that E. Knight underrated the achievements of Taban in respect of some of the stories in The Uniformed Man because she read them literally and not as parodic satires on modernism-post-modernism.

16. For example, Stephen Gray, 'Introduction', EW, p. 11, and Paul A. Scanlon, 'Introduction', SCSA, p. 2.

17. An elaborate discussion of the elements of Taban's parody of modernism is presented in my paper 'Taban lo Liyong's The Uniformed Man: A reconstructivist and metafictional parody of modernism', forthcoming in Language and Style and included as chapter twelve in Tradition and Modernity in the African Short Story, forthcoming.

18. My discussion of the ironies in Achebe's story 'The Madman' is in Okike, vol. 23, 1983, pp. 72-9. It has also been incorporated as chapter eight into Tradition and Modernity in the African Short Story, which also analyses the structural pattern of irony in African short stories as a whole in chapter four.

Language, Ideology, Desire: Rereading Soyinka's *The Road*

Simon Gikandi

Of all Soyinka's works, none seems to present as many 'difficulties' of reading as *The Road*. The play's problem of elucidation has been commented on by critics writing from all sorts of backgrounds: they all seem to agree that its difficulties have to do with language and Soyinka's apparent failure to 'communicate'. As Susan Yankowitz put it succinctly when the play was first published in 1966, *The Road* fails to rise beyond its symbolic level to communicate its meaning, and 'it becomes bogged down in a slough of cabalistic metaphors, unexplained actions, and verbiage'.[1] But why do we demand that a work of art, especially a play on stage, should readily yield meaning to us, or, more specifically, communicate, open up a dialogue with its audience? Isn't it possible for a play to have meaning without communicating directly with its readers or viewers? To answer this question affirmatively, as I hope to do in this essay, we must question certain established notions about reading and language.

In fact, we must begin by questioning some key assumptions underlying linguistic criticism, not least its preoccupation with the laws that govern language use. This concern with laws of language, and linguistic systems in general, has provided common ground for many students of poetics, ranging from the Russian formalists to the structuralists. Thus, as Sunday Anozie has noted, two assumptions underlie the structural-linguistic method:

> The first is the realization that a poetic work contains a system of ordered variants which can be isolated and represented vertically in the form of superimposed levels, such as phonology, phonetic, syntactic, prosodic and semantic. The second is that modern structuralism – especially in the form of its offshoot, generative grammar – provides an adequate theory and method for accounting for such levels and in dealing with the internal coherence of the given work of art.[2]

The analysis of literary forms is hence oriented toward the differentiation of linguistic structures and their subsequent reconstruction into systems of meaning. The reading of a play like *The Road* would, for example, involve, the correlation of what D.S. Izevbaye has termed 'message and method', assuming, I think, that, if we can restore the balance between form and content, we can appreciate the importance of communication in the play, 'not in the sense of something immediately and wholly understood, but in the sense of a play which satisfies our sense of dramatic rightness'.[3]

Izevbaye's need to redefine what constitutes 'communication' is a good indication of the problems we encounter as soon as we seek logical laws in a work of art. A very questionable notion underlies this isolation and reconstitution of linguistic codes and norms – the general belief that the dramatic form requires 'direct and instant communication with an audience'.[4] The theoretical background to this contention is most likely Jakobson's description of the six functional aspects of language as follows:[5]

	Context	
Addresser (A)	Message	Addressee (B)
	Contact	
	Code	

However, communication does not become direct simply because of the comprehensibility of the message sent from point A to B; the analysis of poetic language seems to depend on the critics' or interlocutors' ability to explain the value and importance of linguistic codes within a hierarchical system. Thus Izevbaye isolates certain words in *The Road* as more valuable than others, and then proceeds to develop a hierarchy of usage in which Professor's language seems to be more important to our understanding of the play, and to carry more weight, than that of the other characters. The implication then, is that, if the readers can decode Professor's words, they will have made sense of the play. By extension, to make sense of the play is to account for most of its 'important' words, to develop them into a comprehensible and explicable system of meaning. Thus the mystical 'Word' must be accounted for at every state of the subject's quest, even though, as I hope to show below, it has no determinate meaning.[6]

This desire to rationalize the actions of the literary subject epistemologically, and to unify linguistic codes and structures into one determinate system of meanings, is a major limitation of traditional linguistic criticism. For if we assume that we can fix and classify the language used by characters in a text, and explain it in terms of relationships without questioning the basis on which such relationships are founded, then we are reproducing the world of such characters as if it were natural and innately true. In a play, for example, a reading that aims at overcoming ambiguities and rationalizing deviations is in danger of smothering the very conflicts and tensions which created the dramatic situation, since such conflicts are manifested in language. In fact, I don't think we can study language systems as units of discourse which have only one single meaning, for the very rules that establish the linguistic system reflect the relations of power in the represented situation. To the extent that power is, among other things, the ability to create or determine meaning, the stage is the space in which social relationships (of domination and resistance) are represented or textualized through language. As I hope to show in the following rereading of *The Road*, language is not a natural system of explicable codes, but an arbitrary manifestation of the subject's ideology and desire.[7]

Professor's Word

There is no doubt that *The Road* is a play about language. But what kind of language is Soyinka dealing with? This is a simple question, but language is such a complex system of significations, that every writer must of necessity define the nature of the language he uses.[8] In Soyinka's words, 'language does not operate simply as communication but as matrices of discrete activities including, of course, those of articulation and meaning'.[9] I will deal with the discrete nature of language in a moment, but let me reflect first on the question of articulation and meaning. Professor's vocation is primarily to articulate the unknowable, to interpret the sign to his audience, to rationalize the ineffable. 'I have a new wonder to show you,' he tells Kotonou at the beginning of the play; but for Samson, the man of ordinary language, what Professor posits as wonder, or mystery, can be explained simply as an accident. But is it? Not in Professor's view: 'Are you that ignorant of the true path to the Word?' he wonders. 'It is never an accident.'[10] Who is right? The moment we ask this question, we are confronted by the conflict of interpretations which gives the play its *coup de théâtre*. For what Professor is claiming is a certain privilege as an interpreter, which involves a change in conventional language and challenges the cognitive process. In questioning Samson's right to know and understand the familiar, Professor is also questioning the value we assume that phenomena have on their own. The true meaning of such phenomena is only accessible to Samson through competent speakers, like Professor, who claim to have access to a certain kind of truth. Thus, in reacting to Samson's rather hostile attempt to question his privilege as an interpreter, Professor falls back on the authoritative (in his view) language of religion, which bestows a whole new meaning to the objects of discourse:

> My bed is among the dead, and when the road raises a victory to break my sleep I hurry to a disgruntled swarm of souls full of spite for their rejected bodies . . . you shall be shown the truth of my endeavours. (p. 11)

Within the confines of ordinary language, Professor wouldn't claim to have more knowledge of the road than Samson, the master tout; but, in the area of the supernatural, he is the local specialist.

As a specialist, Professor's quest for the meaning of phenomena is confounded by his determination to represent everything as a mystery. When things are perceived as mysteries, they cannot yield meanings on their own, and must hence be verbalized by a subject to be accessible to us. In this respect, the act of interpretation is also one of representation, for only those who have penetrated the heart of phenomena seem, in Professor's scheme at least, to have the right to re-present reality. In fact, Professor owes his central position in the play to his ability, or claim, to have language to represent everything. In contrast, Samson, the would-be man of the road, is handicapped by his inability to represent anything but that which demands ordinary language. So when Kotonou, on his way to the scene of the latest wreckage, says he is going on a business trip, Samson's response is one of bafflement: 'That is a funny way to talk about a thing like that' (p. 12). And soon after, when Salubi informs him that Kotonou has taken the store over from Burma, Samson can only wonder: 'How could it happen and I not know about it?' (p. 13).

The question, however, is not merely one of seeing or not knowing, as Salubi suggests; it is a question of how certain acts acquire different meanings for certain characters. These differences are inscribed in language. Thus the meaning of words is closely related, and is determined, by the acts they rationalize or motivate. If words precede phenomena, they are motivational; they prefigure what is to happen. We see this happening in Professor's relationship with Kotonou: he exposes the latter to the very accidents that have scared him off the road, and in the process not only succeeds in having the driver as his storekeeper, but also acquires his licence, which he later sells to Salubi. The rationalizational function of language, on the other hand, always comes after the act, so to speak. But it is crucial to Professor's ideology of the road because his desire is to have all phenomena fit into one coherent whole which can be signified by a master code – the Word. For this reason, words acquire their significance only in terms of their articulation; hence the conflict of representation which underlies the dramatic situation.

Take, for example, the opening of Part Two of the play:

> I need a statement form. Here is one . . . now you tell me, you who return empty-handed and empty-minded, what do I write, what do I write? What happened at the bridge? (p. 55)

A statement authenticates what happened with the authority of the eyewitness: it is, as it were, transparent, constituted by the surface language of what was seen – the nothing-but-the-truth of legality. But for Professor, who is seeking the truth of his 'endeavours', the merely descriptive eyewitness account will not do. For the statement is not intended to get Samson and Kotonou off the hook, but to serve as a means of probing the meaning of the unconscious mind – what happened 'before the event' (p. 56). Can the mind be accessory to the event before it happens? Can what happened in the conscious mind before the event acquire meaning without verbalization? Apparently not: as the differing accounts of the accident show, the act of verbalization always re-creates the events anew (p. 58).

Thus, if phenomena in the play are what characters make them be, there is no basis for reconstructing a metaphysical system in which we can read Professor's words and gestures as anything more than distortions. If anything, his pseudo-religious language conceals his whole indifference to the human tragedy around him as he strives to seek meaning beyond the human and humane. Indeed, the play provides the terms by which we as readers can undermine Professor's claim to proper representation. For one thing, we can see how the system of meaning he is reconstructing is dependent as much on an acknowledgement of the realities around him as on a cunning refusal to be sensitive to that which might threaten his image: the visit to the site of the latest accident is hence portrayed as a theological quest, but not as a 'business' trip. Where the 'business' element is acknowledged, it is conveniently coupled with the more acceptable metaphysical quest; thus, in chiding Samson for not bringing loot from the wreckage, Professor speaks as if the spare parts were an integral part of his spiritual strivings: 'You neglect my needs and you neglect the quest' (p. 55). By the same token, he represents the shop as the thing that 'sustains our souls and feeds our bodies' (p. 55). A rereading of the play must hence undermine Professor's attempt to present himself as what he is not by exposing the deceptive nature of his language.

Nowhere is this deception more apparent than in the quest for the Word itself. Those critics of the play who adduce some profound meaning to the quest and accord the Word some ultimate, logical meaning, are them-selves victims of a deception which, fortunately, doesn't seem to affect audiences in the theatre.[11] To avoid falling into this trap, we must begin by acknowledging the fact that Professor does not precisely know what he is seeking; he is involved in a continuous process of defining and redefining the thing that he seeks, more familiar with his desires and motives than his goals. At the beginning of the play, for instance, we see him touting the road sign as a possible signification of the Word, but he is also aware of the arbitrariness of his quest: there is a 'new discovery every hour' (p. 8), and 'anything is possible when I pursue the Word' (p. 9). As the play progresses, we begin to realize that the Word has no fixed meaning; it acquires meaning subjectively, in selective situations, when the subject needs to rationalize his actions. Thus, when his interest turns to Samson's investments, Professor shifts the depository of the Word: whereas earlier he had declared that it was to be found 'companion not to life, but Death', now he says that 'the Word is a living word, not a grave-robber's prayer of appeasement' (p. 40). Whereas before he had promised Samson sanctuary in 'my tower of words', Professor now concedes that he has not yet found the Word, even as he threatens 'to unleash its elemental truths on [Samson's] head' (p. 63).

Professor's notion of the Word is hence tied to momentary needs. The Word cannot be reduced to a single meaning because the path that leads to it is full of turns and twists, and the quester must always be sensitive to the possibility of error. Hence his struggle with ambiguities: recalling his days of evangelical fervour, the subject notes that 'the Word is a terrible fire and we burned [the sinners] by the ear. Only that was not the Word you see, oh no, it was not' (p. 68); and yet he still believes that the Word is in the church, held over the bronze eagle. This mixture of doubt and certainty shakes the credibility of Professor's reliability as a quester: is the Word signified by 'the brazen image' of the eagle (p. 69), or does it defy singular definitions (p. 85)? If the Word signified by the eagle is, like all 'single words', an illusion, why is Professor still attached to it? The Word represents a desire which cannot be fulfilled – the quest for a final truth. And, as Professor wonders in moments of reflection, what, indeed, is the Truth? 'Truth my friend, is scum risen on the froth of wine' (p. 70). Or, as Soyinka has aptly observed, what Professor is trying to do is explicate a *Weltanschauung* from a metaphysical system which is rooted 'more in the very indeterminancy of Truth than upon categorical certitudes'.[12]

Language as Ideology

Although we cannot have any determinate meaning for the Word, we can come to a closer understanding of language in the play through its functions, especially its representation of relations of power. It is through verbal representations that some subjects establish their domination over others. Or, as Barthes has put it more aptly, 'Language is legislation, speech is its code.'[13] Professor seems only too aware of this, for, even when his quest is questionable, he knows that the difference between him and the others is in his mastery of language and the knowledge that comes with this mastery: the layabouts have become dependent on him as the man who forges their documents and writes their statements; in the process, they have become subjugated to his ideology – what he calls 'the course I have drawn for you' (p. 51). Thus, within the political economy of the play, Professor has been designated the intellectual; the rest are manual labourers. The function of this intellectual is, ostensibly, to explain phenomena to those who have no power to probe the mystical, but, in reality, language as ideology is both an instrument of legitimizing the existing relationships of domination, and of concealing the social origins of the conflicts we see on stage. In this respect, the language Professor uses in the few moments when he engages in a real dialogue with the layabouts is a reproduction of the words which have been institutionalized by the hegemonic culture to rationalize exploitation and domination.

Thus, when Samson goes to Professor in search of advice, the latter wants to know whether this is 'a consultation'; within the political economy of signs, 'advice' is given freely, but a 'consultation' is paid for (p. 38). Professor's 'consultation' also tends to be couched in language which, instead of enlightening his students about phenomena, reproduces their false consciousness. Thus the Word can be used as an instrument to put Salubi back in line: 'May the elusive Word crack your bones in a hundred splinters!' (p. 41); the apprentice is not in a position to question Professor's ability to actualize his threat, having assumed that his illiteracy makes that knowledge inaccessible. Similarly, Say Tokyo Kid's uneasiness with the Professor has nothing to do with any real powers the lay reader may have; the curse embodies the unknown, which is powerful precisely because it cannot be decoded. As the thug says to Salubi later in the play, 'Do you want to go blind from things you shouldn't see?' (p. 94).

As part of the discourse of power, the curse 'engenders blame, hence guilt, in its recipient'.[14]

Consequently, the very words whose meaningfulness we have denied Professor constitute his state apparatus; the other agents do not have the verbal power to launch a *coup d'état* against this machine of words. The layabouts cannot demystify Professor's language. Indeed, Samson is right on the mark when he observes that Professor's words always 'mislead a man' and that he is 'a very confusing person' (p. 63). This confusion, I would like to suggest, is the Professor's instrument of exploitation in the sense that it is only by defining and redefining the terms of his relationship with the others that he can delude them about their true interest, the prelude to domination. Take, for instance, the manner in which he expropriates Kotonou's licence: he does not portray this as an act of exploitation, but as a 'solution, a compensation, a redress, a balance of inequalities' (p. 46). The words suggest an equitable act, concealing the simple fact that Professor is the major beneficiary of the transaction. Samson does see through this charade up to a point, but Professor again falls back on language to try and confuse the other's interests: first, the lay reader tries to convince the tout that he and his mate can survive without a driving licence by finding the Word; when this fails, he reminds Samson that he has already worked his spell on Kotonou. By taking the driver to the site of the latest accident, Professor has frightened him off the road for ever: 'there, as the blood and the waste clung to his feet, I knew him. And I tell you, before my eyes, he was touched' (p. 47). To the extent that this kind of language is burdened with the material interests it serves, it is 'practical consciousness'.[15]

Language, Ideology, Desire

But ideology does not always inscribe itself through conscious acts. The relationships of domination which ideology engenders, the set of images and myths carried by language, and the structures of meaning imposed on the layabouts by Professor and the hegemonic culture are as imaginary as they are real.[16] Indeed, one of the central conflicts in *The Road* is between the real and the imaginary, between what the characters are and what they would like to be. Salubi would like to be 'a private driver', but he does not have the licence to drive; Samson would like to see himself as the champion tout, but his self-image has been thwarted by Kotonou's refusal to go back on the road. Thus the way these characters represent themselves is determined as much by their concrete realities (and the consciousness it develops) as by the gap between their needs and demands.[17] Needs which cannot be fulfilled in reality are recreated in language, either as fantasies or as enactments of collective social myths. Thus, as a would-be millionaire, Samson imitates the hegemonic culture and some key aspects of the ideology of capitalism: his imagined situation is one in which human relationships are determined by money ('man wey get money get power') and the forces of coercion (pp. 6–7).

However, the widest gap between needs and demands is in Professor.

His 'abracadabra' with spirits is a manifestation of his desire to enter into a kind of communion with the invisible, and to overcome the gap between the known world of the living and the unknown world of the dead. A greater desire, however, is the desire for authority, a kind of legitimation in the world of ordinary experience. To understand this desire and its centrality in the play, we must turn our attention to what Professor lacks, for desire, as the expression of demand, is always signified in the negative. According to Samson, Professor's conflict with his rival, the bishop, had to do with the former's authority to preach (i.e. to have the exclusive right to explain phenomena), which in the Anglican faith is designated by the BD:

> In fact everybody always said that Professor ought to preach the sermons but a joke is a joke, I mean, the man is not ordained. So we had to be satisfied with him reading the lesson and I'm telling you, three-quarters of the congregation only came to hear his voice. (p. 16)

His desire to have people to dominate through language (a congregation) having been frustrated by the bishop, who casts him out of the church, Professor proceeds to seek the authority of a Word which neutralizes the power of the BD: 'They cannot cast me out. I will live in the shadow of the fort. I will question the very walls for the hidden Word' (p. 44).

But as I have already suggested, there is something illogical about the character's determination to search for the Word in the place where it isn't – the bishop's church – even as he seeks it among the worshippers of Esu. Is Professor then covering all his flanks? or is he simply attached to the other, the Christian church, the source of his alienation? To answer these questions, we have to interrogate Professor, not so much as a knowing subject, one who can confer rational explanations on the unknown, but as a desiring subject, one who wants to reassure himself that his self-image can be imposed on structures of consciousness.

The desires of the subject are, of course, projected into fantasies and manifested in language. Professor's greatest fantasy arises from his desire to understand that which cannot be understood. In Murano, the mute, the quester had thought he had found a 'critical medium' of understanding the numinous territory of transition[18] – hence his confidence that the mute is 'the one person in this world in whom the Word reposes' (p. 44). But how can we be sure of Murano's function as a depository of the Word if his knowledge cannot be articulated in language? Professor's response to this question is not entirely convincing:

> Deep. Silent but deep. Oh my friend, beware the pity of those that have no tongue for they have been proclaimed sole guardians of the Word. They have slept beyond the portals of secrets. They have pierced the guard of eternity and unearthed the Word, a golden nugget on the tongue. And so their tongue hangs heavy and they are forever silenced. (p. 44)

This is a very neat explanation, but it is nothing more than an expression of the role Professor would like Murano to play. No one can really be certain about what Murano really represents; Professor admits as much when he characterizes the mute as 'A shadow in the valley of the shadow of!' - the incompleteness of the phrase suggests definitions which cannot be concluded. For, after Murano is struck by the vehicle, he loses consciousness and retains 'no further link to what he was or where he had been. That, that especially, where he had been' (p. 90).

Professor's desperation at this stage in the play arises from a keen realization that Murano is but a blank consciousness. The quester can only qualify this bitter knowledge with the hope that the mute's 'tongue . . . be released':

> And should I not hope, with him, to cheat, to anticipate the final confrontation, learning its nature baring its skulking face, why may I not understand . . . (p. 90)

'Hope' - a struggle against the reality of Murano's blankness and the finality of death: 'I must hope, even now,' Professor says as the play reaches its climax. 'I cannot yet believe that death's revelation must be total, or not at all' (p. 93). The reality that refuses to be suppressed is that Professor cannot cheat fear by 'foreknowledge' (p. 94). And, when at the end of the play he calls upon the layabouts to power their hands 'with the knowledge of death' (p. 96), he has acknowledged the failure of his quest. For what is death but 'pure silence, pure transcendence, not givable and not given in experience'?[19] And, if Professor cannot find the language to reconstruct the corpus of Ifa, on what authority can literary criticism reconstruct a system of meaning for this indeterminate text? I am not, of course, suggesting a denial of meaning to Soyinka's play. I am only saying that, instead of suppressing those things in *The Road* which do not cohere into one logical meaning, we should read the irrational, the negative and what is not known as 'the unseen motivating force behind the very deployment of meaning'.[20]

NOTES

1. 'The plays of Wole Soyinka', *African Forum*, vol. 1, 1966, p. 132.
2. 'Negritude, structuralism, deconstruction', in *Black Literature and Literary Theory*, ed. Henry Louis Gates, Jr, New York, Methuen, 1984, p. 106.
3. 'Language and meaning in Soyinka's *The Road*', in *Critical Perspectives on Wole Soyinka*, ed. James Gibbs, London, Heinemann, 1981, p. 91.
4. Ibid.
5. Roman Jakobson, 'Linguistics and poetics', in *The Structuralists: From Marx to Lévi-Strauss*, ed. Richard T. De George and Fernande M. De George, New York, Doubleday, 1972, p. 89.
6. Many studies of the play are really attempts to reconstruct Professor's metaphysical system and to accord it a cultural context. See, for example, Oyin Ogunba, *The Movement of Transition*, Ibadan, Ibadan University Press, 1975, p. 132.

7. The notion of arbitrary language underlies so-called deconstruction criticism. See, for example, Jacques Derrida, *Of Grammatology*, trans. Gayatri Chakravorty Spivak, Baltimore, Johns Hopkins University Press, 1976.

8. Although Soyinka has argued that what he aims for is 'operational totality' in the theatre, the language of his plays always registers the difference between the performance and audience. See 'Drama and the revolutionary ideal,' in *In Person: Achebe, Awoonor, and Soyinka*, ed. Karen L. Morell, Seattle, African Studies Program, 1975, p. 90.

9. 'The critic and society: Barthes, leftocracy and other mythologies', in *Black Literature*, op. cit., p. 28. Elsewhere, Soyinka has described language as a seemingly incoherent 'medium of possession'. See 'The choice and use of language', *Cultural Events in Africa*, no. 75, 1971, p. 3.

10. *The Road*, London, Oxford University Press, 1965. All further references made in the text are to this edition.

11. For a discussion of the Word within the Yoruba metaphysical system, see Abiola Irele, 'Tradition and the Yoruba writer', in *Critical Perspectives*, op. cit., p. 64; and J.A. Adedeji, 'Oral tradition and the contemporary theatre in Nigeria', *Research in African Literatures*, vol. 2, 1971, pp. 132–49.

12. See Soyinka's introduction to the 1984 Chicago production of *The Road* in *Stagebill*, April 1984, p. 15.

13. Roland Barthes, 'Inaugral Lecture', in *A Barthes Reader*, ed. Susan Sontag, New York, Hill and Wang, 1982, p. 460.

14. Ibid., p. 459.

15. Karl Marx and Frederick Engels, *The German Ideology*, quoted in *The Marx-Engels Reader*, ed. Robert C. Tucker, New York, W.W. Norton, 1978, p. 158.

16. Louis Althusser defines the concept of ideology, not as consciousness, but as an expression of real relations invested in the imaginary domain. See *For Marx*, trans. Ben Brewster, London, Allen, 1969, p. 233.

17. For a definition of need and demand in desire, see the translator's preface to Jacques Lacan's *Ecrits*, trans. Alan Sheridan, New York, W.W. Norton, 1977, p. viii.

18. *Stagebill*, April 1984, p. 15.

19. Gilles Deleuze and Felix Guattari, *Anti-Oedipus: Capitalism and Schizophrenia*, trans. Robert Hurley *et al.*, New York, Viking, 1977, p. 332.

20. Barbara Johnson, *The Critical Difference*, Baltimore, Johns Hopkins University Press, 1980, p. xii.

Theme & Language in Soyinka's *Madmen & Specialists*

Obi Maduakor

Madmen and Specialists (1971) is the most puzzling, the most challenging and the most elusive of all the plays in which Soyinka has made use of the expressionistic technique as his basic dramatic method. This technique is used in *The Road* (1965) and *Kongi's Harvest* (1967), but the method is most demanding and burdensome in *Madmen and Specialists*. In the expressionistic method, the conventional structure of drama is dissolved into tableaux; the scene is symbolic and not defined in terms of place or time; the characters are not fully individuated but stand as the representative mouthpieces of ideas, emotions and concepts. Nothing is named or explained directly but only hinted at through allusion or insinuation.[1] In an early review of the play, Susan Yankowitz noted that theme replaces plot as the dynamic of the play and characters are sketched rather than fully developed.[2] The play dispenses with Soyinka's favourite technique, the flashback, whereby what has been hinted at might be 'replayed' in retrospect. Pessimism and cynicism have been nurtured to a point in both Soyinka himself and the characters where discussion and meaningful exchange are thought to be unnecessary. Dialogue is esoteric and cryptic, and comprehensible only to the initiate; words reach down to a second unspoken reality which is more potent than the surface meaning. That tendency in modernist drama defined by John Fletcher and James Mcfarlane as the 'aesthetic of silence'[3] has here been stretched to its limit. Who is Old Man? What was he before the war and what did he do at the front? What is the place constantly referred to as 'out there' and 'the other place'? Who are the people referred to as 'they' and as 'faces'? What is meant by 'As'? And where are all these things happening?

The play contains answers to all these questions and herein lies Soyinka's skill as a dramatist – that his plays are self-contained units operating consistently and logically within the ambit of their own universe – but at no point in the play are these answers provided by direct exposition. What we know of the characters' past and of their present roles comes to us in flashes from their casual exchanges and jokes.

Madmen and Specialists is one of those works in which Soyinka has continued to communicate his reaction to social anomy. This reaction began with the October poems of his first verse collection, *Idanre and Other Poems* (1967), in which he mourned the casualties of the social upheavals of 1966. There were at least two military coups in Nigeria during that year. The coups and counter-coups entrenched military dictatorship in Nigeria after it had inflicted a civil war on the country. To Soyinka, the period of military dictatorship and of the civil war will always remain Nigeria's darkest moment. He was critical of the abuse of power and privileges during the era of civilian administration, but those abuses attained an unprecedented climax in the military era. He also suffered personal humiliation under the military, being imprisoned in August 1967 for his effort to organize a third movement which would have taken advantage of the weakening of the power base in the federal structure during the war years to stage a socialist-oriented military coup. Old Man in *Madmen and Specialists* is Soyinka's *alter ego* reacting against the power sadism of military dictatorship in the Nigeria of the war and post-war periods. His counterparts are Ofeyi and the Dentist in *Season of Anomy* (1973). All three subvert the status quo but they differ in their methods. Ofeyi operates through moral conversion, the Dentist by guerrilla violence, and Old Man by cultivating the cult of the absurd, which manifests itself through mockery, self-disgust and cynicism.

Old Man's term for his own method is As. He has formulated its philosophy and has so indoctrinated his followers with its basic principles that their feelings, their psychology and their utterances are permeated by As. This essay discusses the philosophy of As as the play's central theme and the dramatist's engineering of the resources of language to back it up.

The philosophy of As

The meaning of As need not create any problem. What it stands for is unequivocally enunciated by Dr Bero himself. As is the ability to bend nature to one's will (p. 237).[4] But even if Dr Bero had not afforded us this insight, the Mendicants are there to help us. Throughout the play, they do nothing else than demonstrate through parody the method of As. Old Man is evasive all along but at the end of the play he throws off his ironic mask and wants indeed to *demonstrate* by practical example the way As actually operates. 'Let us taste just what makes a heretic tick', says Old Man. That is the voice of As, the language of its agents. As is the radical excision of the cysts that obstruct the efficient working of a socio-political system. In the republic of As, all those who dare to raise a voice of protest against the system are heretics who must be guillotined at the altar of As. That is the lesson to be derived from Old Man's determination to operate upon (the current parlance in the play is 'practise') the Cripple who insisted on being *heard*. Old Man's gesture is a parody which nearly spills over into actuality through his excessive reaction to As as a machinery of oppression. We should see his action as the climax of all the antics in the play that burlesque the method of As.

As is not really a new concept in Soyinka. His works constitute themselves into one long protest against As in its various manifestations. The warrior in *A Dance of the Forests* (1963) who was sold into slavery and was later murdered because he would not fight an unjust war was a victim of As. Eman in *The Strong Breed* (1964), himself a burnt offering on the altar of custom, is a victim of 'sociologic' As. Prophet Jeroboam in the Jero plays has perfected all strategies for making his converts victims of the religious As. *Kongi's Harvest* is one more critique of political As. It is in *Madmen and Specialists*, however, that As has become an over-riding theme. In this particular play, As protects the group interest of a military cartel which Soyinka has called the 'alliance of a corrupt militarism and a rapacious Mafia'.[5] Dr Bero, a one-time medical practitioner now turned military intelligence officer, represents the military wing of the alliance. In Chief Batoki and Zaki Amuri of *Season of Anomy* Soyinka presents the civilian arm of the alliance. *Madmen and Specialists* concentrates on the operations of the military wing of the alliance, just as *Season of Anomy* focuses on the tactics of the civilian power elite. The antics of the new *arrivistes* to power in the bid to perpetuate their positions are identical in both works. Old Man sees through it all and refuses to be deceived like the rest of neglected humanity. As is his pet name for the cartel itself and its tactics. It stands for all forms of dictatorship, oppression, exploitation, injustice, blind pursuit of self-interest, opportunistic expendiency and other social ills.

Old Man's disciples are the Mendicants, whom he elevates above their station by letting them share his insights into human nature. After their indoctrination, the Mendicants begin to *think* and to rationalize. Even the blind ones among them are made to see through human nature with their mind's eye. Blindman, speaking of his own brainwashing, recalls one of his conversations with Old Man:

> You can see me, he said, you can see me. Look at me with your mind. I swear I began to see him. Then I knew I was insane. (p. 243)

Old Man's constant target during his numerous As sessions with the Mendicants is the gimmickry of political power elites. Election manifestos and political speeches are empty words. Behind this political rhetoric languish the real victims, the suffering humanity who choke in silence – the 'underdog', the 'Us' the Dentist talks about in *Season of Anomy*.[6] Old Man's doctrines are extremely popular with the Mendicants. Their mangled bodies are, after all, living testimonies of the reality of As. Old Man's philosophy has helped them to turn their attention away from their misfortunes on to society itself. They scorn self-pity and convert what otherwise would have become a self-destroying disgust with the self into a disgust with society itself. At one point in the play the Mendicants mimic the antics of military dictators who promise all too often to relinquish power if the people so desire but go behind the scenes to stage-manage a vote of confidence for themselves. Aafaa, assuming the role of a military chief executive, intones:

> If there is any one who does not approve us, just say so and we quit. I mean we are not here because we like it. We stay at immense sacrifice to ourselves, our leisure, our desires, vocations, specializations, et cetera. et cetera. (pp. 200–1).

The Mendicants demonstrate the operation of the judicial system in an As regime. Accusations are concocted against a chosen victim, who is subjected to a mock trial. At the end of it all the victim, now a chastened man, is grateful to his tormentors. In the passage that follows, the victim is Goyi. The rest of the Mendicants substitute for Dr Bero and his aides:

AAFAA:	Did we try him?
CRIPPLE:	Resurrect, you fool. Nobody tried you yet.
AAFAA:	You are *accused.*
BLINDMAN:	Satisfied?
CRIPPLE:	Far enough.
BLINDMAN:	Bang!
	[*Goyi slumps*]
AAFAA [*rinsing his hands*]:	Nothing to do with me.
BLINDMAN:	Fair trial, no?
AAFAA:	Decidedly yes.
BLINDMAN:	What does he say himself?
GOYI:	Very fair, gentlemen. I have no complaints. (p. 200)

Because these parodies are not explicit, it is important that the reader should be made familiar with the decoded attributes of As. This need Aafaa satisfies in his alphabetical definition of As (see the section on language).

As has a long history. It was, is and ever shall be. Dr Bero aptly designates it as a god that is both new and old. The satire in the play is directed against the machinations of political As; but there are other forms of As. Old Man names these as scientific As, metaphysic As, sociologic As, the economic, recreative, ethical As (p. 271). The meaning of As changes slightly here from what it was at the beginning, that is, from the machinery of oppression, to the machinery of psychological exploitation: all creeds and dogmas that enslave the mind of man are born of As. This is also true of all excuses that justify man's violation of moral codes.

However, the main emphasis of As in the play is political. It is in the political context that As's relationship to cannibalism becomes immediately meaningful. As seizes human reason and forces man to slaughter his fellow men, thus providing As with its favourite dish, human flesh. Man's history is riddled with wars which have been fought for political ends, and, if so much slaughter is to be permitted all in the name of war, so goes Old Man's Swiftian logic, then we might as well legalize cannibalism. After all, Old Man says, 'all intelligent animals kill for food' (p. 254). The cannibalism theory is Old Man's protest against the senseless wastage of human lives in the name of war. It remains for him the logical conclusion to so much cruelty and inhumanity shown to man by man. Dr Bero, who himself has tasted human flesh, sees the very act as the end of all inhibitions, the conquest of the weakness of man's all too human flesh with all its sentiments. Cannibalism, then, is the ultimate goal of As. It was prophesied in *A Dance of the Forests*[7] that unborn generations would eat one another. That prophecy is painfully fulfilled in *Madmen*.

Old Man's use of As as a means of registering his protest against a corrupt establishment is ineffective, for in practical terms As, as we know it in *Madmen*, is the climax of cynicism and nihilism, the retreat of the ego into an obscure corner where what cannot be changed is ridiculed and mocked at. Soyinka's Marxist critics have denounced this kind of approach to the ills of society as being superficial, defeatist and negative. They charge Soyinka with diverting the revolutionary potentials inherent within the consciousness of the representatives of the masses in his works through ritual and mysticism rather than organizing those very potentials into active fighting forces for the improvement of human society. This tendency in Soyinka is best articulated by Lewis Nkosi in his *Tasks and Masks* (1982):

> Soyinka's greatest achievement has been to find theatrical forms and idioms varied enough to dramatize the frustrations of a certain group in African society; his weakness has been his constant striving after metaphysical formulas which merely mask these frustrations.[8]

Language

The play's most outstanding achievement lies in the area of language. Both Old Man and the Mendicants possess an immense facility for language. Their language is not always rhetorical as Professor's speeches in *The Road* but terse and cryptic and yet profound and far-reaching in its allusions. The ability to twist words into far-reaching nuances is not confined to Old Man but is a linguistic mannerism that is common to the Mendicants as a whole. They have perfected the art of double-talk, which they have learned from Old Man, have mastered his gift for poetry, his flair for verbal witticism and the ability to form new words out of the very core of existing ones.

Aafaa exploits the resourcefulness of his imagination in the attempt to relate As to the alphabet. His attempt stops at the letter *I* but that is no mean feat considering the poetry of the attempt and the appropriateness of its diction. *A* is acceptance: adjustment of the ego to the acceptance of As. *B* is blindness in As. As is all-seeing, all shall see in As who render themselves blind to all else. *C* is for contentment. *D* is for divinity, destiny and duty: destiny is the duty of divinity (d–d–d). *E* is for epilepsy, *F* for fulfilment and *G* for godhead: As is godhead. Aafaa is himself conscious of his power over words. By the time he comes to the letter *H* he is fully inspired. *H* is for humanity: humanity the ultimate sacrifice to As, the eternal oblation on the altar of As.

Aafaa distinguishes himself as the most accomplished acolyte of his master, Old Man. He calls himself 'the quickest of the underdogs' (p. 255). His verbal wit is at its most intensely sustained moment in the one long speech he makes near the end of the play on the history of ecclesiastical schisms:

> there was no hole in the monolithic solidarity of two halves of the priesthood. No, there was no division. The loyalty of homo sapiens regressed into himself, himself his little tick-tock self, self-ticking, self-tickling, self-tackling problems that belonged to the priesthood spiritual and political while they remained the sole and indivisible one. Oh! look at him, Monsieur l'homme sapiens, look at the

lone usurper of the ancient rights and privileges of the priesthood . . . look at
the dog in dogma raising his hindquarters to cast the scent of his individuality
on the lamp-post of Destiny! (pp. 272-3).

We can hear Old Man, the grand rhetorician and eloquent poet, in Aafaa's
verbal jugglery. Old Man dismisses all enemies of As as:

the cyst in the system, the splint in the arrow of arrogance, the dog in dogma,
the tick of a heretic, the tick in politics, the mock of democracy, the mar of
marxism, a tick of the fanatic, the boo in buddhism. (p. 275)

Old Man's trick is to fragment his words into syllabic units and then
convert the most accentuated of the vowel sounds in those units into an
independent sound unit which he juxtaposes with the parent word. In
another instance, he piles up concatenations of rhyming verbals:

do you not defecate, fornicate, prevaricate, when heaven and earth implore you
to abdicate? (pp. 271-2)

In every case the intention is to exploit words for their musical and
rhythmic effects. In Aafaa's long speech cited earlier, he appears at one
point to have lost touch with the main trend of his argument, floating only
on the waves of sound: 'The loyalty of homo sapiens regressed into himself,
himself his little tick-tock self, self-ticking, self-tickling, self-tackling
problems that belonged to the priesthood.'

It is, however, in clever verbal theatricals that the Mendicants have
excelled. This skill is much more than the Mendicants' adroitness with
puns, of which there are many examples in the play. *Rem acu tetigisti*, for
instance, gives us 'rat'. 'Official rat is what I smell,' says Aafaa, which
implies that all along the Mendicants suspect foul dealing in high places;
'dog' gives us 'underdog', 'watchdog' and 'dogma'. 'The end', Old Man
says, 'justifies the meanness' (p. 267); 'disabled' gives us a more serious
deformity, 'de-balled'.

The more obvious case of verbal theatricals emerges in the situations
where words are continuously extended into other dimensions of meaning
where they become relevant to As. Thus, when the Mendicants remark
that when things go wrong it is the lowest who get it first, they recall too
that they are at the bottom of things. The meaning of the word 'bottom'
is immediately extended into As: 'bottomless account'. That reminds us
of the embezzlement of public funds by highly placed public officials, a
phenomenon Soyinka has satirized elsewhere:

Ever-ready bank accounts
Are never read where
Children slay the cockroaches for a meal.[9]

Certain words such as 'smoke', 'flood' and 'elections' serve the Mendicants as cue words whose meanings are to be extended into As. 'Smoke'
gives us 'smoke-screen', and Old Man says that the election manifestos,
the charades and the pious pronouncements are all smoke-screens: 'At the

bottom of it all humanity chokes in silence' (p. 265); and when he looks into the future, he sees 'a faithful woman picking herbs for a smoke-screen on abuse' (p. 267). 'Flood' gives us its counterpart in As: 'running water', by which Old Man means 'running progress', 'faucets' and 'pipes'. The Cripple, who cannot reach the new innovation (the tap-water), says: 'too high', and Old Man 'translates even this secondary motif into As: 'too high like the price' (p. 265). High price does not merely imply the high cost of living, which has made even begging a less profitable concern, but the high price (death) that As exacts from its victims. But the motif of running water recalls more pertinently the running mouths that heap election promises on the people. The word 'elections' in its own turn gives us electricity which in As translates into electrocution and the electric chair. Dr Bero might not have had access to the electric chair, but, whatever means he uses to eliminate his victims, Old Man calls 'Electrodes on the nerve-centre, the favourite pastime of As' (p. 266).

When Old Man evokes the high ideal of patriotism as contained in the Latin aphorism *Dulce et decorum est pro patria mori*, we are meant, of course, to contrast this high ideal with what obtains in the republic of As. What is more becoming and more appealing in As is not to die for one's country but to exploit it. The word 'corum' which is formed from 'decorum' translates into As as: 'quorum'. 'Quorum' reads for some of the Mendicants as a corruption of 'corum', but when they have seen through the irony (that is, when they have perceived its As relevance) it becomes another occasion for *rem acu tetigisti*. 'No quorum, no quorum, that's the damned trouble,' says Goyi as the irony dawns on him, and the Cripple approves: 'Yes Sir, you've banged the hammer on the nail' (p. 261). The word play on 'corum' and 'quorum' points to the increasing emphasis on the 'quorum' even in our national legislatures during the era of civilian government. Because legislators were absentee law-makers, bills depended on the formation of a 'quorum' for their passage. That recalls Old Man's favourite lesson on civic responsibility: 'In ancient Athens they didn't just have a quorum. Everybody was there! That, children, was democracy' (p. 261). The word 'quorum' becomes the Mendicants' euphemism for the seat of political power (the parliament) where the 'national cake' is shared, and they express a desire to be members of that 'quorum':

> Before I join
> The saints above
> Before I join
> The saints above
> I want to sit on that damned quorum. (p. 261)

Certain ethical concepts, especially those connected with 'duty', 'choice' and 'truth', lose their conventional connotation when appro- priated by As. In the very first scene of Part One, the Mendicants' juggling with the word 'duty' indicates that this word carries a meaning that is peculiar to As. 'You may say he is . . . dutiful,' says Goyi, speaking of Dr Bero. Right away the Cripple relates the word to its conventional association: 'Him a dutiful son? You're crazy.' Thereafter, Blindman returns the word to its true meaning in As: 'I know what he means. Bang! All in the line of duty' (p. 220). The stage-directions point to an imaginary victim of As. Goyi, clutching his chest as he drops dead on the floor. To be dutiful in As is to eliminate all suspects, and in the case of Dr Bero to subordinate one's own filial duty to that duty demanded of him by As. Soyinka is careful to situate the tragedy in a domestic context in order to demonstrate the extent that As can go in the bid to dehumanize and depersonalize its agents. Dr Bero did not, indeed, hesitate to assassinate his own father in the service of As.

The meaning of the word 'choice' is also transformed in As so that it bears a meaning that is peculiar to As in its new context. He who chooses is an enemy of As, an agent of subversion. 'As chooses, man accepts,' says Aafaa. This adage is illustrated in a mini-comedy performed by the Mendicants towards the end of Part One. The Cripple has just swallowed a fat bug which he picked from his rags, and Aafaa challenges him on the choice of that particular specimen:

AAFAA: Did you choose it?
CRIPPLE: It chose me.
BLINDMAN: Chose? An enemy of As.
AAFAA: Sure? Not a disciple.
BLINDMAN: An enemy, subversive agent.
AAFAA: Quite right. As chooses, man accepts. (p. 234)

In Old Man's mockery of the concept of freedom of choice in As he suggests to Dr Bero a list of alternatives he can conjure up to camouflage his denial of freedom of choice to his victims:

Shall I teach you what to say? Choice! Particularity! What redundant self-deceptive notions! More? More? Insistence on a floppy old coat, a rickety old chair, a moth-eaten hat which no certified lunatic would ever consider wearing . . . A perfect waterproof coat is rejected for a patched-up heirloom that gives the silly wearer rheumatism. Is this an argument for freedom of choice? (p. 252)

As with 'choice', the word 'truth' has a meaning that is peculiar to As. 'Truth' in As is whatever confessions are extorted from the victim by duress in the torture chamber of As. This kind of truth, the Old Women tell Dr Bero, is easy to come by: 'Truth is always too simple for a desperate mind' (p. 259). The Mendicants have learned to make a mockery of Dr Bero's torture-chamber truth: 'Think not that I hurt you but that truth hurts. We are seekers after truth. I am a specialist in truth' (p. 223). This truth is to be contrasted with the truth which Old Man stands for, the truth that politicians are liars. One recalls that Old Man calls himself 'the one and only truth' (p. 242).

The language of the Old Women has a solemnity that is lacking in the Mendicants' verbal casuistry. Their speech is weighty and their cadence measured: 'We move as the Earth moves, nothing more. We age as Earth ages' (p. 259). Their very personality is identified with Nature herself which indeed supplies them with the ingredients of speech. The herbs and seeds they stockpile in Dr Bero's surgery enjoy an identity with their human body:

> Can I sleep easy when my head is gathering mould on your shelves? (p. 274)

> But my head still fills your room from wall to wall and dirty hands touch it. (p. 274)

Their language has its own ironies and paradoxes but these are of a more sober kind than the Mendicants' verbal gimmickry: 'You never can tell of seeds. The plant may be good; but we'll know, we'll know' (p. 235). The new worthless seed (Dr Bero) is here contrasted with the good parent stalk (Old Man), whose humanity will only be redeemed by the propitious seed (Si Bero). This contrast is more obvious in Iya Agba's remark: 'I haven't burrowed so deep to cast good earth on worthless seeds' (p. 235). Dr Bero metamorphoses rapidly from a 'worthless seed' to a leaking sieve that cannot even hold the grain before it has the chance of being separated into seed and chaff: 'Let him watch it. I haven't come this far to put my whole being in a sieve' (p. 236). The Old Women are natural healers, agents of life-giving forces. It is therefore easy for them to link Dr Bero to butchery and bloodshed:

> Don't look for the sign of broken bodies or wandering souls. Don't look for the sound of fear or the smell of hate. Don't take a bloodhound with you; we don't mutilate bodies. If you do, you may find him circle back to your door. (p. 260)

But by far the most persistent imagery in the play is the religious metaphor which establishes As as a deity. *D* stands for divinity in the alphabetical definition of As, and *I* for 'I am I', a corruption of the biblical attribute for God, 'I am what I am'. If As is a religion, the biblical diction used by its apostles is most appropriate: 'I say this unto you, As is all-seeing. All shall see in As who render themselves blind to all else.' The statement 'I am the one and only truth' stands both for Old Man's truth and the false truth claimed by As. All those who are opposed to the new religion are heretics. Dr Bero's worries are that the Mendicants are provided with a creed but they talk heresy (p. 263).

The play's language is primarily biblical in its diction; but within that diction there are two speech patterns: the solemn, measured language spoken by the Old Women and soaked in grain imagery and animal metaphor when Dr Bero is the subject of their discourse, and the Mendicants' verbal theatricals; and since the bulk of the satire is directed against political As their language derives its force from being rooted in current cant.

NOTES

1. For more information on expressionism see the entry in *Cassell's Encyclopaedia of Literature*, vol. 1, ed. S.H. Steinberg, London, Cassell and Company, 1953, pp. 214–15.
2. Susan Yankowitz, 'The plays of Wole Soyinka', *African Forum*, vol. 1, no. 4, Spring 1966, p. 130.
3. John Fletcher and James Mcfarlane, 'Modernist drama: origins and patterns', in *Modernism*, ed. Malcolm Bradbury and James Mcfarlane, Harmondsworth, Penguin, 1976, p. 507.
4. Wole Soyinka, *Madmen and Specialists*, in *Collected Plays*, vol. 2, London, Oxford University Press, 1974. Subsequent references are to this edition.
5. Wole Soyinka, *The Man Died*, London, Rex Collings, 1972, p. 182.
6. Wole Soyinka, *Season of Anomy*, London, Rex Collings, 1973, p. 104.
7. Wole Soyinka, *A Dance of the Forests*, in *Collected Plays* vol. 1, London, Oxford University Press, 1973, p. 49.
8. Lewis Nkosi, *Tasks and Masks*, Harlow, Longmans, 1981, p. 191.
9. Wole Soyinka, *A Shuttle in the Crypt*, New York, Hill and Wang, 1972, p. 81.

Truth from Contraries: A Study of Form in the Work of Femi Osofisan

Chris Dunton

Femi Osofisan's reputation rests on a series of plays which have marked him out as a leading figure amongst the younger generation of dramatists in Nigeria. Osofisan's first published work was not, however, a play but a novel. This work, Kolera Kolej,[1] appeared in 1975. It remains something of a maverick, being regarded in some quarters as nothing but a shabby little shocker. Yet there is more to Kolera Kolej than its neglect would suggest. In its manipulation of form and language, for instance, it is fairly adventurous. Further, an analysis of its structure reveals a way of thinking – a preoccupation with formal matters – that is dominant in those of Osofisan's works that are highly regarded: that is, in plays like Once Upon Four Robbers and Morountodun. This article attempts to identify the distinctive formal features of the novel and of these two plays, and to assess whether these features are as radical in effect as might first appear.

The story of Kolera Kolej centres on the outbreak of a cholera epidemic on a college campus and on the college's subsequent isolation and transformation into a neo-colonial nation state. Plotting in the novel's first two parts is minimal. Once the campus gains its freedom, a Vice-Chancellor (President) and Senate (Council) are elected. As the economic situation of the mini-state deteriorates, unrest grows widespread; there is a coup d'état, and the Vice-Chancellor is replaced by the Head of Defence, one Dr Paramole.

Osofisan works this material out with a fair measure of comic invention, and in a variety of satirical styles, as the writing veers from the laconic to the extravagant to the downright scabrous. In some episodes, satire is abandoned in favour of domestic farce.

The novel's humour is, then, wide-ranging. Some chapters, however, follow a line of development that has little to do with the novel's satire, and between these and the mainstream comic material there is a very marked disjunction. Kolera Kolej is an audacious piece of work. Its internal disjunctions are constantly stimulating: the narrative voice is one that can tease, lacerate, or turn blunt and earnest, within the space of a few lines. Clearly Osofisan's imagination is taken here with the possibility of creating novel form through the combination of dissimilar materials. In the plays that followed Kolera Kolej, this tendency emerges repeatedly:

81

in the use of contrasting voices and language forms, in the notion of the play-within-the-play. The technique relates, of course, to the process of dialectic: argument progresses through the radical juxtaposition of unlike elements. In *Kolera Kolej*, however, Osofisan's technique has produced a dialectic that is not altogether coherent.

The plays

To date, more than a dozen of Osofisan's plays have appeared on stage. The two discussed below both demonstrate Osofisan's predilection for structuring contrasts: for those disjunctions in register and in dramatic style which enable him to build his argument by a process of contradictions and which lead his audience towards a conclusion only by way of a series of revisions in the judgement-forming process.[2]

The bulk of *Morountodun* is written in a clear, idiomatic English. Occasionally, however, the language shifts into a more intense, heightened register, to express especially forceful emotions, as in the heroine Titubi's comments on the historical figure Moremi;[3] while, for a 'Moremi play' inserted into the main action, Osofisan devises a more decorous and formal style:

> Now Moremi is no longer afraid. Let the women come and we shall dance together, like the procession on a bridal night. Your doubt and your fear have strengthened me. I shall go, and I shall return.[4]

Additionally, there are a dozen or so songs. Most of these spring realistically from the action, but two at least have a special status, as I shall suggest below.

The play contains a large number of disjunctions of various kinds, which are designed to offer fresh perspectives on the action as it proceeds. For the sake of clarity, I have given below a scene-by-scene analysis of the play; the symbol /// marks these disjunctions as they occur.

Morountodun begins with actors preparing to perform a play.

/// Almost immediately, their Director 'step out' (Osofisan uses the Brechtian term) to talk to the audience. From the vantage-point of the present he explains that these actors' preparations were for a play performed at the time of the Agbekoya farmers' uprising in 1969 and taking the uprising as its subject. In fact we never get to see this play. The Director explains that it was condemned as being subversive and in this way the actors became 'part of the [political] problem'.[5]

Preparations to perform the play of 1969 are interrupted by a mob, headed by the young woman Titubi (all that follows from this situation forms the bulk of *Morountodun*: the 'Titubi play'). The crowd enters singing:

> Stand! Stand!
> Fight to be rich
> For happiness . . .

Oh fight for your share
And do not care![6]

Here Osofisan is clearly following Brecht's lead in devising a song which, being beyond character, is self-revealing.[7]

Titubi, the daughter of a powerful market-mammy, tries to have the Farmers' Uprising play banned. She then offers to help the police catch the leader of the farmers' movement. Knowing that the farmers plan to attack the local prison, the police jail Titubi, hoping that she will be 'freed' and will thus infiltrate the farmers' camp.

/// The Superintendent of Police now costumes Titubi as a prisoner. Within the logic of the play, this is a realistic action: she is being dressed to take part in a plot. At the same time, the actor playing the Corporal changes into the costume for the role he will double (the prison Warder). There is a break here with realism, as Osofisan pairs the real and the fictional act of costuming, although it is difficult to see what critical significance this achieves.

/// Almost straight away, the Director reappears. Outside the jail he meets the farmer Bogunde and his comrades. He instructs them to disguise themselves well, since they will not now be playing their 'real roles'.[8]

Within the logic of the Titubi play, Bogunde is disguising himself as a trader, as part of the plot to attack the jail. What, then, is the significance of the Director's remarks? By 'real roles' he is referring to the actors as farmers rather than as farmers disguised as traders. The Director's words remind us that the actors he speaks to now are the same actors who were seen at the beginning preparing to perform the Farmers' Uprising play. Exactly what distancing perspective is Osofisan seeking to achieve? Possibly to point to a parallel between plot and play, and to suggest that the role-playing that is acting *can* be a subversive tactic, just like the role-playing here carried out by the farmer Bogunde.

In the next scene, Bogunde plays his role as trader, while the farmers' leader, Marshal, plays a customer. A public conversation (haggling over fruit) is carried out in pidgin, while their 'real conversation (the passing-on of necessary information) is carried out in standard English: a nice opportunity for 'exposed', versatile acting.[9] Inside the jail, meanwhile, we see Titubi rehearsing with the Superintendent the role she will play when she infiltrates the farmers' camp: that of a convicted murderess. What is striking in this scene is the characterization of the Superintendent: the political function of his work as a policeman is made clear and yet Osofisan allows him to voice – cynically – some harshly realistic comments on Titubi and her mother: '[the] rebels are of your own creation, you who are used to feeding on others', and on the strength of the farmers' movement, whose members are united by hunger.[10]

/// There have been earlier references to the historical character Moremi and to Titubi's identification of her own role with Moremi's struggle to defend Ile-Ife before the invading Igbos.[11] Now Titubi goes into a reverie on the part played by Moremi in that war. Scenes 5 and 6 of *Morountodun* constitute a 'Moremi play', dreamt up and (in the staging) witnessed by Titubi, which shows Moremi insisting on her power to play an effective role in war (like Titubi, she is to infiltrate the enemy camp). This 'Moremi play' ends with Moremi freezing, 'watching the following scene':[12] an intriguing flash-forward, though its exact significance is obscure.

The jail is attacked by Marshal's farmers. Titubi, contrary to her expectations, is freed but not taken with them; she has to pursue them to their camp.

/// An interlude follows: one that does have a clear distancing effect, as – in contradiction to the play's sympathies – the Director praises Titubi's ingenuity and then leads into the Moremi praise-chant.

Scene 9 shows Titubi some weeks later, working as a nurse with the farmers. The following scene shows Titubi's mother with the Superintendent, demanding to know where her daughter is. The Superintendent announces his love of the theatre and his desire to produce a Moremi play of his own: a little acting-out of appropriate roles follows. This (weak) disjunction (weak because the performance arises realistically) suggests the facility with which the Moremi history can be used, and to that extent it throws a critical light on Titubi's identification with Moremi. Then Titubi suddenly appears, with Marshal as her prisoner. She announces that since she set out to capture Marshal she has undergone some kind of change.

/// In a lengthy flashback, designed to explain this statement, Titubi is seen with the village women, learning about the conditions of their lives as they act out two representative instances of their oppression: the first in the form of a satirical burlesque, the second a straight re-enactment of a farmer's defiant speech to a corrupt governor. There is a strong contradiction between Titubi's appearance in this scene and her appearance in the police station with Marshal as her prisoner.

A brief section shows Titubi again in the narrative present, with her mother and the Superintendent, confirming the change that has taken place in her political sympathies.[13]

/// The flashback resumes, but now from a different perspective. The village women are shown teasing Titubi for having fallen in love with Marshal. The play then returns to the present, as Titubi rejects Moremi as a model for her action. This rejection is made in a single, brief speech:

> I am not Moremi! Moremi served the State, *was* the State, was the spirit of the ruling class. But it is not true that the State is always right.[14]

– a dramatic , but surely somewhat perfunctory, disposal of what up to this point has been a major element in the play.

Titubi then condemns the Superintendent and hands her gun over to Marshal. The following scene shows the village women, a fortnight later, with Titubi and Marshal, celebrating their love, and Marshal renaming Titubi – now identified neither as Moremi (a false model) or as Titubi (her name by birth and background, which obscures her true nature), but as Morountodun – that is: 'I have found a sweet thing'. Then Marshal outlines a plan to attack the Central Police Station.

/// The Director appears and abruptly announces the death of Marshal during the failed attack. He then warns the audience not to imagine that the play they have just watched represents the truth:

> The *real* struggle, the real truth, is out there, among you, on the street, in your homes, in your daily living and dying.[15]

The play ends here, with the image of Titubi and Moremi, 'caught in harsh spotlights', staring at each other, the heroine of history confronting the heroine of *Morountodun*. The image suggests: history, myth, tale, and play need to be seen and used – but used critically and clearly, and for a proper cause.

By contrast with the multi-stranded complexity of *Morountodun*, *Once Upon Four Robbers* focuses with fierce concentration on a single idea, establishing armed robbery as an 'apt metaphor' for life in contemporary Nigeria and the armed robber as both product of and moralizing commentator on an 'unjust society'. The public execution of these robbers may mean death and disgrace, 'but so also does hunger, so does unemploy- ent';[16] Osofisan reverses the orthodox morality (that armed robbers are vile) in an attempt to provoke a sharper awareness of those injustices that the establishment prefers to ignore. The play exposes a scandalous disjunction between the public recognition of a symptomatic evil and the systematic neglect of evils that are fundamental.

Osofisan's robbers pour scorn on the mentality of the rich and castigate a system in which menial labour is equated to 'respectability'.[17] The self- seeking individualist is condemned, whether in the person of the army sergeant who embezzles money recaptured after a theft, or in the case of Major – one of the robbers, who betrays the others and is then immediately identified with the absurd, ten-Mercedes-owning rich.[18]

Major's betrayal places a moral gulf between himself and his fellow robbers. He is shown as having betrayed an ideal – the ideal of solidarity practised by the militantly antisocial. Osofisan succeeds in rendering the principle of solidarity convincingly; it is, however, a weakness in the play that he never achieves a *categorical* distinction between Major's solitary acquisitiveness and the group acquisitiveness of the robbers; he never really establishes what the robbers mean by 'justice' or how, except in a sophistic sense, they can claim to be fighting for it.

If the robbers' projection of their own role occasionally rings hollow, other aspects of their characterization have a more solid impact. From the beginning of the play, when he dramatizes their outrage at the public execution of their leader, Osofisan emphasizes their vulnerability to feelings of anger, loss and humiliation. This is particularly the case with the leader's widow, Alhaja, whose awareness of her own life now entering into a decline is very moving:

> It is nothing but ambition
> Nothing but overdaring
> For an old hag to pine and pine
> To be like the swift 'ora' bird . . .[19]

Osofisan stresses the despair that periodically afflicts the robbers: their understanding that finally they are unable to break the system, that all they can do is thrash against it, until the time when they are caught and killed.[20]

As in *Morountodun*, the language norm for the dialogue is idiomatic. Nowhere else, however, is it quite as clear how exciting and varied Osofisan's writing can be. In the opening pages, for instance, when the robbers react to the execution of their leader by reassessing their own position, Osofisan conveys the turbulence of their emotions by showing them constantly shifting from one mood to another: from their initial outrage at the squalor of the public execution, through Alhaja's lament for her husband, which resurfaces again and again, to a gradual livening as they remember their glory days (the pace is faster here, as they swap anecdotes, chime in with praise-names of famous robbers, break into fragments of song) and then back into a bleak depression as they look to the future. The overall impression is of an acute mental alertness amongst the robber characters, as they respond to their situation with a grim, supercharged realism.

In one or two instances Osofisan employs a different style. The soldiers' scene which opens Part Three is played out in its own distinct idiom. A few of the robbers' speeches approach the heightened language used in key speeches in *Morountodun*. One in particular stands out: a passage in which Alhaja enters into a trance, under which she makes a long, agonized speech on the role of the mother, bearing generations of children who will be destroyed in a world of privation. The device of the trance here allows Alhaja to speak beyond character, moving the depiction of injustice beyond the level of the robbers' rhetoric.[21]

As in *Morountodun*, there are songs; here, about a dozen, most of which spring naturally from the action. A Story-Teller's songs provide background and continuity. One other song has a special function, providing a radical disjunction with its surrounding material, as the market-women abandon their official image and shamelessly celebrate their own venality in a large-scale version of the song of the crowd in *Morountodun*:

> Among the crowd
> that's born each day,
> just to sweep the rubbish,
> and scour round like dogs,
> count not our kins! . . .
>
> The lure of profit
> has conquered our souls
> and changed us into cannibals . . .[22]

The sense of theatre is emphasized when Osofisan's (typically inventive) characters indulge in role-playing: the soldiers satirize their Sergeant and his wife, and Alhaja impersonates a market-woman in order to gain the confidence of the soldiers. Osofisan does not, however, emphasize the tactics of theatre as regularly here as in *Morountodun*. What he does, instead, is to develop the plot in a way that 'romanticizes'[23] the robbers' lives and at the same time to set up a series of radical disjunctions between one episode and the next that undermine this very process: the effect is as if he were to admit that the notion of the robbers as moral authorities is outrageous, while simultaneously stinging the audience into recognizing that orthodox morality is unacceptable, too.

The title of the play points to the game. *Once Upon* is the opening formula of a fairy-tale. Magic and fantasy are used to romanticize the activities of the robbers, but at the same time their use is repeatedly circumscribed.

The play opens with the Story-Teller introducing the robbers in a light-hearted song; but the relaxed mood the song establishes is immediately shattered by a realistic staging of the brutal execution of the robbers' leader.

The robbers' grim account of their own lives follows, and the drama of Major's threatened treachery. Then the Story-Teller intervenes again, extracting a series of pledges from the robbers, which make their activities more palatable (they promise not to kill, not to rob the poor, and so on; the unreality of all this is deliberate). In return he teaches them a magic song which, when performed, will reduce everyone around to a state of carnival – during which the robbers can steal anything they please.

After a fairly long section showing two robberies carried out in this way, the play returns to the grim, turbulent mood of its opening. The business of Alhaja's attempt to free Major, who has been captured by the army, is amusing enough, but the mood darkens again as the other robbers reappear, followed by the army, to act out the furious debate that leads to the end of the play. Major begins this, with an angry speech against the establishment:

> today [the] law is on the side of those who have, and in abundance, who are fed and bulging . . . But tomorrow that law will change. The poor will seize it and twist its neck.[24]

Then the robber Hasan enters, at which point the Sergeant recognizes him as his own brother. This is another echo from the traditional fairy-tale; the conventional expectation would be some kind of happy union, or collusion, between the two sides. Now, however, Osofisan turns the convention upside-down. According to Hasan, the fact that the two are brothers only proves the irrelevance of the blood-tie:

> Blood is an accident. It's only our ideas that bind us together, or rip us apart.[25]

And in a repetition of a point made earlier by another robber, Angola, he points out that they all fall amongst either the exploiters or the exploited, and that those who exploit have chosen of their own free will to do so.[26]

A firing squad is set up to execute Major. Then the magic song is heard again: its third and final use. The other robbers have arrived in a bid to save their former colleague, and the action freezes just as the Sergeant gives the order to fire.

Once Upon makes use of fairy-tale conventions, but is clearly not a fairy-tale. The Story-Teller now asks the audience to vote: for the magic song to succeed, or not. The audience have the chance of acceding to the logic of the fairy-tale: that is, to the procedure by which Osofisan has romanticized the robbers – that is, to the logic that argues that the morality which condemns uninstitutionalized robbery alone is not the most perfect morality in the world. If the audience votes yes, then the robbers win. If they vote no, Osofisan requires them to sit through a staging of the shooting of Major and of the other robbers, beginning with Alhaja: a brutal denial of the play's logic and an imitation of the partial morality it condemns.

Conclusion

Behind the works discussed above there is an active political consciousness; there is, especially, an acute sense of *stand*, a sense that men and women are defined in their social lives by those same class affiliations that Hasan describes in *Once Upon Four Robbers* as binding people together or ripping them apart.

Osofisan's imagination is charged with the notion of conflict, with the actual but often unspoken state of war existing between different social classes. His work attempts to articulate this conflict and, in particular, to establish disjunctions – tangible contradictions – through which the *real* relationship between opposing ideologies can be assessed.

The frequency with which Osofisan's work sets up these disjunctions indicates the extent of his imaginative involvement in the dialectical process. The technical expertise he has at his disposal is considerable; hence the variety of means he is able to devise to provoke us into new recognitions: ranging from shifts in language mode, to songs that are, super-realistically, self-exposing, to the creation of model, or the play-within-the-play.

The energy which Osofisan applies to this process makes his work some of the most exciting in the contemporary African theatre. None the less, one or two doubts do arise.

His work is consistently impressive in terms of its technical accomplishment. There is, though, a kind of abstraction – the last quality one might expect to find in the work of a writer with such a marked political commitment: a carrying-out of dramatic strategies that seems oddly remote from the central area of conflict, the basic class struggle to which all his work refers.

It is partly a question of where he chooses to place his emphasis. Osofisan's work very rarely dramatizes the life of the masses; it is the dilemma of the leaders, their psychological development, that seems to preoccupy Osofisan rather than the lives of the people they lead. *The Chattering and the Song*, for example, succeeds as an exciting and inventive play partly because it is a play about exceptionally exciting and inventive people. Further than this, in most cases Osofisan is engaged in a process of special validation: the man in *Kolera Kolej*, Titubi and, to some extent, Sontri in *The Chattering and the Song* are very nearly redundant, or even counter-revolutionary:[27] each has to be shown to have a useful role to play – a large part of the tension in Osofisan's work lies in the process by which the apparent reactionary is revealed finally as a functioning revolutionary. The one piece discussed above that does focus in some sense on the average man is *Once Upon Four Robbers*, in which the masses are approached only very obliquely, as their condition is dramatized through the metaphor of armed robbery. This preoccupation with the leadership role may not be a weakness, but in the work of an avowedly radical writer like Osofisan it is a distinct peculiarity.

Osofisan's technical brilliance also prompts occasional misgivings. Many of the disjunctions he creates do have an obvious, revelatory function: for instance, the abrupt transition to deadly seriousness in the last part of *Kolera Kolej*, or the switches from fairy-tale to grim realism in *Once Upon Four Robbers*. Others seem hardly to relate to a play's thematic development: for instance, much of the emphasis on theatricals in *Morountodun*. Here there is a sense of technique riding free of function; a sense that Osofisan's writerly skills sometimes outdistance his ability to convince that his depiction of the real energies of class conflict is as fleshed-out and thought-through as it might be.

NOTES

1. Femi Osofisan, *Kolera Kolej*, Ibadan, New Horn, 1975.
2. Osofisan's first big success in the theatre, *The Chattering and the Song* is also rich in internal contrasts, with its riddle-games, its use of song, its shifts from idiomatic registers to heightened poetic language and the insertion of an entire one-act historical drama. Yet, in terms of form, the play is more unified than this might suggest, in that these shifts and contrasts tend to reflect the professional skills of the characters involved: songs are performed, satirical sketches are mounted, by characters who are in fact artists and writers; there is little sense of these – even of the striking riddle-game which opens the play – functioning as alienating devices introduced by Osofisan to afford a distanced perspective on his characters.
3. Femi Osofisan, *Morountodun*, in *Morountodun and Other Plays*, Lagos, Longman Nigeria, 1982, p. 20.
4. Ibid., p. 34.
5. Ibid., p. 6.
6. Ibid., p. 27.
7. A close parallel would be the song 'The strong man fights and the sick man dies (and that's a good thing)', from *The Exception and the Rule* (in Bertolt Brecht, *The Measures Taken and Other Lehrstücke*, London, Eyre Methuen, 1977, p. 48.
8. *Morountodun*, op. cit., p. 16.
9. Ibid., pp. 17–18.
10. Ibid., p. 24.

11. Ibid., pp. 14, 20, 25, 26.
12. Ibid., p. 39.
13. Ibid., p. 60.
14. Ibid., p. 70.
15. Ibid., p. 79.
16. Femi Osofisan, *Once Upon Four Robbers*, Ibadan, BIO Press, 1980, p. [viii].
17. Ibid., p. 13.
18. Ibid., p. 33.
19. Ibid., p. 64 (this is from Osofisan's English translation of Alhaja's Yoruba song, p. 9).
20. Ibid., p. 53.
21. Ibid., p. 50.
22. Ibid., p. 28.
23. The word is used in his programme notes, ibid., p. [viii].
24. Ibid., p. 53.
25. Ibid., p. 58.
26. Ibid.
27. See also Akanji in the play *Red is the Freedom Road*: not the traitor he at first appears to be.

Language Pluralism
in Sierra Leonean Drama
in Krio

Julius Spencer

Playwrights in English in Sierra Leone have had to contend with the problem faced by other African playwrights using the same medium, which is that of finding a suitable means of presenting their characters in a way that would reflect the linguistic situation operating in the setting they wish to portray. Alex Johnson, in an insightful study of the use of the English language in West African drama in English, has examined this problem and analysed the approaches of various West African play-wrights to it.[1] While there have been variations in approaches to this issue in the Sierra Leonean theatre, the reactions have generally tended to follow the pattern identified by Johnson in terms of the various functions performed by language through a variety of registers. In this essay, however, we are not concerned with drama in English, but with a much more indigenous manifestation: drama in Krio.

Krio is a creole language found in Sierra Leone which has over the years assumed the status of the lingua franca of the country, being spoken not only in the large urban centres, but also at village level. Drama in Krio owes its present status to the pioneering work of Thomas Decker[2] and its subsequent popularization in the late sixties and seventies by Juliana Rowe (née John),[3] Dele Charley, Yulisa Maddy, Kolosa John Kargbo, Eric Hassan-Deen and a host of others. The use of Krio in the theatre has undoubtedly brought the theatre closer to the average Sierra Leonean than hitherto. This has been due to two major phenomena which the use of Krio has catalysed. In the first place, the theatre, through its use of Krio, has established lines of communication which span a wide spectrum of the Sierra Leonean population. Secondly, there has been a blossoming of drama not only in Krio but in English, for writers are now more confident about using non-standard English on stage, and are therefore more prolific in their output.

The genesis of all this seems to lie in the way playwrights in Sierra Leone have used Krio in the theatre, for while we can easily identify certain plays as being Krio drama, due to the preponderance of that language in the speeches of the characters, the playwrights have by no means limited themselves solely to the use of Krio in these plays. This paper, therefore, is an analysis of the use of language in what has come to be known as Krio drama in Sierra Leone, through an examination of the work of some of its major contemporary playwrights.

Plays in Krio deal primarily with contemporary social issues. These plays are set mainly in urban areas, a reflection of the status of Krio, which is itself mainly an urban-based language, although, as has been pointed out, it does also operate at village level. In order to reflect the linguistic situation in operation in these urban centres in which the plays are based, the playwrights have generally attempted to create a variety of linguistic registers. These registers are used largely as indicators of the educational and social status of the characters.

The various registers created are differentiated mainly on a lexical level, and present a linguistic continuum from English as a second language EL_2 through pidgin to Krio. Some characters, it seems, are differentiated by the amount of English words and expressions in their speech. It is, therefore, not uncommon for a particular character to speak in a purely EL_2 register in a Krio play. Kolosa Kargbo makes quite effective use of this technique in *For Saykah Uman* and *Poyotong Wahala*,[4] two socio-political satires. Mohamed Moses, the lead character in *For Saykah*, who is the President of the Worker's Union, speaks only in an EL_2 register throughout the play. This distinguishes him from the rest of the characters. It seems the motivation for this approach was twofold. The playwright obviously felt the need to present Moses as a highly educated person, and the register he uses obviously reflects this. Secondly, the EL_2 medium was apparently seen as a suitably 'lofty language' in which to express Moses' lofty ideals. This approach, however, stretches situational credibility almost to breaking-point, for, even in the privacy of his own home, Moses consistently responds to his wife, Rebecca, who speaks primarily in Krio, in English. For example, Rebecca says:

> Wɛl, ɔda we nɔ de fɔ ɛp di Mami? We da mɔni we yu se Powers de ɔfa yu, da tati tawzin pɔŋ fɔ mek yu pul an pan yuniɔn biznɛs ɛn lɛf fɔ fɛt fɔ dɛn wokman dɛm.

and Moses replies:

> Rebecca, do you think for one moment that I'll accept such an offer and leave the poor workers at his mercy, to be torn and ravaged, exploited by the establishment? No, woman, that is inconceivable. It's absolutely impossible.

This approach marks Moses as being incapable of speaking Krio.

Another approach which the playwright uses for differentiating characters to reflect educational and social background is the switching from Krio to English within speeches. Mr Hercules Powers, the Industrial Secretary, and Rebecca employ this dual register, for, at certain points in the play, they switch from one to the other. Powers uses English when talking to Moses, but, in the scene where he makes a declaration of his love for Rebecca, they both start off speaking English, then switch to Krio during his declaration and her subsequent rejection of him:

POWERS: [getting up] Look Madam. [He goes to sit beside her] Your husband is dead. Nothing can be done about it. You won't even see the corpse. He will be buried by the prison authorities and then they'll inform you later.

REBECCA: I refuse to believe you. No, you're lying Mr Powers. Mohamed could not possibly die in prison. [She gets up] I'll wait for the letter from the prison authorities.

POWERS: Look Rebecca. Dis nɔto layf. Aw yɔŋ uman lɛk yu . . . luk we yu fayn . . . aw yo go sidɔm fɔ ya tide yu se yu nɔ want man. If na fɔ mɔni, yu no se a gɛt am.

After a short exchange in Krio, Rebecca switches to English to order Powers out of the house.

POWERS: Rebecca, lɛ wi nɔ mek plaba. Fɔgɛt wetin dɔn apin, Naw yu gɛt di ɔpɔtuniti fɔ stat layf ɔl ova egen.

REBECCA: I'll start my life all over again the moment you quit. Will you get out!

POWERS: [Moves over to her] Rebecca a lɛk yu. Bo luk, tri ia naw a dɔn de biɛn yu. Alaw mi fɔ mek a lɔv yu. Yu go bɛnifit.

REBECCA: If your love is all there is in the world, then let me live my life completely unloved, uncared for and hated by you.

This switch from Krio to English effectively reflects a change in attitude on Rebecca's part. It is an obvious reflection of her desire to keep the relationship on a formal level.

The Krio registers used by Powers and Rebecca also display a higher percentage of English lexical items than the registers used by the other characters. This feature serves to further differentiate them on the basis of social status and educational background. Baby Lego, a streetwise character with criminal tendencies, for example, speaks in a register which reflects his background and enhances his characterization. For example, after rejecting an offer of a bribe from Powers to disclose the plans of the union for a crippling industrial action, he says (apparently to the audience):

Nɔ mɛn di dɔg. Na Savisman lɛk mi yu wan ple wit? Wi gɛt fɔ fiks dɛm ɔl ɔp jisnɔ. Na mi yon Baby Lego go dɔn swɛ pan da bad sasa de dɔn a kam tɔk bɔt di plan? Mi nɔ go miks pan da kayn afɔjudi de o. A dɔn lod dis mɔnin. Na klos a de kam go bay na tɔŋ so. A! di joka. Dɛm bebi dɛm sɛf gɛt fɔ ol dɛm yon pan dis brɛd.

In Poyotong Wahala, lawyer Churchill-Sankoh, a political aspirant who fails to win the elections because he is honest, like Moses in For Saykah, speaks in English throughout. He, unlike Moses, only makes two relatively brief appearances, and so the register he uses does not create credibility problems. This approach marks him as being more highly educated than the other characters, while at the same time placing him above the general corruption practised by other educated characters like Bra Lagbaja, a former schoolmaster who wins the election through rigging and is made a minister. Kargbo again seems to have been influenced by the notion of a 'lofty language' to express lofty ideas.

The pastor in Raymond de'Souza George's *Bohboh Lef*, a musical drama, also speaks mainly in English. However, he, unlike the two characters mentioned above, demonstrates competence in Krio by switching to it on rare occasions. For example, he says:

> As our people say, da neba we nɔ bizabɔdi na bad neba. I am only doing my divine duty to the society.

He justifies his use of the English language thus:

> this is one of the reasons I use the English language to communicate with most people, especially the children. Using a foreign language, I find it easy to get them to avoid bad habits even though they don't understand everything I say. It is a psychological weapon. With people like you, it is to show you that there are lapses in human nature which most of us ignore.

The playwright thus seems to have been influenced by a need to distinguish the pastor from the general decadence prevalent in the society.

The technique of switching from English to Krio within the speeches of various characters, as an approach to differentiation on the basis of educational background and status, which was evidenced by Kargbo's *For Saykah Uman*, is used rather extensively by several other playwrights.

In Isaac Randy Wright's *How For Do*, another socio-political satire, it occurs in the speech of almost all the characters, all of whom are educated. Thus, Jolly Boy, the station-master turned bar owner, says:

> Jack, yu de wok, yu get hops fɔ tɔn siniɔ savis. Yu kin kɔntiniu, bɔt fɔ mi, *I will pray to my God* bɔt a nɔ de *forward into any battle*.

The speech of the younger, more educated and more fervent revolutionaries, however, displays a greater percentage of English lexical items. This results in some speeches becoming pidgin, for example:

> For doing sweet nothing! Tell me, how on earth an ex-station master go participate in anything we get fɔ du with krud oil en im bay prodɔkts.

The technique of switching from Krio to English is also evident in Dele Charley's *Titi Shain-Shain*. Here, however, it is limited to the speech of Reverend Hamilton-Douglas, a morally upright character whose wife and daughter are morally bankrupt. This is an attempt to distinguish him from the other characters on an educational and occupational level as well as on a moral level. Thus we find him saying:

> But I also believe that time will speak. Da lif we swit got, na im go mek i get makru ɔ rɔn-belε. No child is too young to learn from the dangerous obstacles of life. Pikin we se i nɔ go gi im mami chans fɔ slip, yu tink se insεf go slip?

In the privacy of his home, however, the Reverend speaks purely in Krio. The Big-Time Boys also speak in a register appropriate to their status as layabouts and 'rare bɔys'. Their speech, therefore, displays lexical items usually associated with this category of people. For example:

BɔN T.: Pɛgi, bang mi wan toga de bɔbs di insay ɛmti.
BAD M.: Wɛn di insay ɛmti, na toga go ful am?
BɔN T.: Bɔbs, mek mi wɔd fɔdɔm na grɔn. A nɔ tɔk to yu.

In *Adopted Pikin*, a play which extols the virtues of family planning and argues for the humane treatment of adopted children, Dele Charley also uses English words and expressions in the speeches of certain characters as a means of distinguishing them from the others on the basis of educational background and social status. The register used by Herbert and Gloria Thorton, a couple that has adopted a daughter, Amy, demonstrates this feature, for example:

HERBERT: When pɔsin lay ɔh tif fɔh du gud to in kɔmpin, i mɔs gɛt gud rizin fɔ 'do evil that good may come'.

Even when apparently speaking purely Krio, their speech is suffused with English lexical items. Thus we find Herbert saying:

Amy na strɔng pikin o, lɛk i bin fɔh bi tu sɛnsitiv, tu withdrɔn ɛn hostayl to pipul dɛm.

This register contrasts sharply with that used by the villagers in the flashback scene, for example:

FOLA: Mansa, a beg. Mansa, yu sabi wetin dɛn wet man na yengema de du if dɛn nɔ want dɛn man dɔg fɔ bɔn pikin wit ɔda dɔg dɛm?
CHIF: Yu tink se na dat di dɔkta dɛm go kam du na ya? Mansa, yu na fɔni man. Sidɔm bo, nɛt de kam.

Here, the playwright avoids, as much as possible, using obviously English lexical items.

Shefunmi Garber also uses the technique of switching from Krio to English within speeches as a means of distinguishing characters on the basis of education and social status. Thus, we find that Regina, Lawrence and their friends, a group of educated young people, in *So Na Mi Mama a Marrade*, speak at times in a register which, because of its constant switching from one language to the other and a high percentage of English lexical items, becomes more of pidgin English than Krio. The following excerpts will serve to demonstrate this:

LAWRENCE: . . . dam it. A nɔ de go ɛni we Regina te yu *unfold* di *agony* na yu bosom. A dɔn *fed up* wit dis *indefinite suspense*. Go kam ɔda tem, go kam ɔda tem. If mi *presence offensive*, a go *apologise later*, bɔt mi, tide yon a nɔ de lɛf yu te a no wetin *responsible* for dis *suspense*.

SYLVIA: Yu dɔn bigin bak ɛn? *Too much thinking, too much crying*. Yu wan tɛl mi se *uptill now*, yu nɔ ebul fit in na di sosayti we yu bɔn into? Yu gɛt fɔ *magnify* ɔl tin we apin to yu?

There are also clear examples of the switching from one stretch of Krio to another of English within a particular speech and among speakers.

EUSTACE: Sure, ɛni human being go jɔj tiŋgs da we de. A min, di bɔy jɛs kam cast a slur on wi.

KPALU: Seriously. A man is known by the company he keeps.

EUSTACE: A fil fɔh su am na kot yu no.

KPALU: Why shouldn't we?

EUSTACE: If mi ɛn Lawrence, wi tu yay mek fo, a min, I'll tell him the bottom of my heart.

KPALU: Eustace, nɔbɔdi kin ful mi. This is intentional, this boy planned it.

SYLVIA: Forces! What forces? Talk sense my dear. Regina tɔk bɛtɛ tɔk bo. Wetin yu gɛt brɛn fɔ? Yu mɛmba se na fɔ kip am ɔp de doing nothing? You use the brain to think, love. Otherwise you are unfit to live. Wɛn yu gɛt prɔblɛms, find solutions to them and stop pressurizing the system . . . wait for me, yu man tɛl mi se if yu mared tide, fada fɔgiv, yu man day tumara, yu go day go mit am?

The other less educated or socially elite characters like Alafia and her mother, Granny, speak in a register which is mainly conventional Krio. Compare the earlier examples with the following:

GRANNY: Wɛl yu nɔ go lɛf man gi am lɛ yu sidɔm saful na yu man os? I bad i bad te, yu pas am, bikɔs yu, Gɔd dɔn bɔta yu brɛd. Im na naw i de fɛn mared.

ALAFIA: Granny, da wan de, aw yu si a dɔn de biyɛn am so, pas a day na im i go mared na dis kɔntri. I tu prawd. Ɔl tɛm i mek lɛkɛ fɔ se i bɛtɛ pas pɔsin.

From the foregoing, a clear picture of the use of language in Krio plays begins to emerge. In the first place, it can be observed that characters are distinguished on a linguistic level only on the basis of educational background and social class. This differentiation of characters is achieved through creating a register for highly educated characters which (1) involves constant switching from Krio to English, and (2) contains a higher percentage of English words and expressions than is normal in Krio speech. This results in their speeches being more of a pidgin than Krio. In some instances, individual characters who stand out above the rest are made to speak exclusively in an EL$_2$ medium.

Secondly, the use of language in these plays is an attempt to reflect the true linguistic situation in Freetown and the large urban centres where Krio is extensively used. The mixture of Krio and English, the switching from one to the other, is a reflection of the actual situation.

It is also observable that some playwrights have been influenced by the prevailing attitudes to Krio and the status of the language in the society. Thus, one finds that certain moods, certain thoughts and certain official activities tend to be expressed either in English or in pidgin.

Language pluralism is, therefore, an important feature of Krio drama. This has undoubtedly contributed to the ability of theatre in Krio to appeal to a wide spectrum of the population.

NOTES

1. Alex C. Johnson, Language and Society in West African Literature: A Stylistic Investigation into the Linguistic Resources of West African Drama in English, unpublished Ph.D. thesis, University of Ibadan, 1981.
2. Thomas Decker's fight for the use of Krio in literary activities has been widely acknowledged, and his contribution in this regard has been documented. See Eldred Jones, 'The potentialities of Krio as a literary language', Sierra Leone Studies, no. 9, December 1957, pp. 40–8; and 'Crusader for Krio', West Africa, 14 August 1965, p. 903. The performance of his Krio translation of Shakespeare's Julius Caesar in 1964 signalled the birth of drama in Krio.
3. Juliana Rowe (née John) was largely responsible for the initial popularity of Krio drama. In 1968 and 1969 respectively, she wrote and directed Na Mami Bohn Am and I Dey I Noh Du, two plays which could be regarded as the first truly popular Krio plays.
4. The spelling used here, as with all other plays titles, is that which appears on the text. Quotations from this and other plays have, however, been transcribed into the standard Krio orthography.

Guillaume Oyono-Mbia: A Bilingual Playwright

Unionmwan Edebiri

Guillaume Oyono-Mbia occupies a significant position among contemporary African writers not only because of his remarkable talent as dramatist but also by virtue of his linguistic resources and the possibilities of his works. In particular, he stands out most distinctly as an accomplished bilinguist who constantly draws on his rich linguistic background to enliven his imaginative re-creations of contemporary experiences – social, political and cultural – of his native Cameroon. Our immediate concern in this essay is not so much the totality of Oyono-Mbia's creative output as his bilingualism and its implications for his art.

Uriel Weinrich defines bilingualism as 'the practice of alternatively using two languages' and qualifies the person who takes to it as 'bilingual'.[1] The bilinguist frequently engages in translation which, according to Eugene A. Nida, 'consists in producing in the receptor language (also called the target language) the closest natural equivalent of the message of the source language, first in meaning and secondly in style'.[2] Nida's definition is appropriate for other forms of translation but it is somehow inadequate for the translation of drama texts, owing to the very nature of drama itself.

Since a play is culture-bound and meant essentially for performance, its translator must aspire to reproduce in the target language the linguistic and cultural elements which constitute its stageworthiness.[3] It is for this reason that the literary translator, in the words of André Lefevere, 'has to be a citizen of two worlds, a member of two civilisations, so that he is able to translate the socio-cultural framework of one world into that of another'.[4] But Lefevere's remark ought to be modified in the case of Guillaume Oyono-Mbia in so far as his plays and translations are rooted in the same Cameroonian culture.

In this regard, he stands apart from a writer like Samuel Beckett, with whom he shares certain affinities mainly on the ground that both of them use English and French in their creative writing and translating endeavours. In fact, it can be correctly argued that Oyono-Mbia, who works within a monocultural background, is even more fortunate than Beckett. Unlike the Irish playwright, who has to render his works from English into French and vice versa, Oyono-Mbia does not have to undertake the tricky and challenging task of translating 'the socio-cultural framework of one world into another'. But, like Beckett, he writes in both of them and translates his works to and from the two languages. It is of particular interest to the student of bilingualism to note that Oyono-Mbia's drama falls into two broad categories. The first category includes plays written originally in French, like *Trois prétendants . . . un mari* (1960) and *Notre fille ne se mariera pas* (1971). (He subsequently translated the former into English as *Three Suitors . . . One Husband* in 1967.)

The second group consists of *Until Further Notice* (1967) and *His Excellency's Special Train* (1969), which he composed in English and later on translated into French, respectively, as *Jusqu'à nouvel avis* (1967) and *Le Train spécial de son Excellence* (1973). Unlike his other plays, whose translations were published as separate texts, *His Excellency's Special Train* and *Le Train spécial de son Excellence* were issued in a single bilingual edition. This practice points to a new trend in Oyono-Mbia and it would be interesting to watch his development of the method, as it seems he will henceforth publish new plays in similar bilingual editions.

Oyono-Mbia's bilingualism is essentially the result of his background and training. His early education was in French, the official language of his native French Cameroon.[5] He began the study of English in the secondary school, and went on to take a combined degree in French and English at the University of Yaounde and a doctorate in European studies at the University of Keele in England. His career both as a university lecturer and as a civil servant kept him in Yaounde, a predominantly French-speaking town. This essay examines his particular brand of literary bilingualism and highlights some of its more important aspects.

Oyono-Mbia is justifiably more concerned with the accurate translation of the meaning of a speech from one language into the other (from English into French, and vice versa) than with paying scrupulous attention to the form and length of the speech. The following examples will illustrate this method:

BIKOKOE MENDEGUE: C'est pour cela! Les grands personnages doivent toujours avoir les meilleures choses de la terre! (*Le Train*, p. 18)

In the English version, he does not bother to translate 'de la terre', which would not add to the meaning of the passage:

BIKOKOE MENDEGUE: Exactly! Great men must always have the best! (*His Excellency's*, p. 18)

In another passage we have:

MISSA MAJUNGA: . . . On ne connaissait pas encore cette vogue de vin de palme et de boissons distillées localement. (*Le Train*, p. 24)

MISSA MAJUNGA: . . . Nobody ever touched palm wine, or any of the locally distilled spirits which have become so popular today. (*His Excellency's*, p. 24)

In the English version, he translates the idea which the character wishes to convey and therefore shuns a literal rendition of his speech. The English version is obviously longer than the French version, as he translates 'vogue', the key word in the French text, by the expression 'have become popular today' in preference to the abstract noun 'popularity' or 'fashion'.

As a good translator, Oyono-Mbia makes allowance for the cultural connotations of apparently ordinary expressions in order to bring out their realistic contextual meanings, as in the following passage:

ATANGANA: Un vrai fonctionnaire ne va pas rendre visite à une femme sans s'être au préalable muni d'une forte somme d'argent. (*Trois prétendants*, p. 17)

ATANGANA: No real civil servant would go courting without a large sum of money in his pocket. (*Three Suitors*, p. 12).

Here 'rendre visite' is not used in its ordinary sense of 'to pay a visit' or 'to visit', but in the sense of 'to woo a lady', 'to ask a lady's hand in marriage'. In the context of this play, therefore, 'rendre visite à une femme' implies a readiness on the part of the man or visitor to pay the customary bride-price, as the examples of Ndi and Mbia clearly show. It follows that he must have enough money on him during such a visit. Thus, the author/translator is right in using 'go courting' to translate 'rendre visite à une femme'.

Oyono-Mbia respects the language register of the passages he has to render in one or other of the two languages. For instance, he translates the vulgar French in this passage into a correspondingly vulgar English:

BIKOKOE MENDEGUE: . . . En tous cas il faut que moi, j'aille un peu pisser. (*Le Train*, p. 27)

BIKOKOE MENDEGUE: . . . Anyway, I must go and have a pee. (*His Excellency's*. p. 27)

The reader observes a number of differences between the French and English versions of Oyono-Mbia's plays. These differences are due to his additions to, deletions from or slight alterations of the original texts in the course of his translation. Generally, the additions are simple amplifications while the omissions hardly detract from the meaning of the original lines. The author/translator's reasons for lengthening, shortening or slightly modifying the original texts are easily understandable in some cases, while they are very difficult, if not impossible, to explain in others.

For instance, in the following translations the words in italics are additions to the original passages:

ABESSOLO: Your younger sister Matalina has just come back from overseas with her great man! They could easily pay back your husband! (*Until*, p. 96)

ABESSOLO: *Sois tranquille, Ada! Aussi vrai que je suis Abessolo, fils d'Essindi, neveu de la noble tribu des Essamkom, tout va bientôt s'arranger!* Matalina ta soeur cadette arrive cet après-midi avec son grand homme. Ils vont rembourser à ton mari l'argent qu'il nous avait versé! (*Jusqu'à*, p. 24)

In this example, the genealogical facts which Abessolo gives about himself do not add to the meaning of his speech in English. It is therefore impossible to understand Oyono-Mbia's intention in introducing the new details. A similar device in his French rendition of the English version of Mezoe's speech is difficult to explain in the following:

MEZOE: She promised! Besides, she wants to work in a big, modern hospital like the one in Yaounde, where she would only give orders to the less educated girls. (*Until*, p. 102)

MEZOE: Elle a promis de suivre mes conseils! *D'ailleurs elle même n'a aucune envie d'aller travailler en brousse, loin des cinémas et des magasins de produits de beauté.* Elle préfère travailler dans un grand hôpital moderne comme celui de Yaoundé: c'est là qu'elle se contenterait de donner des ordres aux filles moins instruites qu'elle. (*Jusqu'à*, pp. 32–3)

The addition states her preference for work in the town where she can go to the cinema and buy the cosmetics she needs whereas the original statement stresses only her position in her place of work and the influence as well as the authority which goes with it. Thus, the addition contains an entirely new and different fact which has no clear logical connection with the meaning of the original.

But the author/translator's addition to Meka's speech in this example merely amplifies it by stating clearly why he used to give her some cocoa whenever she was about to return to school:

MEKA: And I always said to her: 'Go to the kitchen, my daughter. Ask your mother Makrita to give you one kilogramme of cocoa. You'll sell it on your way to Metet, in Awae.' (*Until*, p. 99)

MEKA: Et moi, je lui disais, toujours: 'Va à la cuisine, mon enfant! Demande à ta mère Makrita de te donner un kilo de cocoa sec: tu le vendras au marché d'Awae, *pour t'acheter des cahiers et des crayons à Metet.*' (*Jusqu'à*, p. 28)

Also, in the following excerpt where Nkatefoe and Abessolo discuss the latter's former wife, Oyono-Mbia's additions in his translation provide more information about her beauty than is in the original. In fact, apart from their logical connection with the original, the additions underline her beauty:

NKATEFOE: [*with surprising sensuality*] Hmm! . . . She was a woman!
ABESSOLO: A woman! And what a good land too! That's where women never speak when men are speaking, and you can cut your wife's head off if she dares to turn her back on you in bed during the night . . . No missionaries, no . . . (*Until*, p. 106)

NKATEFOE: [*Avec une sensualité un peu surprenante*] Hmm! C'était une femme! . . . *Sa poitrine n'était pas encore pleinement formée, mais* . . .

ABESSOLO: *Elle n'avait encore que des épines de fromage sur la poitrine, mais c'était une vraie femme!* [*Un temps, il continue sur une note encore plus nostalgique*] *Et quel beau pays, ah Nkatefoe! C'est là que les femmes ne parlent jamais quand les hommes parlent. Tu peux très bien couper le cou à ta femme si jamais elle ose te tourner le dos au lit pendant la nuit . . . pas de missionaires, pas de . . .* (*Jusqu'à*, p. 38)

There is one addition in his translation of *His Excellency's Special Train*:

THE STATIONMASTER: Your special train should normally have been two hours late, Your Excellency. But . . . [*with a military salute*] thanks to my relentless and tireless efforts, I beg to officially inform you that the delay has been reduced to 120 minutes exactly. (*His Excellency's*, p. 57)

LE CHEF DE GARE: Votre train spécial avait, officiellement, deux heures de retard, Excellence. Mais . . . [*avec un salut militaire*] grâce aux efforts *inlassablement dignes d'éloges* que j'ai inlassablement déployés j'ai le respectueux honneur de vous annoncer officiellement que ce retard a été réduit à cent vingt minutes. (*Le Train*, p. 59)

Oyono-Mbia's addition to the Stationmaster's speech is meant to emphasize how great his efforts have been to ensure that His Excellency is not kept waiting for the train for too long.

Similarly, Oyono-Mbia's translation of *Trois prétendants . . . un mari* contains only one addition:

ONDUA: [*méthodique*] Il me faut, pour moi . . . euh . . . un grand lit en fer . . . un matelas en coton . . . euh . . . une armoire, des cou . . . (*Trois prétendants*, p. 42)

Here the author/translator adds 'ten cases of red wine, twenty bottles of' presumably white wine, or any other imported liquor, to Ondua's demands.

It is not only through additions that Oyono-Mbia incorporates changes of varying degrees in his translations. Sometimes, he makes deliberate omissions as can be seen in the following examples:

MEKA [*impatiently*]:   Patient? You want us to be patient! Don't you realise that man will soon be getting both his own and the salary of the daughter whose education we paid for? *Why do you think he wants to take her to that hospital somewhere in the bush? He wants to stop us . . .* (*Until*, p. 102)

MEKA [*impatiemment*]:   Patience? Tu nous dis de prendre patience? Tu ne vois pas que cet homme-là va bientôt toucher son propre salaire en même temps que le salaire de la fille dont nous avons nous-mêmes payé les frais d'instruction? (*Jusqu'à*, p. 32)

In the French translation, aside from Meka's uncompleted sentence, Oyono-Mbia also deletes the rhetorical question which serves to reinforce the main point of his speech. In doing so, he thinks that such emphasis is not really necessary. In *Three Suitors . . . One Husband*, he makes this rather long excision:

KOUMA: Pas encore! En fait, il leur reste encore bien des bouteilles d'arki à vider! Et le chef de village m'a dit: 'Mon fils, viens saluer Mbia, ton beau-frère! C'est lui le grand fonctionnaire qui vient de payer deux cent mille francs de dot pour ta cousine Juliette. *Dorénavant, si tu vois un de ces vauriens de collégiens tourner autour d'elle, dis-lui que Juliette est une femme mariée . . . Mon genre Mbia nous a versé deux cent mille francs . . .*' (*Trois prétendants*, p. 55)

KOUMA: Not yet! They still have quite a few bottles to empty, as a matter of fact. And the headman said to me: 'Come and greet Mbia, your brother-in-law! . . . He, the great civil servant from Sangmelima who's just paid two hundred thousand francs for your cousin Juliette!' (*Three Suitors*, p. 40)

It is difficult to explain why Oyono-Mbia deletes from his translation this passage, which throws light both on Abessolo's contempt for young students who cannot pay bride-prices for girls whom they want to marry, and on his joy that his family has found in Mbia a rich prospective son-in-law.

Discrepancies of the kind discussed above in Oyono-Mbia's plays are not limited to dialogue alone; they are to be found also in the stage-directions. For example, just at the moment when Juliette asks her parents if they really expect her to refund the school fees they paid for her, in the course of the discussion during which they try to persuade her to marry the rich civil servant, Mbia, the author gives this stage-direction in connection with the arrival of Mbia's car:

[*Ici, on entend le bruit caractéristique d'une grosse Mercedes Benz qui s'arrête sur la route, mais les acteurs sont trop scandalisés par la réplique de* JULIETTE *pour faire attention*] (*Trois prétendants*, p. 25)

This stage-direction, which relates to how Mbia carries himself and speaks during his visit to his prospective parents-in-law, is absent from the English version of the play. Moreover, the English translation omits the comparative clause and is not as precise as the French original:

MBIA: [*Se lève majestueusement et parle avec autant de solennité qu'un sous-préfet le jour de l'indépendance*] (*Trois prétendants*, p. 31)

MBIA: [*stands up majestically and speaks solemnly*] (*Three Suitors*, p. 22)

Differences also exist between the stage-directions in *Until Further Notice* and its French translation, *Jusqu'à nouvel avis*. For instance, early in the play, where Abessolo orders Mezoe to get some drinks for the elders of the village who have gathered to await the arrival of Matalina and her husband, the dramatist provides the following direction:

[MEZOE *goes to fetch a calabash of palm-wine at the far corner*] (*Until*, p. 97)

In the French text, this is given as:

[MEZOE *se dirige vers les calebasses de vin de palme tandis que* MEKA *allume sa pipe à l'aide d'allumettes empruntées à* ABESSOLO. NKATEFOE *regarde tout ceci d'un oeil désapprobateur*] (*Jusqu'à*, p. 25)

Thus the French text is longer as it contains information about Abessolo and Nkatefoe which is not in the original English text. The English text also specifies the location of the palm-wine whereas the French does not. Then, as Abessolo recalls with a feeling of nostalgia his former wife and her country (probably Equatorial Guinea or Fernando Po), the author observes in French:

[*Un temps: il continue sur une note encore plus nostalgique*] (*Jusqu'à*, p. 38)

This stage-direction is an addition to the French translation since it is absent from the original English text (*Until*, p. 106).

Finally, the stage-directions which bring the play to an end describe the light-hearted mood of Abessolo, the Driver and his Companion, who have been feasting themselves on Abessolo's palm-wine, which, in the words of the old man, is 'the best palm-wine in the whole Fong region'. These stage-directions read as follows in English:

[*The three of them burst out laughing heartily. Their laughter is soon covered by* MEKA'*s enthusiastic message on the talking drum, and the curtain falls a few moments later*] (*Until*, p. 113)

In the French text, we have:

[*Tous trois partent d'un énorme éclat de rire qui est bientôt couvert par le message de* MEKA *au tam-tam, derrière la maison principale. Lorsque le rideau tombe quelques instants plus tard, nous avons une brève et dernière vision d'*ABESSOLO *versant à boire au* CHAUFFEUR *et à son* COMPAGNON, *la mine réjouie de ces derniers montre clairement que le vin de palme d'*ABESSOLO *est sans conteste le meilleur dans tout le pays Fong*] (*Jusqu'à*, p. 48)

It is evident from the examples discussed so far that Oyono-Mbia incorporates changes of varying degrees when he translates his plays. Although these changes are fairly numerous, they are none the less generally minor and do not, in the final analysis, amount to such profound modifications as to make the translated versions of his plays distinctly different from the originals. Even so a translator other than the author himself would expose himself to charges of infidelity to the original if he made such changes.[6] But the charges of infidelity cannot be levelled against Oyono-Mbia since both texts originate from the author. Thus, Oyono-Mbia takes more liberties with his own material than another translator would and in the process makes it more dynamic.

Any serious consideration of Oyono-Mbia's bilingualism must take into account his ability to transfer the comic quality of his social comedies from one language to the other as a few examples will show. The following speech of the Stationmaster, striving to ingratiate himself with His Excellency at all costs, is as amusing in French as in English:

LE CHEF DE GARE: Votre train spécial avait, officiellement, deux heures de retard, Excellence. Mais ... [avec un salut militaire] grâce aux efforts inlassablement dignes d'éloges que j'ai inlassablement déployés j'ai le respectueux honneur de vous annoncer officiellement que ce retard a été réduit à cent vingt minutes. (Le Train, p. 59)

THE STATIONMASTER: Your special train should normally have been two hours late, Your Excellency. But ... [with a military salute] thanks to my own relentless and tireless efforts, I beg to officially inform you that the delay has been reduced to 120 minutes exactly. (His Excellency's, p. 57).

Oyono-Mbia conveys the amusing element in the Stationmaster's speech in both languages, first, by the officialese or elaborate language which he uses in order to impress His Excellency favourably but which is not effective because it betrays its intention, and, second, by his smart attempt to claim credit for having influenced the reduction of the train's delay of two hours to one hundred and twenty minutes, expressing the same period of time in minutes instead of in hours!

Similarly he brings out the obscene humour in the following remark in which Bilomba insinuates that Folinika is still sexually virile in spite of her claim to old age:

BILOMBA: ... D'ailleurs, tout le monde sait que lorsque c'est ton tour, le pauvre Missa Majunga ne parvient plus à fermer l'oeil de la nuit. (Le Train, p. 22)

BILOMBA: ... Besides, we all know you're still managing to keep Missa Majunga very warm and very active in bed, eh? (His Excellency's, p. 22)

In Until Further Notice, the ignorance exhibited by Abessolo and his wife about the difference between a doctor and a midwife provokes laughter:

CECILIA: ... Matalina also went there to become a doctor, you know!
MEZOE [sitting down]: A midwife.
CECILIA: What's the difference?
ABESSOLO: A doctor is a man; a midwife is his wife. (Until, p. 98)

Oyono-Mbia's French translation also brings out the ridiculous nature of Abessolo's explanation:

CECILIA: ... Matalina est allée là-bas pour devenir docteur elle aussi, vous savez!
MEZOE: ... Sage-femme, Na Cecilia.
CECILIA: N'est-ce pas la même chose?
ABESSOLO: Non évidemment: les docteurs sont des hommes: les sage-femmes sont leurs femmes. (Jusqu'à, p. 26)

It is pertinent to point out that Oyono-Mbia's works are not totally devoid of grammatical errors, which can be explained in most cases by linguistic interference. For instance, he translates 'nostalgique' (*Le Train*, p. 24) by 'with a touch of nostalgy' (*His Excellency's*, p. 36). This is a case of 'false friendship' for, needless to say, 'nostalgy' does not exist in English. 'Nostalgique', of course, can be rendered in English by 'nostalgically' or 'with nostalgia'.

Whereas Oyono-Mbia uses tautology in the following sentence:

MATALINA: Tu ne marcheras plus jamais à pied. (*Trois prétendants*, p. 27)

he translates it correctly in English thus:

MATALINA: . . . You'll no longer have to walk. (*Three suitors*, p. 19)

His translation of each of the following sentences is incorrect:

BIKOKOE MENDEGUE: Atangana lui avait égorgé deux porcs bien gras. (*Le Train*, p. 38)

BIKOKOE MENDEGUE: Atangana killed him two fat pigs. (*His Excellency's*, p. 37)

A correct translation should read: 'Atangana slaughtered two fat pigs for him' or better still: 'Atangana slaughtered two fat pigs in his honour.'

He uses 'justly' to translate 'j'avais raison' in the following sentence where 'with some justification' or 'confidently' is more appropriate.

ATANGANA: En l'envoyant au collège, j'avais bien raison de dire à tout le monde: 'Un beau jour, cela me rapportera.' (*Trois prétendants*, p. 15)

ATANGANA: When I sent her to secondary school, I was justly saying to everybody: 'Some day I'll benefit from that!' (*Three Suitors*, p. 11)

Finally, Oyono-Mbia mixes up the correct French expression 'être né sous une bonne étoile'.

MATALINA: Ma cousine est vraiment née avec une étoile sur le front! (*Trois prétendants*, p. 16)

He goes on to translate it word for word, thus mixing up the well-known English equivalent of the French expression:

MATALINA: My cousin was definitely born with a star on her forehead. (*Three Suitors*, p. 11)

The correct French and English expressions are, respectively: 'Ma cousine est vraiment née sous une bonne étoile' and 'My cousin was definitely born under a lucky star.'

However insignificant the grammatical flaws cited above may appear, they cannot be ignored in a study which examines Oyono-Mbia's bilingualism – they appear more in his English than in his French, a natural result of his background. He nevertheless expresses himself with sufficient ease and competence in both languages to qualify as a true bilingual playwright.

NOTES AND REFERENCES

I have used the following abbreviations in the quotations in this article:

Trois prétendants – *Trois prétendants . . . un mari*
Three Suitors   – *Three Suitors . . . One Husband*
Jusqu'à   – *Jusqu'à nouvel avis*
Until   – *Until Further Notice*
Le Train   – *Le Train spécial de son Excéllence*
His Excellency's   – *His Excellency's Special Train.*

1. Maurice van Overberke, *Introduction au problème du bilinguisme*, Bruxelles, Labor, and Paris, Feru and Nathan, p. 119.
2. Rene Haeseryn, 'The role of specialized non-literary translation in the development of general and specialized language', *Babel*, vol. 23, no. 3, 1977, p. 103.
3. The importance of translating drama texts with performance in view and the recognition of the changing nature of acting styles and concepts of drama have led some critics to suggest that the translation of a play should be undertaken every fifty years. See Georges Mounin, 'Traduction au théâtre', *Babel*, vol. 14, no. 1, 1968. pp. 7–11.
4. 'The translation of literature: an approach', *Babel*, vol. 16, no. 2, 1970, p. 79.
5. Cameroon was a German colony until the First World War. After the war, the eastern part was administered by the French while the western part was administered by the British under the trusteeship of the League of Nations. Both parts were reunited to form the Federal Republic of Cameroon on 1 October 1961.
6. Ekundayo Simpson, *Samuel Beckett: traducteur de lui-même: Aspects de bilinguisme littéraire*, Publication B-79, Quebec, CIRB/ICRB, 1978. I found this work particularly helpful in writing the present article.

BIBLIOGRAPHY

Trois prétendants . . . un mari, Yaounde, Editions CLE, 1964.
Three Suitors . . . One Husband/Until Further Notice, London, Methuen, 1968.
Jusqu'à nouvel avis, Yaounde, Editions CLE, 1970.
Le Train spécial de son Excellence/His Excellency's Special Train, Yaounde, Editions CLE, 1979.

Graphology & Meaning in the Poetry of Christopher Okigbo

Modupe Olaogun

This article explores the graphological patterns of Okigbo's poetry as a means of relating the form of that poetry to its content. It aims, in other words, to examine the way Okigbo tries to 'mean' graphologically; how graphology is a source of 'obscurity'[1] in the poetry; and how an understanding of the graphology can help in unravelling this obscurity. In so doing it will be providing a complementary alternative to the usual focus on the verbal source of Okigbo's obscurity. The first part of the article explores graphology within the context of linguistic representation. It also explores graphology as a grammatical, semantic and tonal resource in poetry. The insights yielded by this exploration provide, in a sense, a fulcrum for the analysis which follows in the second part. This section will chart graphological patterns in Okigbo's poetry, taking samples from different stages of his poetic career.

I

Graphology refers to the physical appearance of the text on the page. Here graphology is given the kind of interpretative potential that would be ascribed to phonology, lexis and syntax in linguistic analysis. The category is taken to include 'orthography, punctuation, and anything else that is concerned with showing how a language uses its graphic resources to carry its grammatical and lexical patterns'.[2]

Graphology has often been disregarded or subordinated to phonology in much analysis of processes of signification, the argument usually being that it is merely a way of representing speech. But, as Angus McIntosh demonstrates in a seminal study of graphology,

> an organised written system of language has a status equivalent to any spoken 'opposite number' it may have; it simply manifests *language* in another substance – one which appeals to the eye rather than to the ear. In other words it is not a mere second-degree system in the way implied by Aristotle in *De Interpretatione* when he says that written words are the symbols of spoken words ... [W]ritten language and spoken language both symbolise mental experience but ... written language, by virtue of its graphological system, *also* symbolises spoken language.[3]

Indeed, one need only look at the Chinese ideographs to demonstrate McIntosh's point. In the scribal tradition, the emblematic poems of George Herbert and Dylan Thomas,[4] or, more strikingly, the calligraphic poetry of Guillaume Apollinaire,[5] as well as the 'concrete' poetry of Ian Finlay, Emmett Williams and Nichols[6] also readily prove McIntosh's point.

Taking a different route, Jacques Derrida in his reappraisal of the rhetoric of philosophy also reinstates writing to a position of equal, if not greater, respectability vis-à-vis speech. Derrida's strategy is a vigorous questioning of the assumption of 'the Western metaphysics of presence', which grounds itself in the myth of origin and consequently pursues an ultimate, transcendental signified. This erstwhile logocentric tradition, Derrida proves, had bestowed on speech a supreme value based upon its supposedly inherent capability to embody intention, hence its unique privilege to ideal objectivity. In contrast, writing is presumed to bear the taint of mediation or, at best, to be a lifeless token of expressive, content-filled speech. In Derrida's deconstructive project, which entails the exposure of the illusion of a determinate meaning predicated upon presence, the term 'writing' is applied not simply to the graphic notation of language but also to the more insidious inscriptions of language that are generated by a complex historical–intertextual process within which an utterance or a text is located. The active ingredient in Derrida's appreciation of language is a feature which he terms 'differance'. According to Derrida, 'differance' is evoked not so much as a word or a concept but as 'the *strategic* note or connection . . . which indicates the closure of presence'.[7] Stated differently, 'differance' indicates the lack of immediate and total accessibility to meaning by virtue of the fact that language entails a canny and interminable interplay of deferral and difference.

The implications of Derrida's arguments cannot be fully investigated here,[8] but their point of interest for the present study derives from the exposure of the constructed nature of the prioritization of speech as repository of meaning. Also, Derrida's investigation demonstrates the active, rather than passive, interaction of texts in the sense of a critical dialogue of a text with itself as well as with other texts. The former marks the text's self-deconstructive propensity and the latter its intertextuality.

Concomitant with Derrida's demystificatory project is a relocation of meaning not in immanent and immutable terms, but in more human and sceptical terms. But, for all its breakthrough in the discussion of the rhetoric of language, Derrida's deconstructive theory, with its over-wrought attention to the 'textness' of the text, has been seen as a ruse for escaping the actuality of the world and its political urgencies. Edward Said's corresponding appreciation of the text's public nature, its political circumstantiality or 'worldliness',[9] reaffirms the text's cardinal relations to palpable politics. The present focus on graphology is not riveted to just the 'textness' of the text but anchors the text within its circumstantiality.

The study does not preclude references to the other levels of language. The various levels, after all, do often collaborate in the making and meaning of poetry. The interrelationship of the various levels will be seen, for example, in the harmony between phonology and graphology in much rhymed poetry. The placing of the rhyme at the end of a line is an announcement through graphology of the phonological significance of the line. It is also impossible to think of a strict dichotomy between graphology and syntax in the complex inversion that is characteristic of the poetry of Gerard Manley Hopkins, Wole Soyinka and most characteristically, Okigbo. The semantic aspect comes in when it is realized that any poetic arrangement is ultimately a mode of meaning, or a physical purveyor for a more generalized or abstract kind of meaning.

Often a poet manipulates a text graphologically to make it easily distinguishable as poetry: traditionally, poetry has a 'characteristic' lineation which has no equivalent in prose. Within the genre of poetry are various kinds with different styles of lineation. In the sonnet, for example, variations in the thought-pattern are mediated through lineation: in the Petrarchan type, the situation or problem is stated in the octave, with the resolution taking place in the sestet. The ballad has stanzas whose lines are metrically regulated to achieve a musical tempo. Free verse, without the traditional accoutrements of rhyme and uniform metre, achieves through graphology similar and other important effects. By merely 'playing' with the line poets evoke symbolic shapes for the ideas they try to convey. George Herbert's supplications in 'Easter-Wings' float on the poem's visual wings. Dylan Thomas draws attention to the complementarity of the two parts of 'Vision and Prayer' through their shapes. The graphological architecture of this poem is suggestive of the mortise and tenon. The shapes could, however, also be seen as diamonds, hourglasses and wings.[10] Through graphology, Dylan Thomas heightens the ambiguity of his poem.

The line, too, serves as a punctuation mark for some poets. By isolating a word or a word group, the poet draws attention to it. The line becomes a warning system to the reader about the significance of the word or word group, as in the poem titled 'Luo Plains' by Wole Soyinka:

Plague
Of comet tails, of bled horizons
Where egrets hone a sky-lane for
Worlds to turn on pennants

Lakemists
On her shadeless dugs, parched
At waterhole. Veils. Molten silver
Down cloudflues of alchemist sun . . .
A lake's grey salve at dawn?

That dawn
Her eyes were tipped with sunset spears
Seasons' quills upon her parchment, yet
The hidden lake of her

Forgives!

For she has milked a cycle of
Red sunset spears, sucked reeds of poison
To a cowherd's flute. The plains

Are swift again on migrant wings
And the cactus
Flowers the eagle sentinel[11]

A violent concourse of expressive and archetypal phenomena, the scene
captured by this poem breaks forth in the impressionistic description. The
confluence of forceful words and their arrangement produces a picture
of grand, yet raw, energy. The staccato appearance of some of the words
fits the general purpose of recording impressions. The lexical items
'plague' and 'lakemists', which are segments of larger grammatical
units, are given special focus by being linearly isolated from their post-
modifiers – one a genitival-prepositional phrase, the other a preposi-
tional-locative. The nominal group, 'That dawn', is linearly amplified to
take a central place in the poem: it becomes the theme from the third
stanza to the end. The dawn is both setting and, in its archetypal role as
the sun's consort, accomplice in the sexual violence which dominates the
poem: 'Her eyes were tipped with sunset spears/Seasons' quills upon her
parchment'; 'For she has milked a cycle of/Red sunset spears, sucked
reeds of poison'. The cycle of relentless craving and pain is sustained by
the singular act of forgiveness. This gesture of extenuation is underscored
graphologically by isolating the word 'forgives' and putting an exclama-
tion mark after it. The verb, separated from its grammatical subject by
enjambment, is so placed that it calls attention to itself.

Through the use of the more conventional punctuation marks various
lyrical effects are achieved by poets. Rather than be seen as sheer
eccentricity, Emily Dickinson's dashes seem to be devised as a means of
preventing the reader from racing through the lyrics without pondering
the words. Dickinson, in addition, imbues words with majesty through the
capitalization of the initial letters.

Also through the employment of punctuation, Atukwei Okai is able to
bring to the reader's ears the *tomtomfrom* which throbs in the background
of his poetry. The drum rises to a frenzied crescendo in his invocation of
each historical or literary figure, and continues to pulsate as he assumes
his lament, in 'Lorgorligi Logarithms':

jawa apronti, ARE YOU THERE?!
ayikwei armah, WHERE ARE YOU?!
atta britwum, ARE YOU THERE?![12]

In Okigbo's poetry, tonality, laconicism, ambiguity, symbolism and
lyricism are among the chief effects of the exploitation of graphology. An
attempt to achieve some or all of these effects in one breath often leads
to obscurity, but sometimes it simply heightens the density of the poetry.

II

Okigbo's concern for the graphological shape of his poetry is perhaps
suggested by his acknowledgement, on more than one occasion, of his debt
to Ben Obumselu, then of the University of Ibadan, 'for criticisms which
led to improvements in phrase and structure'.[13] The poems themselves

are strong evidence of this concern. From the early poems, including 'Four Canzones',[14] to *Path of Thunder*,[15] there is a technical adventurousness, climaxed in the *Transition* 'Distances',[16] which contains visually striking architectonic shapes. The Heinemann 'Distances',[17] as well as many of the 'revised versions' of the other poems, shows considerable trimming at the grapho-syntactic level.

Perhaps Okigbo's famous declaration that he was a poets' poet[18] was meant to suggest that he aimed at utilizing to the fullest, and going beyond, the licence ordinarily granted to poets. His predominant choice of free verse would seem appropriate because it offered the least restrictions, especially graphologically. Okigbo grew up in the ferment of the influence of T.S. Eliot, Ezra Pound and Dylan Thomas – poets who had immediate recognition for their inventiveness. This inventiveness cannot be fully investigated here, but suffice it to mention the salient features of the trio's poetry: grammatical deviation, syntactic inversion, allusiveness, verbal terseness and tonality. Like these poets and others before him, Okigbo honed his poems until the gem remained. Graphology bore the brunt of this sculpturing.

One of Okigbo's earliest poems is 'Song of the Forest', published as part of the 'Four Canzones'. Ostensibly based on Virgil's *Tityrus*,[19] the derivation is not one of literal correspondence or subservience and, indeed, Virgil's poem is a model in a very broad sense. Omolara Leslie has already indicated Okigbo's formal departure in terms of the pointed brevity of the poem and also his transposition of the pastoral to a modern Nigerian scene in which a city-dweller feels an acute sense of alienation from rural life. Leslie tacitly attributes the formal simplicity of 'Song of the Forest' to Virgil's example in the eclogue.[20] However, 'Song of the Forest' also shares with some of the other earliest poems, without bringing in Virgil,[21] a graphological and syntactic simplicity that makes them easy reading.

'Song of the Forest' 'translates' Virgil on Okigbo's terms. It begins characteristically with the capitalization of the first two words:

YOU LOAF, child of the forest,

The capitalized words gain focus typographically and rhetorically as a nominative of address. Commas are used, quite conventionally, as a device for appositional elaboration and, more strikingly, for tonality. Through well-measured pauses the commas produce a majestic melody:

YOU LOAF, child of the forest,
beneath a village umbrella,
plucking from tender string a
    Song of the forest.
Me, away from home, run-
away, must leave the borders of our home
land, fruitful fields,
    must leave our homeland.

But you, child of the forest,
loaf beneath an umbrella,
teaching the woods to sing a
    song of the forest.

The commas are integral to the depiction of the dramatis personae of the poem. The two 'characters' are contrasted pronominally. Through appositional elaboration the one emerges as a denizen and the other as a fugitive. The commas make the syntax easy to follow. The lexical items are generally everyday, not arcane. One of such everyday words, 'runaway', is exploited graphologically – through hyphenation – to direct the interpretation of the poem along more ambiguous lines. Because it is compound, and located at the end of the line, 'runaway' presumably has a basis for being split. By separating the suffix 'away' from the root 'run' (5th and 6th lines), the suffix is given an independent status, and consequently acquires a similarity with the first 'away' in the 5th line. This intensifies the adverbial quality of the preposition 'away', and places the focus on the uneventful situation of the fugitive rather than on the act of escape.

Although published together with 'Song of the Forest' in the 'Four Canzones', both 'Lament of the Flutes' (1960) and 'Lament of the Lavender Mist' (1961) are remarkably different from the first poem. By this time Okigbo tended to be less lavish with words, resorting more frequently to ellipses, and designating the connective 'and' by a sign. In addition, he breaks off sentences with dashes and paradoxically employs these dashes as a means of connecting fragmented units or of forcing connections between independent clauses or thought units.

'Lament of the Flutes' traces memories of some catalytic experiences in the poet's development. Apprehension about the reliability of the apparatus of recall is pre-empted in the elliptical marks which take over soon after the poem begins:

TIDEWASH . . . Memories
fold-over-fold free-furrow,
mingling old tunes with new.
Tidewash . . .

The elliptical marks convey the vagueness and fragmentary nature of memory, just as words serve as a regulatory device:

Ride me
memories, astride on firm
saddle.

Elliptical marks accompany the refrain until the end of the poem when they are dropped to affirm the transformation in the poet's sensibility. The tentativeness and dilatoriness found in the refrain at the beginning:

Sing to the rustic flute:
Sing a new note . . .

gives way to a more positive assertion as the poet's probing progresses to a finale:

Shall I offer to *Idoto*
my sandhouse and bones,
then write no more on snow-patch?

Sing to the rustic flute.
Sing a new note.

Nearly every kind of punctuation mark employed in 'Lament of the Flutes' will be found in 'Lament of the Lavender Mist', but the latter poem is much more complex. The poem's complexity is jointly accounted for by collocational deviation and graphology. The poem begins as follows:

(i)
BLACK dolls
Returning from the foam:
Two faces of a coin
That meet afar off ...

Sea smiles at distance
        with lips of foam
Sea walks like rainbow
        beyond them.

The style established by these lines is very much sustained throughout the poem. The salient aspects of that style are: a propensity for separating grammatical elements which are often proximate in discursive formations; ellipsis; and a profuse use of dashes. Take, for instance, the construction beginning 'And voice' ending 'wakes us ...', which, considered as a sentence, displays a number of interruptive elements. The line, 'Air, sun, blood ...' bears no discursive continuity with the construction, yet its appearance in that particular spot will have to be accounted for. Generally, dashes serve as an elaborative and a parenthetic device, and it is not difficult to discern these traditional roles of dashes. However, within the entire graphological layout of the poem the dashes and ellipses appear to derange the syntax, as illustrated by the sequence,

And voice
Returning from a dream,
Descends, rejoices –
Air, sun, blood ...
        And wakes us ...
DOLLS ...
Forms
Of memory,
To be worshipped
Adored
By innocence:
Creatures of the Mind's eye
Barren –
Of memory –
Remembrance of things past.
            [Okigbo's ellipses]

The poem presents what Annemarie Heywood describes in a study of *Labyrinths* as a 'building up of compulsive series of significances'.[22] Through a configuration of the 'significances' which she identifies in *Labyrinths*, Heywood is able to determine that Okigbo's poetry is 'ritual' in the sense of being 'in itself a ritual instrument'. It is indeed possible to sort out the various themes, motifs and so on in Okigbo's poems and reconfigure these to arrive at some kind of overall significance of the poetry. However, this structural remoulding of the poetry underplays, or even disregards altogether, whatever significance is generated by the space relations governing the various configurations.

'Lament of the Lavender Mist' (1961) prefigures later poems, particularly 'Limits' and *Path of Thunder*, as prophetic poetry. The graphological evidence of the poem supports this reading. First, the poem evokes phases from precreation to apocalypse. Secondly, it recalls and projects aspects of cultural history. The inchoate, precreative state is captured in such surrealistic images as 'Sea walks like rainbow/beyond them', and in more straightforward descriptions and allusive phrases such as 'abyss', 'the wind and the waves' and 'Echoes of the waters of the beginning'. The apocalypse is hinted at in 'Shadows of the fires of the end'. Between the polar stages of birth and death the poem enacts the intervening phases, mostly initiatory and exploratory. These are engendered by the act of worship and through the protagonist's metaphysical experience with the female figure, the 'Lady of the lavender-mist'.

As Okigbo explores the events of the individual's life cycle from birth to death in the poem, so does he proclaim on public events. The black dolls are cultural icons of childhood and of the incarnative/image-making propensity. The historical pith of the dolls is projected not simply through the cultural specificity implied by 'black' but, by virtue of its allusion to Leon Damas's poem 'Limbe', the phrase evokes the context which generated Damas's journey back to his childhood and the reaffirmation of his original cultural values.[23] Okigbo's poem is more a reappraisal of African cultural and historical experience. The re-vision in 'Lament of the Lavender Mist' is graphically realized through the repetition of dolls and in the modulated form, 'Of masks, black masks, idols'. The reverberation is effected through the elliptical marks and dashes – punctuation marks which will ordinarily be perceived as anacoluthic (interruptive) agents. An exception, Dan Izevbaye remarks of ellipsis in Okigbo's poetry that it is 'an invitation to conjecture and deduction'.[24] No doubt, the ellipses in Okigbo's poetry proclaim semantic openness; however, they frame meaning in a less chancy and schematic manner than might be implied in Izevbaye's suggestion. In 'Lament of the Masks' the ellipses kindle circumspection even as they invite interpretative openness. The poem invites circumspection of the 'forms of memory' presented by the black dolls:

BLACK dolls
Returning from the foam:
Two faces of a coin
That meet afar off . . .

and

> And voice
> Returning from a dream,
> Descends, rejoices –
> Air, sun, blood . . .
>   And wakes us . . .
> DOLLS . . .
>   [Okigbo's ellipses]

Like the inspired medium which arouses worshippers and bereaved relatives in the ceremony of souls,[25] or the charged voice of the Old Testament prophets, 'voice' descends in Okigbo's poem and memory is awakened. The pre-vocal barrenness associated with mind gives way to remembrance; and mind, released from the prison of abstraction, opens up to extraordinary perceptions. The protagonist wakes up into the 'abyss of wonders'; he encounters the multiform lady of the lavender-mist, who as earth mother is supremely constituted in 'Dance of the Painted Maidens'.[26] In the latter poem exact phrases identified with creation and apocalypse in 'Lament of the Lavender Mist', namely 'waters of the beginning' and 'fires of the end', define the earth mother. The metaphysical 'Lady' is the instrument by which the protagonist undergoes the vital initiations, the passages through the various stages of life's cycle from birth to death.

As vision and pre-vision of public events, perhaps the poem's most remarkable line is: 'Eagles in space and earth and sky'. This line recurs in both 'Limits' and *Path of Thunder*. By examining its recurrence or reverberations it will be demonstrated how the line is generated into a leitmotif of public prophecy in Okigbo's poetry.

In 'Limits' the metaphor of the eagles occurs in the poem titled 'Fragments out of the Deluge', specifically in sections VIII and X. 'Limits VIII' presents the sunbird iterating from the oilbean tree a vision of a fleet of eagles ominously parading their strength and splendour. The eagles, ostentatious and vexatious, are identified with the bronze metal. They bedazzle the landscape with their strength. 'Limits X' projects the eagle metaphor again as it recounts an outrage committed by an invading fleet. The invaders had spitefully desolated the community by murdering its gods and the prophetic sunbird.

The sunbird overlooking the landscape from the sacred oilbean tree in 'Limits VIII' is easily placed as a priest-prophet. Read against the events of the day the eagles in the sunbird's utterance may be matched with the power-brokers of Nigeria's first republic. Historical interpolations imposed by the tense of, and the kind of details in, 'Limits X' identify the set of eagles here as the colonizers, but Okigbo's metaphor fuses into one archetypal image both sets of participants in the two historical references.

In *Path of Thunder* the metaphor of eagles is resonant in these lines:

> Statuettes of legendary heroes – iron birds
>   ('Thunder Can Break', *Labyrinths*, p. 63)

Magic birds with the miracle of lightning flash on their feathers . . .
('Come Thunder', ibid., p. 66)

AND THE HORN may now paw the air howling goodbye . . .

For the Eagles are now in sight:
Shadows in the horizon –

THE ROBBERS are here in black sudden steps of showers, of caterpillars –

THE EAGLES have come again,
The eagles rain down on us –
('Elegy for Alto', ibid., p. 71)

The most prominent occurrence of the eagle metaphor is in 'Elegy for Alto', where eagles are explicitly made to stand for politicians. The politicians, who are called robbers, are identified here with iron, symbol of inexorable strength and, in classical mythology, of ultimate degeneracy.

If Okigbo's poetry were to be read backwards, from *Path of Thunder* to 'Lament of the Lavender Mist', the line 'Eagles in space and earth and sky' would be more readily recognizable as an important prognostic leitmotif in his mytho-history. The linguistic accuracy of 'Lament of the Lavender Mist' comes from Okigbo's archetypal apprehension of both individual and cultural history, as well as his assured mythopoeic dispensation of language. But, whereas 'Lament of the Lavender Mist' functions as prophecy through its intuitive apprehension of cycles of individual and cultural history, *Path of Thunder* defines prophecy in terms of forecast and forewarning. The latter is consequently far less recondite grapho-syntactically.

The most striking feature of *Path of Thunder*, explicitly subtitled 'poems prophesying war', is the extendedness of the utterance units in contrast to the highly compressed form of 'Lament of the Lavender Mist'. Words come forth more freely; verbs are not frequently suppressed; and there is less collocational confusion. The proximity of clause elements aids intelligibility. The themes are repeated within and across the poems which make up *Path of Thunder*. Again there is a profuse use of elliptical marks and dashes, with the former bearing reverberative echoes and the latter being generally elaborative or anacoluthic (i.e. interruptive), for instance:

The General is up . . . the General is up . . . commandments . . .
the General is up the General is up the General is up –
condolences from our twin-beaks and feathers of condolence

and

thunder fells the trees cut a path
thunder smashes them all – condolences . . .

THUNDER that has struck the elephant
the same thunder should wear a plume – condolences
('Elegy for Slit-drum', *Labyrinths*, pp. 68–70)

Nearly every one of the poems in *Path of Thunder* ends in ellipses, the poems solemnly trailing into apprehensive silence. Silence is Okigbo's metaphorical exploration of 'the music to which all imperishable cries must aspire'.[27] *Path of Thunder* in fact shares with the poems in the sequence titled 'Silences'[28] a deep anguish that words seem unable to give adequate shape.

The foregoing reveals the close relationship of 'Lament of the Lavender Mist' to 'Limits' and *Path of Thunder* despite the pervasive tendency to overlook this seminal poem in discussions of Okigbo's poetry; or to sketchily identify it, when it finds rare mention, with Okigbo's more self-exploratory poems in *Labyrinths*.

The poems which Okigbo published with Heinemann as a volume titled *Labyrinths* are compositionally placed between the 'Canzones' and *Path of Thunder*. Generally, the poems in *Labyrinths* have some affinity with 'Lament of the Lavender Mist' – in their tendency to be cryptic. The fact that the poems are often very allusive, coupled with the complex inversions and a ruthless economy through a suppression of verbs and other graphic resources, accounts for the difficulty associated with reading these poems. The problems identified here are perhaps as intense as those created by Okigbo's 'revisions' of the poems which eventually make up this volume. To illustrate both sets of difficulties I shall examine 'Distances', which presents the most striking variants, each of which I shall denote by their means of publication, as *Transition* 'Distances' and Heinemann 'Distances'. Of Okigbo's poems it is also 'Distances' which I find to be the most compelling – by virtue of its extraordinary construction of the perennial subject, death; in Heinemann 'Distances' Okigbo's lyrical genius attains its peak.

Transition 'Distances' presents an attempt at a conflation of shape and meaning while Heinemann 'Distances' shows a dependence on ordinary lineation and the sheer collocational force of words to project meaning. Like George Herbert, Okigbo constructed graphological shapes which emulate architectural structures in *Transition* 'Distances IV':

And at the archway	T
a triangular lintel	HE
of alabaster	ONL
enclosed in a square	YWAY
inscribed in a circle	TOGOT
with a hollow centre	HROUGH
above the archway	THEMARB
yawning shutterless	LEARCHWA
like celestial pincers	YTOTHECAT
like a vast countenance	ATONICPING
	PONGOFTHEEV
	ANESCENTHALO

     the only way to go
     through the marble archway
     to the catatonic pingpong
     of the evanescent halo . . .

and beyond the archway
like pentecostal orbs

resplendent far distant
in the intangible void
an immense crucifix
of phosphorescent mantles:

AFTER

WEHAD

THENONLYTHEFORMSWEREFORMEDANDALLTHEFORMSWERE

AFTER

OURFO

RMING

after we had formed
then only the forms were formed
and all the forms were formed
after our forming . . .
(*Transition*, vol. 4, no. 16, 1964, pp. 11-12).

In Heinemann 'Distances', Okigbo is content with ordinary lineation and does away with the emblematic use of graphology. *Transition* 'Distances IV' is actually verbally similar to Heinemann 'Distances IV', the basic difference being the absence of the iconic shapes which are constructed of words taken from the italicized lines of the poem.

The entire *Transition* 'Distances' shows a very important structural difference from the Heinemann 'Distances' in the former's use of the connective 'and' to provide narrative continuity. This connective is replaced by the function word 'for' or sometimes expunged altogether in several structurally confluent positions in Heinemann 'Distances', as indicated by the following excerpts:

I
For [And] in the inflorescence of the white
chamber,

II
For [And] the wind, eternal suitor of dead leaves,
unrolled his bandages to the finest swimmer . . .

[And] It was an evening without flesh or skeleton;

III
[And] In the scattered line of pilgrims

VI
[*for*] the goat still knows [*will know*] its fodder
[*and*] the leopards [*leopard*] on its trail . . .
For [And] it is the same blood
through the same orifices
                    [My italics and interpolations –
                    to indicate *Transition* version]

Also as a means of maintaining structural continuity in *Transition* 'Distances', there is consistency in the denotation of the white chamber as the physical location where the experience takes place. But in Heinemann 'Distances' the white chamber gives way to Shibboleth in section III. Finally, five lines which begin section VI of *Transition* 'Distances' are excised in Heinemann 'Distances':

And in the intimacy
of the evanescent halo,
the symbol, forsaken
in a cloud of incense,

delivers herself of her bandages . . .

These lines, which begin with the ubiquitous 'and', provide a double-edged form of continuity between this section and the rest of the poem, dwelling as they do on the ambience of the phantasmic experience. They evoke symbols of death's realm and of the initiate's experience.

The implications of all these structural differences will lead to a suggestion that, rather than be seen as versions of each other, *Transition* 'Distances' and Heinemann 'Distances' are indeed two separate poems. To elaborate, in *Transition* 'Distances' the word 'and' functions variously in the manner of the connective temporal adverbials 'then', 'thereupon', 'next', 'afterwards', 'in addition'. In Heinemann 'Distances' the word 'for', also conjunctive, is understood to function as an explanative: 'wherefore', 'since', 'because'. The word 'and' projects a sequential manner of revelation and it is an invitation to a paratactic apprehension of experience. On the other hand the situations introduced by the word 'for' need not be diachronically related to the situations described by their grammatical antecedents. In fact, Heinemann 'Distances' reinforces a complex synchronicity in the apprehension of the ethereal experiences delineated by this poem. Whereas the strophes in *Transition* 'Distances' are more laterally connected to each other, the strophes in Heinemann 'Distances' are technically more independent of one another but in fact interact both laterally and vertically. Heinemann 'Distances' is more liable to greater structural looseness and multivalency. Okigbo's achievement in this respect is comparable to that of Guillaume Apollinaire, who substituted graphically evocative shapes and disruptive structures for linear and discursive forms to project his concept of 'simultaneity'. By his practice Apollinaire was inviting an active engagement of the reader with the process of synthesis involved in poetic representation.[29]

The reference to Shibboleth in section III of Heinemann 'Distances' retains the poem within the context of purgative death. But paradoxically it widens and inscribes this context through the mytho-religious archetype. On the other hand, the white chamber employed throughout *Transition* 'Distances' is imbued with associative freedom although that freedom is also circumscribed by the identification of 'white' and 'chamber' with the ubiquitous female figure who tortures and redeems the poem's protagonist.

Overall *Transition* 'Distances' tends towards structural explicitness. As already demonstrated above, the particular structural connective employed in the poem proclaims a paratactic style. The poem's graphic icons may also be seen as a demystificatory scheme. For one thing the vision is very abstract, but it presents geometrical shapes which are quite definite. And for all their superfluity the shapes do incarnate this very abstract vision. The two graphic shapes represent symbols which are identified with religion and geometry; the one is a speculative or metaphysical field, the other traces very precise and definite outlines. But the speculativeness of the one is belied by the forceful, palpable position it occupies in human activity; while the imaginative disposition of the other is not occluded by its precision. The tension between these two symbolic polar values is what this section of the poem is about. All through the section images of three-dimensional experience jostle with fourth-dimensional reality, the palpable with the ultra-fine. The vision is, after all, death's portal and the transitional nature of the experience is suggested in the fusion of the two symbolic representational modes.

The potential for greater ambiguities in Heinemann 'Distances' will be acknowledged. Without the emblematic shapes, the poem is tighter and more brief. The lines which provide the bricks for the architectonics in *Transition* 'Distances' are, after all, italicized in both poems. The italicization constitutes in itself a form of highlight, so that the emblematic shapes might be taken as an over-representation. Conversely, intensity rather than a mid or *sotto voce* effect might have been intended, taking into account the musical terms on which the poem invites appreciation, from the implicit analogy with music in section I:

> For in the inflorescence of the white
> chamber, a voice, from very far away,
> chanted, and the chamber descanted, the birthday of earth,
> paddled me home through some dark
> labyrinth, from laughter to the dream.
>   (from Heinemann 'Distances')

In fact, read as a musical score, Heinemann 'Distances IV' does not have the strongly contrapuntal suggestiveness of *Transition* 'Distances IV'. However, the rest of Heinemann 'Distances' shows a more assured cadence than does *Transition* 'Distances'. As illustration, the lines above are more finely and elegantly modulated than the following, which constitute the equivalent in Transition 'Distances':

> And in the inflorescence of the white chamber,
> a voice, from very far away, chanted, and the chamber descanted
> the birthday of earth, paddling me home through
> some dark labyrinth, from laughter to the dream.

The greater tonality of Heinemann 'Distances' can be related to the greater relaxation towards the subject of death which this poem conveys overall. This effect is partly a product of the semantic import of the structural connective 'for', which has been partially commented on. This word is suggestive of 'the already and always': 'since' 'because'. It is attended by knowledge and retrospection. Thus, 'the goat still knows its fodder,/the leopards on its trail' rather than the *Transition*'s 'the goat will know its fodder/and the leopard on its trail'. The situations which advance the protagonist to death are then welcomed with greater assurance and faith. The end of *Transition* 'Distances',[30] with its largely unvarying rhythm, dulls the arrival of the protagonist while the finale of Heinemann

'Distances' bespeaks a triumphal but solemn arrival through its superb, varied measure:

> And at this chaste instant of delineated anguish,
> the same voice, importunate, aglow with the goddess –
>
> unquenchable, yellow, darkening homeward
> like a cry of wolf above crumbling houses –
>
> strips the dream naked,
> bares the entrails;
>
> and in the orangery of immense corridors,
> I wash my feet in your pure head, O maid,
>
> and walk along your feverish, solitary shores,
>
> seeking, among your variegated teeth,
> the tuberose putrescent laughter;
>
> I have fed out of the drum
> I have drunk out of the cymbal
>
> I have entered your bridal
> chamber; and lo,
>
> I am sole witness to my homecoming.

The foregoing, while unravelling the graphological features of 'Distances', has also put in a different perspective the troublesome issue of the different editions of Okigbo's poetry. In discussions of the so-called different 'versions', there has tended to be an appeal for ultimate resolution in Okigbo's prefatorial comments in Heinemann *Labyrinths* that the poems in that collection were a 'final' version. But suppose the first published editions of Okigbo's poems were actually 'intended' and the subsequent 'revisions' a peace-offering to critics? Considering the fact that Okigbo had a penchant for rewriting/rereading his poems, how can we be sure that he would not have undertaken another rewriting/ rereading had he lived? This point will, however, not obscure the truth that Okigbo did develop his skills. *Path of Thunder*, as already demonstrated, is generally easier to read and more lyrical than a number of Okigbo's earlier poems. Similarly, Heinemann *Labyrinths* is divested of the Latinisms and the enigmatic lines which were common in the earlier Mbari version. The Latinisms of Mbari *Labyrinths* portray Okigbo as being, like Ezra Pound, eclectic. In addition, in Mbari *Labyrinths* there are some private orthographic inventions denoting private references which are spliced with Latinisms. These are simply vexatious for their unnecessary attempt to mystify; indeed, they have been mistaken for the expression of some grand revelation by at least one critic.[31]

The allusive nature of Okigbo's poetry cannot be glossed over. It accounts in part for the reflexivity of the poetry. Another contributory factor to this reflexivity is Okigbo's situation at the juncture between orality and writing. How does this reflexive aspect of the graphology of Okigbo's poetry call attention to the larger context of writing?

One prevalent attitude to the allusions, echoes and other forms of linkages to other texts in Okigbo's poetry has been to regard such as material evidence of Okigbo's derivativeness. A pithy statement by the semiotician, Roland Barthes, might serve as a riposte to this kind of perfunctory source-hunting. According to Barthes, 'to search for the "sources of" and "influence upon" a work is to satisfy the myth of filiation'.[32] Upon close examination it will be revealed that this attitude posits a certain ultimate origin of ideas, linguistic formulations, and so on. The parallel to this ultimate origin will be the transcendental signified which Derrida identifies as the chimera of the 'metaphysics of presence'. Barthes's formulation which follows upon his observation is worth quoting, for pointing yet again to the possibility of a proto-writing antedating both writing and speech:

> The quotations from which a text is constructed are anonymous, irrecoverable, and yet *already read*: they are quotations without quotation marks. [Barthes's emphasis]

An appreciation of this feature of the intertext, and of the intertextuality of Okigbo's poetry, may prevent the sometimes misleading interpretation attendant upon a monistic construal of Okigbo's poetic resources. In this respect, an article by Catherine Acholonu appears to be a reductionist reading of Okigbo's poetry which ignores all signposts against such reductionism. In the article titled 'Ogbanje: a motif and theme in the poetry of Christopher Okigbo', Acholonu suggests that 'Okigbo's life-style was a classical [sic] example of what the Igbo people refer to as ogbanje.' The ogbanje, as Acholonu indicates, are the semi-human and semi-spirit people of Igbo mythology, 'who are fated to die young and if they grow into adulthood . . . [die] at a momentous period of their lives'. Acholonu deduces from Okigbo's reference to the images of the drowning virgins and Gilgamesh an indication of Okigbo's own ogbanje status. The introductory lines of 'Heavensgate' and 'The Passage' (two poems in *Labyrinths*) are inferred by Acholonu to be a proleptic mourning of Okigbo's death. Acholonu also identifies the female figure(s) that feature(s) in Okigbo's poetry as 'a water spirit' with whom Okigbo has a 'love affair' and equates the silent sisters of Okigbo's 'Silences' to the 'seven ogbanje girls' of folklore, 'who brandish their beauty to attract suitors, while concealing the fatality of their existence'.[33] Also, there is a widely held view that Okigbo owes those of his lines which carry themes of reincarnation to Wordsworth's 'Ode: Intimations of Immortality'.[34] Let us at this point examine in greater detail the self-reflexivity and intertextuality of Okigbo's poetry.

Beginning with the suggestion that Okigbo's poetry is reflexive of his destiny as an *ogbanje*, what is the relation of the poet Okigbo to the subject generally denoted by 'I' in the poetry? What are the shared aspects of this subject and the situation of the set conjured by such figures as the drowning virgins and Gilgamesh?

Indeed a common link between the drowning virgins, Gilgamesh and the protagonist of Okigbo's poetry may be their death, but the point to be made embraces not just the essence, but also the significance, of this death. Through an extensive build-up of the sacrificial image which describes Okigbo's protagonist he is actually made to share this much with Gilgamesh. But just as the virgins dream of death (and pursue it as a means to martyrdom) so does Okigbo's protagonist show an ardent fascination with death, so that death here is a form of adventure. The *ogbanje*, on the other hand, dies as a matter of course: no adventure motivates him/her; no mission of redemption urges him/her. He/she is, therefore, precluded from the anguish and elation that must attend the desired death of Okigbo's protagonist.

Neither 'Heavensgate' nor 'The Passage' can be taken so extemporaneously as a proleptic mourning of Okigbo's death. The following lines can hardly be taken as a vision of 'darkness, gloom and chaos':

DARK WATERS of the beginning.

Rays, violet, and short, piercing the gloom,
foreshadow the fire that is dreamed of.

Contrary to the claim that the picture painted here is a gloomy portent of a young man's fated death, the vision suggests a supersession of gloom by light. The idea projected by these lines has an intertext to which others similar to it belong, for instance, the Biblical account of creation. These lines or modifications of them are also used in connection with the 'Lady of the lavender-mist' and the 'earth mother' of 'Dance of the Painted Maidens'. This intertextual reference certainly carries some significance. 'Heavensgate' is expressly about the subject's confrontation with Idoto, a female figure comparable to both the 'earth mother' and the 'Lady of the lavender-mist'. Idoto, identified as the village stream, also bears a connotative relation to the 'maid' of 'Distances VI', whose 'pure head' provides the channel whereby the subject's ultimate deliverance is realized. Wherever these four functionally related figures feature, the theme is one of redemptive yearning on the subject's part. The figures are subsequently celebrated in archetypally powerful terms, as for example in the lines quoted above.

The number seven features in 'Dance of the Painted Maidens' in the lines, 'From the seven quarters of the globe,/Past the seven seas past the seven/Distant deserts, bearing beads of coral and/kolanuts fit for a queen'. The context of this poem, which is a celebratory welcome of the earth mother by her handmaidens, puts the figure seven in an eminently positive connotation. It is inconceivable that the number would be consigned to absolute evil. In fact, seven functions in Okigbo's poetry as a symbol of consummate energy.[35]

Let us briefly examine 'Lament of the Drums' and its evocation of the figure seven. The immediately relevant lines are:

We are tuned for a feast-of-seven-souls . . .
        (*Labyrinths*, p. 45; Okigbo's ellipsis)

But distant seven winds invite us and our cannons
To limber our membranes for a dance of elephants . . .
        (Ibid., p. 46; Okigbo's ellipsis)

The distant seven cannons invite us
To a sonorous
Ishthar's lament for Tammuz
            (Ibid., p. 49)

'Lament of the Drums' features an anthropomorphized chorus of drums
who begin their 'lament' by invoking their constitutive elements, basically
flora and fauna which imprint the drums' strength and efficacy. The
drums announce their pressing task, contained in the lines quoted above.
Certainly the drums' lament recalls that of the 'silent sisters', in the profound anguish for the tragic events which occasion their lament. But there
is nothing to suggest that the number seven specifically denotes the 'silent
sisters'. The activities of both the drums and the sisters cannot be simply
termed evil. The prescient disposition of both choruses is employed for a
positive (and optimistic) engagement with the tragic events of their lament.
Thus, after outpouring their grief, the 'Crier' and the 'Chorus' intimate
an exultant vision in 'Lament of the Silent Sisters':

I hear painted harmonies
From the mushrooms of the sky –

Silences are melodies
Heard in retrospect:

And how does one say NO in thunder?
            (Labyrinths, p. 59)

In 'Lament of the Drums' Palinurus is metaphorically counterpoised with
Tammuz to indicate the complexity of the grief. Of Palinurus the drums
intone:

Tears of grace, not of sorrow, broken
In two, protest your inviolable image.

But no exultant tone surges through 'Ishthar's lament for Tammuz', in
which the focus is the pain of deprivation (brought about by death) rather
than death's tansformative aspect:

The wailing is for the fields of men:

The drums' lament is:
They grow not . . .
            [Okigbo's ellipses]

    If the sheer matter of death provides a link between Palinurus, Tammuz
and the ogbanje, the question again is, what kind of death? Because the
ogbanje is caught in a relentless cycle of death, it might be suggested
that death is the ogbanje's destiny. The major part of Palinurus's and
Tammuz's identity is that their death constitutes an aperture for society's
new beginning.
    It cannot be presumed, as is frequently the case, that a one-to-one
correspondence exists between the central subject of Okigbo's poetry and
the poet Okigbo. The most overtly self-reflexive section of Okigbo's poetry
is Path of Thunder, where the subject is dramatized as follows:

> If I don't learn to shut my mouth I'll soon go to hell
> I, Okigbo, town-crier, together with my iron-bell.
>   ('Hurrah for Thunder', Labyrinths, p. 67)

> the mythmaker accompanies us (the Egret had come and gone)
> Okigbo accompanies us the oracle enkindles us
> the Hornbill is there again (the Hornbill has had a bath)
> Okigbo accompanies us the rattles enlighten us –
>   ('Elegy for Slit-drum', Labyrinths, p. 69)

The explicit reference – 'I Okigbo, town-crier' – in these poems is invariably welcomed by explicators of Okigbo's poetry as the infallible revelation of the identity of the 'I' as the real Okigbo. This hazy equation leads to the kind of logically confusing statement presented by the following:

> In 'Path of Thunder', Okigbo witnesses the actualization of the death and destruction he has so long prophesied and clamoured for . . . Okigbo the town crier discards his 'iron bell' and makes way for the ogbanje, who bids the world 'a howling farewell' and prays to be allowed to perish with his dying folk, and the poem ends with his voluntary martyrdom.[36]

The poet Okigbo did die shortly after writing this poem and no one will deny the poem's premonitory hint. However, the passage is logically confusing. To clarify the confusions we need to examine more closely the relationship between the graphic symbol, 'Okigbo', and its referent(s). Graphic substitutes for 'Okigbo' include 'I', 'town-crier', 'mythmaker' and 'Hornbill'. All of these nominals do not exhibit the same deep-structure status. 'Town-crier', 'mythmaker' and 'Hornbill' are metaphorical in varying degrees, and in this respect contrast with 'I', which is in turn imbued with selfness – an awareness of possession of a personal individuality (to paraphrase Webster's New Collegiate Dictionary, 1973). The metaphorical fluidity of the nominals, with the exception of 'I', makes it possible to enlist other nominals from Okigbo's entire poetry with which they bear functional similarity, namely 'wagtail', 'sunbird'. The 'I' equally enlists another epithet, 'prodigal' (from Labyrinths), and the string of associations can grow indefinitely. Because it is the functional or attributive role of these various substitutive nominals which is being engaged, the correspondence is not in toto. The metaphorical substitutes are temporally mediated. For instance, the prodigal image, which is implied in 'Song of the Forest', is prominent in Labyrinths, and then fades off in Path of Thunder. Similarly, 'Limits X' records the killing of 'the Sunbird', but it is clear that the victim here is not the 'Okigbo' of the poem. Also, it is known that the real Okigbo was employed in different occupations but not as an actual town-crier. The 'I, Okigbo, town-crier' is thus a mythical construct. Its relation to the real Okigbo is conceptual rather than actual. The 'I' serves as a construct of continuity to enforce this conceptual relation.

The reference 'I, Okigbo, town-crier' indeed serves as an index to a reading of Okigbo's poetry as 'metapoetry', that is, 'poetry that includes within itself a commentary on its own poetic and/or linguistic identity'.[37] An awareness of this metapoetic feature should provoke a more self-conscious and critical disposition to the analysis of the poetry. 'If our knowledge of this world is now seen to be mediated through language,' thus reasons one narratologist, 'then literary fiction (*worlds constructed entirely of language*) becomes a useful model for learning about the construction of "reality" itself.'[38] Quite so; my emphasis.

The foregoing has not sought to be an inclusive commentary on the graphology of Okigbo's poetry, but, by concentrating on salient aspects of the graphological patterns, it has attempted to lay bare some of the veiled meanings of that poetry. Through a close attention to the graphology of the earlier poetry, for instance, we discover Okigbo's prognostic leitmotif and find a striking link between the early poem, 'Lament of the Lavender Mist', and *Path of Thunder* which has not hitherto been acknowledged. The problematic of the various 'versions' of Okigbo's poetry has also been re-examined; through an exploration of the implications of the graphological differences of the two 'versions' of 'Distances' we are led to a startling discovery, that these two so-called versions are more accurately described as two separate poems. The graphology has also been demonstrated to be very revealing of the self-reflexivity and intertextuality of the poetry – features whose recognition prevents the pitfalls of a monistic search for filiation. Okigbo's exploitation of the graphological possibilities of poetry has produced very dense, poignantly lyrical and tonal poetry. Occasionally the poignancy flags but this does not overall detract from the striking achievement of the poetry. Graphology is one of the pre-eminent hallmarks of Okigbo's style.

NOTES

1. This is the general manner in which Okigbo's poetry is regarded. But as Eldred Jones, in his preface to no. 7 of *African Literature Today*, observed '[Okigbo] was once so "obscure" but . . . now – thanks to persistent examination – is far less of a closed book even to non-poets.'
2. M.A.K. Halliday, A. McIntosh and P. Stevens, *The Linguistic Sciences and Language Teaching*, London, Longmans, 1964, p. 50.
3. Angus McIntosh, ' "Graphology" and Meaning,' *Archivum Linguisticum*, vol. 13, no. 2, 1962, p. 108.
4. Notable among the emblematic poems of George Herbert (early seventeenth-century English poet) are 'The Altar' and 'Easter-Wings', both of which may be found in *The Poetical Works of George Herbert*, London, James Nisbet, 1865, pp. 27 and 49. Dylan Thomas's more elaborate iconic poem is titled 'Vision and Prayer' and may be found in *Dylan Thomas: The Poems*, ed. Daniel Jones, London, J.M. Dent, 1974, pp. 180–5). 'Vision and Prayer' was first published in 1945.
5. Guillaume Apollinaire (French poet, 1880–1918) developed the term '*calligraphie*' for his innovative, visually striking poetry, which aimed at provoking instant and multidimensional awareness of the object. He applied the term 'simultaneity' to this practice in his poetry. His outstanding collection in the mode is titled *Calligrammes* (completed in 1912–13), Berkeley, University of California Press, 1980. Apollinaire's original calligraphy is retained in this text.

6. For examples of the 'concrete' poetry of Finlay, Williams and Nichols, see the entry 'concrete poetry' in *Twentieth-Century Poetry and Poetics*, ed. Gary Gedes, Toronto, Oxford University Press, 1973.

7. Jacques Derrida, 'Differance', in *Speech and Phenomena and Other Essays on Husserl's Theory of Signs*, trans. David B. Allison, Evanston, Northwestern University Press, 1973, p. 131.

8. Evaluations of Derrida's theory of deconstruction, and its subsequent application by other critics, can be found, among others, in Christopher Norris, *Deconstruction: Theory and Practice*, London, Methuen, 1982; *The Deconstructive Turn: Essays in the Rhetoric of Philosophy*, London and New York, Methuen, 1983; David Carroll, *Paraesthetics*, New York, Methuen, 1987.

9. See Edward Said, 'The Text, the World, the Critic', in *Textual Strategies: Perspectives in Post-Structuralist Criticism*, Ithaca, Cornell University Press, 1979, pp. 161–88.

10. See William York Tindall, *A Reader's Guide to Dylan Thomas*, New York, Farrar, Strauss and Cudahy, 1962, pp. 239ff.

11. Wole Soyinka, *Idanre and Other Poems*, London, Methuen, 1967, p. 13.

12. Atukwei Okai, *Lorgorligi Logarithms and Other Poems*, Accra, Ghana Publishing Corporation, 1974, p. 13.

13. See Christopher Okigbo, 'Distances', *Transition*, vol. 4, no. 16, 1964, p. 9; 'Lament of the Masks', in *W.B. Yeats, 1865–1965: Centenary Essays*, ed. D.E.S. Maxwell and S.B. Bushrui, Ibadan, Ibadan University Press, 1965, p. xv.

14. Christopher Okigbo, 'Four Canzones', *Black Orpheus*, vol. 11, 1962, pp. 5–9. 'Four Canzones' is reproduced in *Collected Poems*, London, Heinemann, 1986.

15. *Path of Thunder* was posthumously published with the volume *Labyrinths* by Heinemann, London, in 1971. The volume was simultaneously published in the United States by Africana Publishing Corporation and has lately been reproduced with other poems in Christopher Okigbo, *Collected Poems*, op. cit.

16. Christopher Okigbo, 'Distances', *Transition*, vol. 4, no. 16, 1964, pp. 9–13.

17. 'Distances', *Labyrinths*, op. cit.

18. When asked on one occasion what he conceived as his audience, Okigbo replied that he 'was writing for other poets all over the world'. See Okigbo's interview with Lewis Nkosi, in *African Writers Talking*, ed. Dennis Duerden and Cosmo Pieterse, London, Heinemann, 1972, p. 135.

19. Okigbo states beneath the title of 'Song of the Forest' that it is based on Virgil's *Tityrus*.

20. Omolara Leslie [Molara Ogundipe-Leslie], 'The poetry of Christopher Okigbo: its evolution and significance', in *Critical Perspectives on Christopher Okigbo*, ed. Donatus Nwoga, Washington, DC, Three Continents Press, 1984, pp. 291–2.

21. See, for example, 'On the New Year' and 'Debtors' Lane', in 'Four Canzones', op. cit.

22. Annemarie Heywood, 'The ritual and the plot: the critic and Okigbo's *Labyrinths*', in *Critical Perspectives on Christopher Okigbo*, op. cit., p. 209. Heywood's article was first published in 1978.

23. O.R. Dathorne rightly indicates that Okigbo has transformed Damas's dolls but does not demonstrate how. See 'Ritual and ceremony in Okigbo's poetry', in *Critical Perspectives On Christopher Okigbo*, op. cit., p. 264. Damas's 'Limbe' (first published in 1937) may be found in *Pigments*, Paris, Présence Africaine, 1972, pp. 43–5.

24. Dan Izevbaye, 'From reality to the dream: the poetry of Christopher Okigbo', in *Critical Perspectives on Christopher Okigbo*, op. cit., p. 327.

25. The ceremony of souls is a soul-cleansing ceremony whereby the living confront the dead to enable each party to proceed with living or after-life responsibilities. A very poignant dramatization of the practice and concept is

provided by George Lamming in *Season of Adventure*, London, Allison and Busby, 1979; first published 1960.

26. Christopher Okigbo, 'Dance of the Painted Maidens', *Collected Poems*, op. cit., pp. 83-6.

27. See Okigbo's 'Introduction to *Labyrinths*', *Labyrinths*, London, Heinemann, 1971, p. xii. The first 'version' of *Labyrinths*, published by Mbari (Ibadan), 1962, did not contain an introduction.

28. 'Silences' is one of the sequences which make up Heinemann *Labyrinths*.

29. See note 5 above. See also the 'Introduction' by S.I. Lockerbie, *Calligrammes*, op. cit., pp. 1-20.

30. The following lines usher the protagonist into the final redemptive stage in *Transition* 'Distances':

> And at this chaste instant
> of delineated anguish,
> the same voice, importunate,
> aglow with the goddess –
> unquenchable, yellow,
> darkening homeward
> like a cry of wolf
> above crumbling houses –
> strips the dream naked,
> bares its entrails;

The unvarying rhythm, the monotone, does not project the tension and the thrill of this penultimate instant.

31. For instance, one critic, Wole Ogundele, in a peculiar interpretation assumes one of such *mélanges* to be speaking of 'that Elysian past when harmony between man, nature, and god obtained'. The lines quoted by Ogundele, which include 'etru bo pi alo a she e anando we aquandem . . .' have been revealed to be a conflation of a childhood corruption of 'Little Bo Peep' and phrases from Catholic liturgy, as well as an account of Okigbo's boyhood imitation of birds' songs. See Wole Ogundele, 'From the labyrinth to the temple: the structure of Okigbo's religious experience', *Okike*, vol. 24, 1983, pp. 61-2. Compare O.R. Dathorne, 'Ritual and ceremony in Okigbo's poetry', in *Critical Perspectives on Christopher Okigbo*, op. cit., p. 263.

32. Roland Barthes, 'From work to text', in *Textual Strategies: Perspectives in Post-Structuralist Criticism*, op. cit., p. 77.

33. Catherine Acholonu, 'Ogbanje: A motif and a theme in the poetry of Christopher Okigbo', *African Literature Today*, no. 16, 1988, pp. 103-11.

34. This effete view has recently been revived, for instance, by Robert Fraser, *West African Poetry: A Critical History*, Cambridge, Cambridge University Press, 1986, p. 133; Catherine Acholonu, op. cit., p. 107. The relevant lines in Okigbo's poetry are 'The man embodies the child/The child embodies the man.' Wordsworth's famous epigram begins with the line, 'The Child is father of the Man.' Wordsworth's line could easily pass for a translation of a Yoruba truism, 'Omo ju Baba', literally 'The child is greater/older than its father.' This expression appears to 'have always been' because it is attributed to no one. But to suggest any kind of vertical passage of the Yoruba expression to Wordsworth is to succumb to an unfruitful solipsism. Okigbo's lines record a paradox that any culture might have recognized long ago from observations of cycles of regeneration. They belong to an intertext of pithy expressions of cycles of regeneration.

35. Although Okigbo is sometimes almost exclusively situated within the Igbo

mythic tradition, his wordlore was not woven from Igbo mythology alone. For instance, Okigbo lived and worked among the Yoruba, in the cities of Ibadan, Fiditi and Lagos, where he composed a substantial part of his poetry. In Yoruba linguistic cosmology seven is evoked as a figure of expansivity and climactic activity. Okigbo acknowledges both explicitly and implicitly several other cultures which had provided materials for his poetry.

36. Catherine Acholonu, op. cit., p. 110.
37. This operational definition is an adaptation of Linda Hutcheon's definition of 'metafiction' in *Narcissistic Narrative: The Metafictional Paradox*, Waterloo, Wilfrid Laurier University Press, 1980, p. 1.
38. Patricia Waugh, *Metafiction: The Theory and Practice of Self-Conscious Fiction*, London and New York, Methuen, 1984, p. 3.

From Rhetoric to Occultism: The Word as Music & Drama in Okigbo's *Labyrinths*

Catherine O. Acholonu

For Baudelaire, Rimbaud and Mallarmé, the flag-bearers of the French symbolist movement, the purist goal of poetry was the state of music. Paul Valéry maintains that all art aims ultimately at attaining purity, that kind of unity and wholesomeness which is attainable only through music.[1] In Christopher Okigbo's *Labyrinths* music and drama play a vital role in the poet's attainment of his ultimate goal of fulfilment. The musicality of language, the recurrent patterns and variations upon the same theme, the accumulating images of infrastructure and dramatized experience, function as carriers of the poet's vision. Through music, the poet attains a state of abstraction in his pursuit of the artistic ideal of purity, of the perfect identification of matter with form.[2]

In *Labyrinths* there are two main personalities through whose voices the poet's vision becomes apparent. These are the persona 'I' and the chorus. Through these personalities or characters, the audience is brought nearer to the inner world of the poem. The reader or audience is made to believe in the action and spectacle of the poem because it is what the persona 'I' and the chorus see. In this sense, Okigbo's poetry is a poetry of experience in the Nietzschean sense of 'a poem which originates in song and passes temporarily through drama in order to articulate the song and refer us back to the song for meaning'.[3]

Labyrinths starts as the 'broken monody' or dirge of a young bird whose language is characterized by uncertainty:

On one leg standing
in silence at the passage
the young bird at the passage[4] (p. 4)

The persona is standing before the shrine of mother Idoto, praying for purification. 'Heavensgate' is a death-in-life poem, its characters are living dead encountered by the persona in the erring early period of his existential journey. All the tunes heard in the language of 'Heavensgate' are more echoes of the poet's unworthy past, a past characterized by illusion:

where the players of loft pipe organs
rehearse old lovely fragments, alone

> for we are listening in cornfields
>   among the windplayers,
> listening to the wind leaning over
>   its loveliest fragment (p. 5)

and by 'errors of the rendering' (p. 8) such as the song of Jadum, a half-demented village minstrel, 'from Rockland'.

As the Newcomer emerges with a new life and a new identity, the persona begins to identify with his native religion and his native culture, while the sound of the bells of the angelus begin to recede:

> softly sing the bells of exile
> the angelus
> softly sings my guardian angel (p. 17)

and are replaced by the thundering drums and cannons that accompany the ascending spirit in the palm grove:

> Thundering drums and cannons
> in palm grove
> the spirit is in ascent. (p. 16)

The first signs of the dramatic lyric are seen as early as 'Heavensgate', as the persona introduces his characters and even puts words into their mouths:

> So comes John the Baptist
> with bowl of salt water
> preaching the gambit:
> life without sin, without/life; (p. 6)

Jadum, the mad minstrel, comes with words of advice and caution from Rockland. He sings to shepherds with a flute on his lip:

> Do not wander in speargrass
> After the lights
> Probing liars in stockings,
> To roast
> The viper alive ... (p 8)

Then comes Upandru saying:

> Screen your bedchamber thoughts
> with sun-glasses,
> who could jump your eye,
> your mind-window, (p. 9)

to which the persona of the poem makes a reply, creating an occasion for verbal exchange or *dialogue* thus:

> And I said:
> The prophet only the poet.
> And he said: Logistics.
> (Which is what poetry is) ...

And he said to the ram: Disarm.
And I said:
Except by rooting,
Who could pluck yam tubers from their base? (p. 9)

Another element of drama which is found in *Labyrinths* is *action*, with or without dialogue. Physical action or movement can be observed from the persona's encounter with the watermaid:

BRIGHT
with the armpit-dazzle of a lioness,
she answers,

wearing white light about her;

and the waves escort her,

Downward . . .
the waves distill her;
gold crop
sinking ungathered. (p. 11)

In the 'Newcomer' we see a sure-footed protagonist standing above the bridgehead as large as life, so real, so vivid; and we can hear the rippling of the waters as they flow by:

I AM standing above the noontide,
Above the bridgehead;

Listening to the laughter of waters

I am standing above the noontide
   with my head above it;

Under my feet float the waters
Tide blows them under . . . (p. 19)

The use of the present tense – 'I am standing', 'listening', 'blows' – in this episode helps to strengthen the dramatic element; the element of uncertainty which had earlier characterized the language of the hero now gives way to more surety and self-confidence.

The combination of the dramatic and the musical in poetry results in a genre known as the dramatic lyric or the lyrical drama as the case may be. The lyrical drama or the dramatic lyric 'began with those poets of the neoclassic age who, in trying – as a counterpoint to the satirical and didactic poetry of the time – to be lyrical, found it necessary to give their lyrical poems a dramatic setting, to draw their feelings and reflections out of the observation of a scene remarkable for its beauty and picturesqueness'.[5] The music is the music of the poet's soul, the music of evolution and continuity; the drama, a drama of the poet's experience. The quest hero in this journey is an observer who seeks out incidents and establishes among them a sequence, however illogical, with the power of his experiences. Also the references to biographical elements such as the poet's personal experiences and personal relationships help to strengthen the message of the poem and lend it a validity which otherwise might have been lost as a result of the vagueness of the events and the illogicality of their sequence. The question of validity is a rhetorical question. In a dramatic lyric a new validity is created, a new logic out of non-logic, for it is not just the description of optical perceptions as they are in true life, or as they appear to the narrator, which is significant, rather, it is the re-creation of these observed objects. They assume a new life, a new significance, through the poet's imagination, through the music of the poet's soul. The dramatic element is a sign that the experience is really taking place, that the object is seen and felt –

I am standing above the noontide . . .

Under my feet float the waters . . . (p. 19)

– and not just remembered as an abstract idea or point of view. The experience has more validity because it is dramatized as an event, a palpable experience, rather than formulated as an abstraction. The poet's perspective, even though extraordinary, and his imagery, even though far-fetched, are made palpable by the musicality of his rendering. Every living being on earth responds to music, there is music in growth, in movement, in stillness, even in silence. This is what Okigbo refers to as the 'music of the firmament' (p. 41).

Labyrinths is made musical not only through the usual musical elements of verse such as rhythm, metre, onomatopoeia, consonance, assonance, etc., but also through the adaptation of its structure to such musical structural patterns as leitmotif, symphonic form (movements), orchestration, the musicality of recurrent patterns, of accumulating images, of infrastructure and dramatized experience. These function as rhetorical devices, as objective correlative carriers of the poet's vision, unifying his diverse experiences and the different variations of the same themes by the force of the voice and personality of the persona 'I'.

Labyrinths was originally conceived as a musical experience; it is, like classical music, made up of movements. In addition, it is a drama whose performance is to be accompanied by traditional Igbo musical instruments like the drums (*ekwe*), the flutes (*oja*), *ubo* (the Igbo equivalent of the guitar) and the *ogene*. Okigbo's distribution of the musical accompaniments for his poetry is most elaborate in his early publications, especially in the 'Four Canzones', published in *Black Orpheus*, no. 11. But, even though these arrangements are not clearly spelt out in *Labyrinths*, the musical quality of these poems is in no way minimized. The first thing that strikes a reader of *Labyrinths* is the measured cadence of syllables, lines and stanzas, and the resultant rhythm and melody, as in the following stanzas:

1. A   Before you, mother Idoto,
        naked I stand;
    before your watery presence,
        a prodigal

   B   leaning on an oilbean,
    lost in your legend.

A   Under your power wait I
        on barefoot,
     watchman for the watchword
        at *Heavensgate*;

B   out of the depths my cry:
     give ear and hearken . . . (p. 3)

2. A   And to the Distant – but how shall we go?
         The robbers will strip us of our tendons!

    B   For we sense
         With dog-nose a Babylonian capture,
         The martyrdom
         Blended into that chaliced vintage;

    B   And savour
         The incense and in high buskin,
         Like a web
         Of voices all rent by javelins.

    A   But distant seven winds invite us and our cannons
         To limber our membranes for a dance of elephants . . . (p. 46)

The graphological arrangement and punctuation of these lines equally enhance the musical effect. Other musical patterns prevalent in *Labyrinths* are onomatopoeia, consonance, assonance, metre and pitch. All these together give the effect of orchestration, as in the lament of the drums:

  – So, like a dead letter unanswered
    Our rococo
    Choir of insects is null
    Cacophony . . .

  – But the antiphony, still clamorous
    In tremolo,
    Like an afternoon, for shadows; (p. 49)

It is necessary to note that these lines are supposed to sound like the beating of the Igbo drum; they echo and re-echo with a sonorous invitation to Isthar's lament for Tammuz. Words like rococo, cacophony, tremolo, antiphony, clamorous are onomatopoeic, but also they are well chosen for their consonance (rhyming of consonants) and assonance (rhyming of vowels). But the reader of *Labyrinths* must learn to recognize where sheer rhetoric and artistic embellishments end and where occultism begins. In fact very often rhetoric and occultism run concurrently in Okigbo's poetry. Through the activity of the imagination, the poet fuses 'opposite and discordant qualities', of creation and destruction, life and death, just and unjust, the idea and the image, and thus establishes the paradox of his creative or Promethean ego as the vehicle of tragedy in the Nietzschean sense. By the original title of his book *The Birth of Tragedy Out of the Spirit of Music*, Nietzsche declares tragedy to be, 'not the illustration of an idea of the world, of an objective order of values, but a birth, a natural growth from the unarticulated life-surge, from what he calls the "Primordial Unity" or "Primordial Pain", of which music is an expression'[6] – Okigbo's 'music of the firmament'.

Okigbo's first attempt at achieving this primordial unity can be seen in 'Siren Limits', as the creative artist 'feeling for audience' is seen 'straining thin among the echoes':

> Into the soul
> The selves extended their branches
> Into the moments of each living hour ...
> And out of the solitude
> Voice and soul with selves unite
> Riding the echoes ...
> And crowned with one self
> The name displays its foliage (p. 24)

Anozie has remarked that 'the poet's "soul" which is said to disintegrate into "moments of each living hour" seems to have been installed as the One or the Primeval Being (Supreme Being) itself. "Selves", as used above, by virtue of its plurality, may be said to be already fragmentalized. Each fragment is perhaps one ideal Self?'[7]

This Promethean or creative realization of the poet's ego strengthens him for a larger task yet to follow. The triumph of the creative ego equals the discovery of a new voice, a new language, a new vision – 'the name displays its foliage':

> Horsemen of the apocalypse
> And crowned with one self
> The name displays its foliage (p. 24)

It is very significant that this point marks a milestone in the poet's development. This new voice that 'displays its foliage' in 'Siren Limits II' is already put into action in 'Siren Limits III', the very next poem. For the very first time, musical leitmotifs occur in *Labyrinths* in the form of refrain:

> and the mortar is not yet dry ...
> and the mortar is not yet dry ... (p. 25)

The music is becoming louder and the voice stronger, in fact the poet finds it difficult to control the current of sound issuing from his soul:

> And the voice that is reborn transpires
> Not thro' pores in the flesh
>   but the soul's back-bone (p. 25)

The protagonist now nears the destination of his journey; the speed is increased especially for the hero's second self who is nearing his end:[8]

> Hurry on down –
>   Thro' the high-arched gate –
> Hurry on down
>   little stream to the lake;
> Hurry on down
>   Thro' the cinder market

Hurry on down
   in the wake of the dream . . . (p. 26)

This second self which, like Gilgamesh's Enkidu, represents the limitations
of mortal man, is eventually destroyed in 'Fragments out of the Deluge'
and the hero is thus finally freed of all earthly limitations.

In 'Silences' this new-found voice burgeons into a new life with a new
vitality and insistence. In the 'Lament of the Silent Sisters' music and
drama actually spring into life. The dramatic lyric of *Labyrinths* suddenly
metamorphoses into lyrical drama, a performance whose characters are
the silent sisters – the crier and chorus. Theirs is a triumphant dirge that
unifies life and death, through memories, through the silent music of the
soul:

Crier: I hear sounds as, they say,
         A worshipper hears the flutes

Chorus: The music sounds so in the soul
         I can hear nothing else

Crier: I hear painted harmonies
         From the mushroom of the sky

Chorus: Silences are melodies
         Heard in retrospect: . . . (p. 43)

The Crier represents the narrative voice of the persona of *Labyrinths*; the
Chorus represents the gods. As such the chorus lends wisdom and sacredness to the language of *Labyrinths*. Through them, the lyric is transformed
into a dramatic evocation of the psychic union of the 'I' of the poem (the
narrator) with the infinite power that nurtures all creation.

In 'Silences' Okigbo's language becomes incantatory due to the fusion
of music with actual drama, something akin to what Rimbaud refers
to as 'Alchimie du Verbe' and what Anozie refers to as 'incantatory
lyricism'.[9] The 'I' of the lyricist, the 'we' and 'our' of the crier and
chorus, sound from the abyss of being. It is an invocative 'I' and is further
made potent by the 'plastic music of words reaching out now into the
silence of the night, now into the mountain cataracts; now conjuring up
twisted forms mirrored from the sea, now invoking a panorama of vague
but symbolic images'.[10] The following incantatory images are from the
'Lament of the Silent Sisters':

For as in sea-fever globules of fresh anguish.
   immense golden eggs empty of albumen
   sink into our balcony . . .

Where is there for us an anchorage;
A shank for a sheet, a double arch

   scented shadows above the underrush (p. 39)

So, one dips one's tongue in the ocean, and begins
To cry to the mushroom of the sky (p. 40)

And there will be a continual going to the well
Until they smash their calabashes (p. 40)

Unseen shadows like long-fingered winds
Pluck from our strings (p. 41)

Wild winds cry out against us . . .
We shall wear the green habit of kolanuts . . .
The kingfisher gathers his ropes in the distance
The salt water gathers them inward (p. 42)

In traditional African religion, religious practice is evocative; as in the religion of the Negro spiritual, faith is expressed through the invocation of a god. In this ritual, which is a form of occultism or magic, three main vehicles abound. These are: dance, drum (flute, or other musical instruments) and the spoken word, which is recited or sung. The dance is a form of dramatic performance, the drum a musical instrument and the incantation is still music. Thus, whichever way we approach it, we still arrive at the two poles of drama and music which are essential in the practice of the African cult. Mbiti has observed that 'Music, singing and dancing reach deep into the innermost parts of the African peoples, and many things come to the surface under musical inspiration which otherwise may not be really revealed.'[11] And Janheinz Jahn observes that 'drums and other percussion instruments are indispensable for the practice of an African cult . . . particular gods are invoked by particular drum-beat formulas. These formulas are the *nommo* names with which the gods are invoked.'[12] Jahn describes the African culture as 'a culture in which invocatory poetry is simply word magic: not the written word but the word which is sung and danced'.[13] This is the evolutional point in Okigbo's poetry. In 'Silences' the written word gets transformed into cultic language. The 'swan song' and 'jubilee dance' of the silent sisters, the lament of the drums, all these are essential ingredients to transform the written word into magic, which is still a prerogative of the poet. He invokes, by the power of this magic word, the goddess of the sea, the hidden face of the dream who becomes one with Idoto, the watermaid, the poet's mother Anna, the lioness, the silent sisters and even the drums (which incidentally are female drums: Okigbo refers to them as mother and daughter drums in his introduction to *Labyrinths*). The song of the silent sisters is a lament, a song of death (swan song).

This is our swan song
This is our senses' stillness . . .
This is our swan song
This is the sigh of our spirits (p. 41)

(The swan is a death bird in European mythology; its equivalent in Igbo is the owl or *ajo nnunu*). Their dance is a dance of death, a 'jubilee-dance above the carrion' (p. 39).

This female essence which is destructive is also creative. It destroys the hero's second self so that his immortal soul might surface with greater creative power. She is the poet's muse, and through her he gains the power of prophecy; thus in the 'Lament of the Silent Sisters' and in the 'Lament of the Drums' we see glimpses of future events such as war:

> What cast-iron steps cascading down the valley
>   all forged into thunder of tanks
> And detonators cannoned into splintered flames
>   in this jubilee dance of fire-flies (p. 40)

betrayal:

> And bearded Judas
> Resplendent among the dancers (p. 43)

and oppression:

> For the far removed there is wailing:
> For the far removed;
> For the Distant . . .
>
> The wailing is for the fields of crop:
>
> The drums' lament is:
> They grow not . . .
>
> The wailing is for the fields of men:
>
> For the barren wedded ones
> For perishing children
>
> The wailing is for the Great River
>
> Her pot-bellied watchers
> Despoil her . . . (p. 50)

Thus the poet's use of cultic language can be said to be positive rather than negative, useful rather than harmful.

The climax of this ecstatic experience of the poet is in 'Distances', where the poet, having lost all consciousness, compares this new state to that of 'sensual anaesthesia':

> From flesh into phantom (p. 53)
>
> And the eye lost its light
> and the light lost its shadow (p. 54)

From now on the poet no longer 'describes' images and scenery that are symbolic of the idea; rather, he formulates the idea itself: this new vision of Primeval Unity, in a visionary language devoid of rhetorical embellishments. This new language is precise; it is mathematical and architectural rather than merely rhetorical:

> And at the archway
> a triangular lintel
> of solid alabaster
> enclosed in a square
> inscribed in a circle
> with a hollow centre
> above the archway
> yawning shutterless . . . (p. 57)

Through ritual and invocation, through music and drama, Okigbo, the poet from a lineage of priests of the water cult (Idoto worship), roots his poetry in African traditional cultic religion, where word magic is not simply the written word but the word which is chanted and danced to musical accompaniments; the word which links man with God; through which the creative process is accomplished:

> In the beginning there was the word
> And the word was with God
> And the word was God . . .
> Through him all things were made . . .

Language ceases to be mere rhetoric and assumes a cultic stance. The dramatic hero who has now become one with the Supreme Being experiences what Coleridge refers to as the 'synthetic and magical' power of the imagination made manifest through the spoken word. Symbolism deepens into occultism – the 'Alchimie du Verbe'.

Finally, in 'Path of Thunder', the soothsayer – priest of the water cult-emerges from the cocoon of the creative artist, takes up his iron bell and moves through the streets as town-crier, prophesying impending war.

NOTES

1. Paul Valéry, 'Pure Poetry', *The Art of Poetry*, trans. Denise Folliot, New York, 1958, pp. 184–5.
2. See Wayne C. Booth, *The Rhetoric of Fiction*, Chicago, University of Chicago Press, 1961, p. 95.
3. Robert Langbaum, *Poetry of Experience*, Harmondsworth, Penguin, 1974, p. 228.
4. Christopher Okigbo, *Labyrinths*, London, Heinemann, 1971. All further quotations are from this edition.
5. Langbaum, op. cit., p. 32.
6. Ibid., p. 226.
7. Sunday Anozie, *Christopher Okigbo*, London, Evans, 1972, p. 75.
8. C.O. Acholonu, 'From Ritual to Politics: Christopher Okigbo and the Loadstone Myth', paper presented at the Unical International Conference on Literature and the Teaching of English, 1–6 May 1984.
9. Anozie, op. cit., p. 103.
10. Ibid., pp. 102–3.
11. John Mbiti, *African Religions and Philosophy*, London, Heinemann, 1980, p. 67.
12. Janheinz Jahn, *A History of Neo-African Literature*, London, Faber, n.d., p. 159.
13. Ibid.
15. St. John, I:1.

The Rhetoric of J.P. Clark's *Ivbie*

Isaac I. Elimimian

J.P. Clark's *Ivbie* is a rhetorical *tour de force* which has not received the attention that it deserves. It is not that critics have not read it and tried to explore its meaning. Far from it! Indeed, many critics[1] have either analysed the poem or commented upon it, but on the whole their approach has been aesthetic (poetic) and not rhetorical.

I do not mean to suggest that any discussion of a literary work which has no rhetorical import has no claim to validity. My argument is simply that, the aesthetic consideration of a literary artefact is distinct from the rhetorical consideration of it: the one will afford us the opportunity to examine the work's internal structure; the other will offer us the opportunity to examine not only the work's internal apparatus but its implication for the author and the audience as well.

Part of the problem which *Ivbie* poses as a work of art, however – a problem which apparently accounts for the dearth of rhetorical criticism of the poem – is that it does not represent a unified picture or development of thought.[2] Although Clark groups the poem into six 'movements', perhaps to give it a rhetorical impact, it is, in fact, a hodgepodge of experience whose focus centres around three thematic considerations which are only dimly interrelated: namely, the beauty and glory of the indigenous culture, colonialism in Africa and Clark's polemics on his own inadequacies.

Consequently, because the poem fails to enact one central theme, and because the three themes explored employ different kinds of rhetoric (namely, the ceremonial, the forensic and the political) in advancing their argument, the poem has a complex rhetorical framework which is bound to bother many critics. To have spoken with one tone or voice by concentrating on, say, one of the three kinds of rhetoric, to advance the poem's themes, would have given the work not only an organic unity but also a rhetorical appeal.

In discussing *Ivbie*, therefore, this essay will not only consider the poem's rhetorical perspectives in light of the three themes explored but will take the liberty of speculating on the relative purpose which the poem's complex structure is designed to serve.

In his handling of his first theme – the beauty and glory of the indigenous culture – it is well to remember, first of all, that here (and to some

141

extent in the other themes treated) Clark not only deals with the contemporary situation but seems to be retrospective in his approach, in the sense that he is trying to recapture with some verisimilitude a passing phase or what has gone before.

Secondly, the nature of this kind of discourse necessarily calls into play the rhetorical strategy appropriate to it, that is, the ceremonial or epideictic oratory which, Aristotle explains, 'either praises or censures . . . concerned with the present, since all men praise or blame in view of the state of things existing at the time, though they often find it useful also to recall the past and to make guesses at the future'.[3]

Throughout his treatment of the theme under consideration, Clark focuses on certain fundamental values in traditional African society. Briefly stated, they centre around a cosmogonic universe in which everything is organically ordered: a world of myths, legends and tales; a world in which the ancestors and the gods play a significant role in the affairs of men.

Regarding the use of myth, Richard Chase's definition of the word is pertinent in appreciating its aesthetic significance for Clark. 'Myths are told in order to preserve the meaningfulness and purposefulness of social customs and institutions.'[4] To Clark, traditional institutions and beliefs are so important that any violation of them is bound to have dire consequences. Thus when Oyin, 'the Creator, the ultimate being in Ijaw myth', remonstrates:

> Fear him, children, O fear the stranger
> That comes upon you
> When fowls have gone to roost
> Fear him his footfall soft light
> As a cat's, his shadow far darker
> Than forest gloom or night
> And flimsy like matter in the mist
>
> O fear the dragon smoke-cloud
> That hangs bloated, floating over
> Roof-thatch mangoes and lime
> Fear him that wreath-curling fetish-tree
> Seeth-writing beyond lofts
> It turns out no less than him of the spots[5]

she has at the back of her mind not only the need to resist foreign incursions, or the necessity to protect and preserve indigenous beliefs, customs and traditions, but more importantly the calamity which would follow if the warning is not heeded.

Relying on the rhetorical device of contraries, Clark deftly parallels foreign influence and the indigenous culture, showing not only that the former is pernicious and hypocritical but that it is inferior to the latter. The negative effect of the former Clark highlights through his employment of the following images: 'footfall soft light/As a cat's', 'shadow far darker/ Than forest gloom or night', 'flimsy like matter in the mist' and the 'dragon smoke-cloud'.

Accordingly, he employs positive images to characterize the indigenous culture: 'children', 'fetish-tree', 'Roof-thatch mangoes and lime' and the 'lofts'. In African culture, not only are children regarded as the light of the family, they also serve as touchstones for assessing a man's social worth, which explains the fact that anyone without them is often considered to be unfortunate. The 'fetish-tree' is a sacred object, usually an object of devotion or divine worship, or a place of ritual sacrifice. The 'Roof-thatch mangoes and lime' and the 'lofts' suggest the natural and peaceful setting of the typical African farmhouse, dwelling-house or homestead. Clark's love of the peace and quiet of the indigenous culture is reflected later in the poem, when he laments that it is under external threat:

> Yet in my father's house I cannot sleep
> Nor shut myself up in peace
> But loud knocks,
> Absorbed in the thick of shocks,
> Come beating back on my door
> Crying: 'Sleep no more'
>
> (*D.T.*, p. 30)

In addition to Oyin, other indigenous myths and legends which feature in the poem include Ifa, 'the Yoruba oracle'; the dead, who have the mystical power of life after death (especially in 'Ijo and Urhobo myth', *D.T.*, p. 25); and finally, the 'communal' gods who, apart from being the spiritual conductor between the living and the dead, are the 'be-all' and 'know-all' of virtually every event affecting human destiny. Thus when, for instance, the poet cries out derisively at the gods for their passivity in confronting colonialism:

> Say, you communal gods at the gate
> Has the whiff of carrion crept
> Past your bars while you slept?
> Did it roll-blowing gain the village
> And without as much as a fight
> From you? Did he brow-beat,
> Bribe-beat you into our plight?
>
> (*D.T.*, p. 27)

he obviously is not only drawing our attention to their immense power and significance, nor is he only calling attention to the atmosphere that enhances his developing logos of myth, he is also challenging his audience to accept the sincerity of his argument. The lines, indeed, combine the dynamics of persuasiveness, commitment and action: they engage us logically, ethically and emotionally; they suggest Clark's own commitment or involvement in the subject of his discourse; they serve as a call to action to all concerned to appreciate and defend their cultural heritage.

Another aspect of the indigenous culture which Clark highlights centres around animal and bird stories. In particular, the poet cites the 'ram', 'kites', the 'owl' and the 'hen' (*D.T.*, pp. 27, 28, 29, 31). Although the narratives connected with these creatures are superstitious, they none-the less serve as an index or mirror-image in interpreting the value system of the people.[6]

There are, of course, the African culture symbols (dating to the cosmogonic period) which were looted:

> *Rare works of art discovered in*
> *Tin mines! Another in Benin*
> *Of great historical*
> *Interest in London! Moscow!*
> *New York!*
> *And still more from Olumo*
> *Rock,*
> *All before the flood*
>   *(D.T., p. 24)*

'Treasures, so many and beautiful', Clark eulogizes, that Bartholomew Diaz and Sir John Hawkins had a feeling of amazement upon first sighting them. Indeed, it is not only the natives who cherished or derived interest from the African art works, or the poet himself – a fact suggested by his italicizing the lines quoted above – but even the colonizers who, motivated by prejudice, initially failed to appreciate their intrinsic value.

Clark also praises such traditional institutions and places as 'our virgin jungle', 'occult groves', 'ivory bust' and the 'shrines of Ifa' (D.T., pp. 23, 24, 25). And he celebrates the charm and mystique of indigenous objects and preserves:

> How can they in the fixity
> And delirium of a glance
> How can they catch the thousand intricacies
> Tucked away in crannies
> And corners perhaps known only to rats?
> How can they tell the loin-cloth
> Cast away in the heat of desire
> The shifts hanging in the wind
> Now groins want oiling?
> The sanctuary of things human is swathed
> In menstrual rags, not in the market place.
>   (D.T., p. 24)

Nor can one fail to be moved by some of the other traditional elements to which the poet nostalgically alludes: for instance, the cheap 'cow-dung' used for polishing floors; and the locally brewed 'gin', more efficacious than 'tea' (since, in addition to its power to evoke sleep, it is also capable of generating wakefulness).

Of what rhetorical significance are the sources cited thus far – myths, legends and tales, the ancestors, the gods, culture symbols, etc.? First, as materials for ceremonial discourse (because they are invaluable or of interest to others), they are worthy of praise. Second, they highlight the aspirations and beliefs which inspire or unite a people. Third, they further the poem's theme. Fourth, because they are external aids to invention (the 'non-artistic means of persuasion'), not only do they serve as an additional source of information for the poem, but through them the audience is irresistibly drawn into the poet's argument. Finally, they dramatize Clark's commitment to his roots and consequently invest his discourse with significance. As Abiola Irele observes, 'what gives a special character to literary creation in Africa today is the movement to establish and to maintain the sense of tradition'.[7]

Coming now to the second theme, European colonialism in Africa, it is important to emphasize the fact that, unlike the first, where the poet employs ceremonial oratory, here Clark's argument is fundamentally forensic. Forensic oratory, explains Aristotle, 'either attacks or defends'; it is concerned, moreover, with 'establishing the justice or injustice of some action' (*Rhetoric*, 1358b).

In *Ivbie*, Clark's primary objective is to censure or highlight the injustice wrought by colonialism. Consequently, almost every part of the poem's six sections has one negative thing or another to expound about the colonial system. For example, the first section introduces us to 'Visitors from across the seas' as they penetrate the hinterland 'like therapeutic rays'; the second section speaks of how the 'Visitors catch their host napping'; the third section highlights the economic ambition of the colonialists, who 'go toot/Tooting in mad rush for loot'; the fourth section speaks of the pride and arrogance of the colonialists who 'spat/Straight on our ancestral seat'; the fifth section describes the pernicious effect of colonialism on 'The white-collar generation, more white than white'; while the sixth section emphasizes the 'missile-hurled' speed with which colonialism swept across every area occupied by the native population.

In developing his theme, however, Clark singles out three aspects of colonialism for attack: its economic drive, exemplified in its mineral and human exploitation; its pride and arrogance, symbolized in its wanton destruction or desecration of sacred institutions; and its missionary evangelical fervour.

Regarding the colonialists' economic drive, Clark early on in the poem names those foreign agents who participate or are interested in exploitation: the likes of Bartholomew Diaz, Sir John Hawkins, Mr and Mrs Gamp and Austin Herefords. And he details, as the following passage illustrates, the mode and manner of imperial operation:

> Those unguent gums and oils
> Drawn in barrels off to foreign mills
> The soil quarried out of recognition
> As never would erosion another millennium
> The blood crying for blood spilt free
> From keels away on frothing sea
> The dark flesh rudely torn
> And grafted on to red fetid sore
> Breeding a hybrid lot
> To work the land of sunset
>
> (*D.T.*, p. 26)

Here, the imagery of 'unguent gums and oils' symbolizes Africa's natural resources which the colonialists siphoned off to their respective countries. Elsewhere, Clark documents the other natural resources which fascinated the colonial exploiters: 'Works of art', 'Tin mines', 'ivory bust', 'mahogany', and 'gold' (*D.T.*, pp. 24, 25, 27).

Professor R.N. Egudu has some reservation about the last four lines of the above-quoted passage. 'One feels reluctant to probe these lines,'[8] he writes. But if the truth must be told and if we are to appraise the ubiquitous harm perpetrated by colonialism, no less than the poet's indictment of it, I think that the lines deserve elucidation. The expression, 'The dark flesh rudely torn/And grafted on to red fetid sore', the most chilling image in *Ivbie*, suggests the unhealthy amalgam of irreconcilable polarities: the forcible taking away of the Africans from their ancestral home through slavery to foreign lands where they not only were made to work against their innate desire, but were – more often than not – mercilessly beaten until blood, tears and putrid sores became their common dower. The expression 'hybrid lot' is a metaphor for the offspring of slaves, who suffered almost the same fate as their ancestors, while the 'land of sunset' connotes the West, where the slaves were initially transported.

In furnishing proof for his discourse and eliciting sympathy from the audience, Clark relies heavily on the general topos of cause and effect: for instance, the mad rush for 'oils/Drawn in barrels off to foreign mills' results in the 'soil' being 'quarried out of recognition'; also the imagery of 'blood crying for blood spilt free' suggests the perennial oppression of man by man simply because there was no one to question the unrighteousness of slavery. Clark also employs the enthymematical device constructed from probabilities, as when he earlier in the poem hints at the suffering that has been the lot of the downtrodden since antediluvian times:

> In the irresolution
> Of one unguarded moment
> Thereby hangs a tale
> A tale so tall in implications
> Universal void cannot contain
> The terrible immensity
> Nor its permanence dissolve
> In the flux wash of eternity
> (*D.T.*, p. 25)

Clark's indictment of colonialism runs the gamut of modes between exposé and satire. Unlike David Diop and Kofi Awoonor, for example, who are uncompromisingly critical and harsh in their denunciation of colonialism (for instance, see, respectively, 'The Vultures' and 'The Cathedral') and whose criticisms exhibit traces of malevolence arising from anger or ill will or both, Clark achieves a rhetorical feat by leading his audience to believe that he is either exposing the evil inherent in human exploitation or, on the other hand, ridiculing those agents who engage in exploitation.

Clark is, nonetheless, unmistakeably clear in his repudiation of the pride and arrogance of the colonialists, who, for instance, 'Walk as on . . .

tarmac our occult groves/With alien care and impunity'; 'Dig well below wild opensteads/Dig well below dry riverbeds'; '. . . wreath-curling fetish-tree/Seeth-writhing beyond lofts' (*D.T.*, pp. 23, 25, 29). And, as the colonialists become more and more nefarious in their attitude towards indigenous cultural values, Clark equally adopts a more radical stance in his discourse:

> A snake-bird fell down early flat
> In the market-place
> Clinging quick to earth on his belly
>
> Digging with his bristle fangs
> Open communal graves amid confused clangs
> Of race and riot
> Fear the poison passed out or spat
> Straight on our ancestral seat
> Fear it though a trickle or dot
> Fear it, the corruption
> That dissolving, will deluge all the earth
> (*D.T.*, p. 29)

The image 'snake-bird' is employed to dramatize human viciousness. The 'snake-bird', as presented above, digs 'Open communal graves' and pollutes the air; worse still, it spits on sacred places, the embodiment of traditional values. But the imagery conveys more than this. Of particular interest is the use of the word 'snake'. As a rhetorical device, that is, a satiric allegory, it aims to highlight the evils, the travesties of colonialism. By analogy, colonialism, much like the biblical snake, is deceitful and sinister, and has all the implications of desecration, dislocation and destruction. If the analogy is stretched further, it can be said that colonialism and neo-colonialism, much like the biblical snake which ushered in 'sin' and 'death', are the source of much of the evils of contemporary civilization. Consequently the poet, fully aware of the colonialists' wicked design, admonishes the native population through repetitive employment of the injunction 'fear': 'Fear the poison . . ./Fear it . . ./Fear it . . .'

Sometimes, the poet's admonition (initially rendered through the native god, Oyin) recalls an imminent struggle and disaster:

> So come in children
> An unlaid ghost
> Has come into the village
> Tonight out of the coast
> I hear his wings flapping in the twigs
> I smell the dank sweat
> Brine of his breath
> Heavy on plantain leaves and palm
> They crinkle dry up and die
> (*D.T.*, p. 28)

At other times, it is simply one which hints at the end, not the continuum:

'Dirt and death'
And all along only the owl
Safe in her magic cowl
Saw all
I the white bearded woman
Of night fame saw all
But men heeded not my hooting
Placed instead penalty in warning
And finality in brief omen.
                    (D.T., p. 29)

The first passage above dramatizes, through its imagery of 'plantain leaves and palm' which 'crinkle dry up and die', the terror and violence of the colonial system. The second passage vividly mirrors, through its imagery of 'finality in brief omen', the price which a people must pay for disobedience.

Three sub-topics of importance upon which the forensic rhetorician usually depends in developing his argument are: *an sit*, that is, whether a state of justice or injustice exists; *quid sit*, what the justice or injustice is; and *quale sit*, the motive for it. In *Ivbie* Clark clearly establishes, through the poem's subtitle ('a song of wrong'), that a state of injustice exists. He also shows, from our discussion thus far, that colonialism is responsible for the injustice. As for the colonialists' motive, the following account by Ernest Bradford not only explains what they were about but also serves as prefiguring in appreciating Clark's indictment of the colonialists' missionary activities:

> The inherent contradiction in human slavery had always generated dualisms in thought, but by the sixteenth century Europeans had arrived at the greatest dualism of all: a devotion to the principles of liberty coupled with an economic expansion rooted in the exploitation of slave labor in the colonies. Thus their expansion was made possible by the monstrous acts of dehumanizing others, particularly Africans, perpetrated in the name of Christianity . . . The Church educated its constituencies (church membership, colleges, universities, seminaries, hospitals, missions, and publications) in thought and act.[9]

Yes, Christianity, which for ages had been used as a vehicle for proclaiming salvation, was now being employed by the colonialists as a tool for subverting the tradition and promoting selfish socio-political and economic paradigms. That is precisely Clark's argument in *Ivbie*:

For does not the Holy Writ
Loud peddled abroad
To approve imperial flaws and fraud
Does it not say true:
'Knock it shall be opened unto you'?
                    (D.T., p. 31)

Earlier, he reflects:

At the office desk, we clapped
Ourselves on the back;

So well-fed on sweet quotations and wine.
Were we, with pride, we said:
'Forget O forget . . . to forgive is divine'.
                    (*D.T.*, p. 30)

Chaos, ironic reversals and contradictions in intent, no less than the struggle between good and evil, are woven into the fabric of the above passages: and this, Clark seems to be saying, is the bane of contemporary Christianity. The injunctions 'Knock it shall be opened unto you' and 'Forget O forget . . . to forgive is divine' are cardinal tenets of the Christian religion; but, as it were, they are in trouble because of the ever-increasing pursuit of materialism. Obviously convinced that things are in a state of confusion, the poet expostulates:

Is it truce or ruse
That peace which passeth all
understanding
O big brother in heaven!
                    (*D.T.*, p. 26)

Further pained by contemporary religious inadequacies, and anxious to know what has become of the orthodox Christian ideals, he remonstrates:

Now where are the lightning-spokes
That quivering should dance
Ten thousand leagues into the limbs of things?
Where are the broadways
Of oriflamme that opening wide
should lance
Into the heart of darkness
As when trembling like a fresh
Maid before her man
Moonlight distils fluorescent submarine seas?
                    (*D.T.*, p. 27)

These lines must represent some of Clark's best poetry, in which we find the peculiar blending of *epiplexis*, or asking a series of questions in order to show anger or indignation; *anacoenosis*, or seeking the listener's response through questioning; and *exuscitatio*, or emotional statements which stir the listener to deep feelings. Finally, the resourceful use of sound effect arising from the careful weaving of sibilant sounds, especially in the lines 'Ten thousand leagues into the limbs of things?' and 'Moonlight distils fluorescent submarine seas?', is a daring stroke.

Equally interesting is the fact that not only does Clark speak here with authority, his questioning recalls pulpit oratory. The 'lightning-spokes' and the 'broadways/Of oriflamme' are supposed to perform magic wonders; apparently they have not. As religious images they connote, on the one hand, the age-old Christian tenets of redemption, hope, forgiveness, healing and love. On the other, they suggest the promises made and broken, the ideals sought but unattained. Perhaps having at the back of his mind the early Christian missionaries who leaped into 'the heart of darkness' in furtherance of noble ideals (e.g. Albert Schweitzer and David Livingstone), Clark's rhetoric here is not only to call attention to the lapses of colonialism, but apparently also to urge allegiance to indigenous religious beliefs or, in the absence of this, a return to orthodox Christianity which upholds spiritual responsibility and a compelling humanitarian ethos.

There are three classes of audience which Clark addresses in *Ivbie*: the African audience, the colonialist audience and the general, rather uninvolved audience. His message to the first group is to fight for its rights; to the second, to desist from its nefarious practices; and to the third, to serve as witness to, if not contain, the catalogue of atrocities perpetrated by colonialism. Apparently it is in recognition of the fact that none of these categories of audience is ready to act that the poet decides, in the long run, to undertake the onerous task of salvaging the indigenous culture. And here he is employing the deliberative or political oratory, which, says Aristotle, 'urges us to do or not to do something' (*Rhetoric*, 1358b).

This kind of rhetoric, moreover, is concerned with 'ways and means', with 'establishing the expediency ... of a proposed course of action' (*Rhetoric*, 1358b). Thus, unlike the first two themes discussed above, where the poet mostly employs the second-person pronoun 'you', here he employs the first-person narrative 'I':

I cannot sleep I cannot sleep
. . .
And you say I ought to on this cup of tea
. . .
And if I open unto them in haste
. . .
And if I fail
                    (*D.T.*, pp. 30–1)

Although Clark is often criticized for not distancing himself from the poem's action[10] by observing what T.S. Eliot characterizes as the 'impersonality of the author', the fact remains that, in this poem, a rhetorical situation is presented which demands a rhetorical response: the poet needs to say whether 'to do or not to do something'. Besides, he has to weigh the pros and cons of the situation ('Balancing the right and wrong of it', *D.T.*, p. 31) before taking a decision. The following lines, for instance, highlight the degree to which the poet ponders the situation:

Talk then round the point,
Hamlet, do talk on.
The Niger, long ago,
Faced with a similar lot,
Hedged round and till tomorrow
Goes on spinning whirlpools

The cocks begin again to crow
The night is old
And I am cold

So cold I know
Right in my bones the fear
Electrical in an old woman's breast
As new kites appear
Swooping in from the west.
I cannot sleep nor act
And here I pace her bastard child
A top twirling out of complexity
'Gnawing at my finger-tips deep perplexity'.
                    (*D.T.*, pp. 31–2)

The Hamlet who talks 'round the point' is a reference to Shakespeare's tragic character, who gets lost in the labyrinth of his delusions. The expression 'The cocks begin again to crow' recalls Peter's reflections on the prophecy that he would have denied Christ upon the cock's crow. The lines 'The night is old/And I am cold', parallel Prufrock's initial musings and predicament. By echoing these literary stereotypes, the poet indicates that he is aware of the pitfalls of others and will, if possible, try to overcome them.

Other expressions in the passage have underlying meanings. The allusion to the 'Niger' which 'Hedged round and till tomorrow/Goes on spinning whirlpools', the 'fear' which grips 'Electrical' as 'in an old woman's breast', the confessional statement 'I cannot sleep nor act', and the metaphor ' "Gnawing at my finger-tips deep perplexity" ' – not only do they all suggest the difficulties which account for the poet's equivocation, but, more importantly, they bespeak his sincerity, depth of feeling and strong critical faculty. And when finally he exhorts colonialism to have its way:

Pass on then, O pass on, missile-hurled
In your headlong flight to fool the world;
Being self-turned, how could you have heard
Above our wild herd
And market murmur of assembled waves
A song strange fallen out of night-caves
Like a star all of a sudden from the sky?

I
Reared here on a cow-dung floor,
From antediluvian shore
Heard all, and what good it did!
'Magnificent obsession' now
magic chords are broken!

Pass on in mad headlong flight
O pass on, your ears right
Full of throttle sound,
So winding up your kaleidoscope
Leave behind unhaunted
An innocent in sleep of the ages
                    (*D.T.*, p. 32)

because of the perspective of its military strength ('missile-hurled'), we are not taken by surprise but, rather, are satisfied that he has acted judiciously. Aristotle explains the motivation for deliberative action: 'men choose their means with reference to their ends' (*Rhetoric*, 1366b). Elsewhere, he elaborates: 'we are bound to act if the action is possible, easy ... this is true even if the action entails loss, provided the loss is outweighed by the solid advantage' (*Rhetoric*, 1399b).

We come now to the clustered structure of the poem, in which, as I pointed out at the beginning of this essay, Clark not only divides the poem into six incongruous 'movements' but employs different thematic and rhetorical strategies in developing his argument. By classifying the poem into six 'movements', Clark probably had the intention of organizing his discourse into the traditional six-part sequence of *exordium* (introduction), *narratio* (circumstances of a discourse), *divisio* (the parts), *confirmatio* (proof), *confutatio* (refutation of dissenting views) and *peroratio* (the conclusion) which the Roman rhetoricians employed in oratory. But *Ivbie's* rhetoric departs from this schema. If a defence can be made for the poem's illogical structure and the clash of theme and form, it is that the poet, aware of the complex nature of contemporary civilization and modern man's predicment, seeks to reflect these accordingly.[11] For, as he says plaintively at the end:

> And here I pace her bastard child
> A top twirling out of complexity
> (D.T., p. 32)

Against the above background, it must be admitted without paradox that *Ivbie* has some integrated structural design. Although the experience presented is diffused, the poet's voice serves as the link uniting the poem's diverse thematic and stylistic features. Also, the poem, by recreating the values of the African past, offers a perspective through which we assess our gains and losses against a backdrop of the past, present and possibly the future.

No doubt, the diverse critical views on *Ivbie* suggest that it has almost limitless possibilities for African literature. For example, M.J.C. Echeruo characterizes it, along with Nwanodi's *Icheke* and Okigbo's *Four Canzones*, as 'our nearest to the epic';[12] Dan Izevbaye sees it as 'a lament dealing with the infiltration of the white man into the household of the African because the gods who should be guarding the gates have been taken unawares';[13] Donatus I. Nwoga says 'parts' of the poem 'are undigested Hopkins';[14] and Romanus Egudu praises it as 'great'.[15] The poem can be all of these, but I think also that it will perhaps best be remembered as a work whose rhetoric centres around the poet-persona's patriotic struggle to salvage the indigenous culture from the shattering effects of colonialism.

NOTES

1. See, for instance, the following: N.J. Udoeyop, *Three Nigerian Poets*, Ibadan, Ibadan University Press, 1973, pp. 70-6; Romanus N. Egudu, *Four Modern West African Poets*, New York and London, NOK, 1977, pp. 47-55; Thomas R. Knipp, '*Ivbie*: the developing moods of John Pepper Clark's poetry', *Journal of Commonwealth Literature*, vol. 17, no. 1, 1982, pp. 128-42; W.H. Stevenson, 'The Horn: what it was and what it did', in *Critical Perspectives on Nigerian Literatures*, ed. Bernth Lindfors, Ibadan and London, Heinemann, 1978, pp. 215 and 222: Ken Goodwin, *Understanding African Poetry*, London, Heinemann Educational Books, 1982, pp. 62-3.
2. As Professor John Povey observes, 'In this poem there are the same apparently haphazard sequences which mirror the muddled and dissonant range of experience.' See 'The poetry of J.P. Clark: two hands a man has', *African Literature Today*, vol. 1, 1968, p. 38.
3. Aristotle, *Rhetoric*, trans. W. Rhys Roberts, New York, The Modern Library, 1954, 1358b. All references to Aristotle come from this edition: subsequent quotations from it are included parenthetically in the text and designated simply as *Rhetoric*, followed by the section(s).
4. Richard Chase, 'Notes on the study of myth', *Partisan Review*, vol. 13, 1946; as quoted by Charles Nnolim, 'From nostalgia to myth: an archetypal interpretation of Camare Laye's *The Dark Child*', *Nigerian Journal of the Humanities*, no. 2, September 1978, p. 47.
5. J.P. Clark, *A Decade of Tongues*, London, Longman, 1981, pp. 28-9. All references to and quotations from *Ivbie* come from this edition. Further quotations from the poem are included parenthetically in the text and designated as *D.T.* followed by the page number(s).
6. Even where it is obvious that an object is an abstract phenomenon, such an object is still considered important in the African cultural context. Oladele Taiwo, *An Introduction to West African Literature*, London, Nelson, 1967, pp. 127-8, explains the nature and significance of superstitious beliefs:

> To what extent are the superstitious beliefs and ritual practices of Africans capable of opening up to us fresh perspectives? ... The African himself is superstitious and believes very strongly in mystic rites. He reconciles himself to these forces and treats them with reverence and dignity. He believes that his every action is guided and directed by spirits ... Every fetish or object which is feared and respected has two faces: the first which is visible to the human eye but is inanimate to the devotee, and the second, "the replica", which is not perceptible by humans, but which for the devotee is the essence of life and the controller of the first. It is this second face which is endowed with force and strong will-power, and which merely employs its superficial or inanimate counterpart in directing or controlling the affairs of human life.

7. Abiola Irele, *The African Experience in Literature and Ideology*, London and Ibadan, Heinemann, 1981, p. 174.
8. Egudu, op. cit., p. 50.
9. Ernest Bradford, 'Toward a view of the influence of religion on Black literature', *CLA Journal*, vol. 27, no. 1, September 1983, p. 18-19.

10. To be sure, this is one area of the poem in which Clark receives his severest criticism. For example, Professor Povey criticizes him for 'taking sides' (op. cit., p. 44); Thomas R. Knipp says: '*Ivbie* is not detached . . . Clark personalizes . . . in an effective way that stops short of the self-indulgent' (op. cit., p. 129); Dathorne castigates him for 'melodramatically' articulating his 'personal plight' (p. 198).

11. As Douglas Ehninger, in *The Rhetoric of Western Thought*, ed. James L. Golden *et al.*, Iowa, Kendall Hunt Publishing Co., 1976, p. 19, says: 'the collective rhetorics of a period are culture-bound'.

12. M.J.C. Echeruo, 'Traditional and borrowed elements in Nigerian poetry', *Nigeria Magazine*, vol. 89, June 1966, pp. 149–50.

13. Dan Izevbaye, 'The poetry and drama of John Pepper Clark', in *Introduction to Nigerian Literature*, ed. Bruce King, Lagos and Ibadan, University of Lagos and Evans Brothers, 1971, p. 154.

14. Donatus, I. Nwoga, 'Obscurity and Commitment in Modern African Poetry', *African Literature Today*, no. 6, 1973, p. 35.

15. Egudu, op. cit., p. 54.

Dimensions of Language in New Nigerian Poetry

Ezenwa-Ohaeto

Nigerian literature is often taken as the representative voice of African literature. Although this may be disputed, it is largely true in relation to Anglophone African literature. Few countries have witnessed so many writers within so short a time and fewer still have produced so many distinguished writers. The names of Achebe, Soyinka, Okigbo, Clark, Okara, Munonye, Emecheta, Aluko, Nwapa, Ike and Amadi are well known in Africa. However, there is both danger and hope in this trail-blazing role in the sense that either negative or positive influences could be generated. That uncertainty notwithstanding, Nigerian writers have led the way in the refinement of an authentic African literature. Bernth Lindfors comments that Nigeria has produced a number of remarkably talented creative artists. He also feels that:

> Through these agents and their works, Nigeria has probably contributed more to international awareness of modern Africa's literary and cultural achievements than any other nation.[1]

Nigerian poetry is part of this literature.

It is rare to encounter a commentary on African poetry that ignores the merits of Okara, Clark, Soyinka, Okigbo and Achebe but few readers are aware of the poets who have recently emerged on the Nigerian literary scene. This lack of awareness becomes a serious issue when it leads to such accusations as Kofi Awoonor's that, 'beyond Okigbo, Clark and Soyinka, there seems to be a cul-de-sac, a verbal arid land where the same half-arsed clever poems are being written';[2] then the issue becomes urgent. In effect Awoonor feels that new Nigerian poets have taken the failures of the elder poets and are trying to transform them into regional virtues. The glaring error in Awoonor's review is that he considers too few poets, just the two poets: Kalu Uka, author of *Earth to Earth*, and Pol Ndu, the author of *Songs for Seers*.

There is hardly a society where poetry is static. The view that poetry has the ability to communicate 'some new experience, or some fresh understanding of the familiar, or the expression of something we have experienced but have no words, which enlarges our consciousness or refines our sensibility',[3] takes care of its vitality and pulsating life. Any diligent reader would discern through at least the pages of *Okike*, which Chinua Achebe edited, that numerous poets with fresh voices and poetic vigour are constantly appearing. The only difficulty might be that of intellectual laziness which militates against careful consideration of their efforts. Moreover, it is ironic that Awoonor praises the same older poets that Chinweizu, Jemie and Madubuike regard as writing with 'old-fashioned, craggy, unmusical language; obscure and inaccessible diction; a plethora of imported imagery; a divorce from African oral poetic tradition, tempered only by lifeless attempts at revivalism'.[4] It is such a conflict of judgements that has prompted this study and we shall examine three new Nigerian poets, Chinweizu, Aig-Imoukhuede and Osundare, in order to perceive whether there has been an improvement, especially in their experimentation with language forms and their thematic concerns. We shall also note Nwoga's injunction that domesticated African poetry in English is that 'which talks to as many Africans as possible about issues of greatest relevance in Africa's ongoing development'.[5]

Experimentation with language and the need to talk to as many Africans as possible about issues of relevance are interwoven in the poetry of Chinweizu. The desire to make language a model of a culture and an adjustment to the world is also discernible in his poetry because 'language is the primary and most highly elaborated form of human symbolic activity'.[6] However, as a poet, he does not use language in the normal prosaic form. He rather writes both complexly and idiosyncratically. His poetry is therefore distinct due to its intensity and ability to illuminate his perceptions of life.

Chinweizu's perceptions and also his concept of poetry are clear in his collection *Energy Crisis and Other Poems*.[7] It is interesting also that Chinweizu, who, in the company of Jemie and Madubuike, criticized and condemned obscurity in modern African poetry, has produced a collection of poems that can be used to assess his views. Maduakor seems right to observe that readers 'would naturally expect his own poetry to embody the virtues of simplicity and of transparent lucidity in the use of image and symbols which he advocated in his essays on poetics'.[8] The poet therefore uses language that illustrates simple uncomplicated syntax.

The poetic territory of Chinweizu is large. His wit and humour are derived from Africa, America and Europe. He infuses our consciousness with new ideas through the transformation and modification of words. Words are enlarged to incorporate subtle nuances of language. Perhaps he knows that nothing really is new except the manner in which it is presented and this may account for the poem titled 'Originality', which says:

> He who must do
> Something altogether new
> Let him swallow his own head (*Energy Crisis*, p. 37)

The philosophy of life embeded in that poem is that nothing is new under the sun. The freshness of Chinweizu's poetry, however, arises through his ability to make poetry simple and also substantial. This is a feat that

eludes many poets who strive to formulate adequate poetic forms for
sustaining their poetry. He succeeds in this venture because he conveys
poetry to a level accessible to the largely intellectually lazy Nigerians.
This feat is also what the American poet Don Lee achieves in his poetry
when he writes:

i ain't seen no poems stop a. 38
i ain't seen no stanzas brake a honkie's head,
i ain't seen no metaphors stop a tank,
i ain't seen no words kill.[9]

Apart from the sarcasm and irony in this poem, Don Lee has artistically
introduced the peculiar Chicago street language into the realm of poetry.
It is in this wise that he shares something in common with Chinweizu.

Chinweizu, however, combines elements from the American and
African cultures in the creation of his poems and this can be seen in the
title poem 'Energy Crisis' in the section, 'Wild Oats Farm'. He uses the
notorious fuel shortage of the seventies, which was felt keenly in America,
to signify a sexual experience. Women are imbued with the imagery of
vehicles as they are likened to 'sleek Cadillacs', 'Chevrolets', 'pick-ups',
'Volkswagens' and 'banged-up Volvos'. It is the apt mixture of humour,
irony and colloquialisms in this poem that transforms it into a unique
exposition of reality. The satire is corrosive, signifying the timeless truth
that pride goes before a fall. What Chinweizu has done is to take poetry
to the familiar terrain of colloquial communication. In this terrain words
may appear simple but not simplistic because even the everyday words
we use are not bereft of vivid imagery. This is why the poet can write of
love, for instance, without boring his readers.

The love poems show relevance to the impatience inherent in human
nature. The poems treat contemporary issues like divorced marriages,
infidelity caused by poverty, deceitful love and also pleasant memories of
love. In 'Faithful Mary Lou', the poet uses a woman who is caught with
another man to comment that hunger obliterates faithfulness. The woman,
Mary Lou, tells her husband:

Ah only slept with his name;
Ah only slept with his color;
Ah only slept with his money not with him.
Ah ain't been unfaithful to you, can't you see?
(Energy Crisis, p. 26)

It is quite clear that Chinweizu has successfully adapted the thought-
patterns of American blacks. The words 'ain't' and 'Ah only' are typical
of the Americanisms that have crept into the English language. The vigour
in this poem arises from the adept use of irony and humour and a familiar
theme. The irony is in the idea that a woman can 'sleep' with the colour,
the name and the money without 'sleeping' with the man himself. Furthermore the poet successfully avoids the pitfalls of overt preaching. In
another interesting love poem, 'The King Fisher', the poet turns to another

dimension of love where he uses a kingfisher that waits patiently for its meal as an insightful symbol to caution that impatience appears to be a destructive element.

It is clear that, in whatever guise the poet appears, it is the humour that ameliorates the vulgar connotations that could be derived from the poems. Moreover, he uses familiar symbols that do not militate against effective understanding. This is the problem that Okigbo arouses when he writes for instance:

> mystery which I, initiate
> received newly naked
> upon waters of the genesis
> from Kepkanly.[10]

The symbol of Kepkanly here is not familiar and the fact that he is a half-serious, half-comical primary-school teacher of the late thirties is not immediately obvious. Chinweizu avoids this kind of personalism in his poetry by using familiar symbols.

The poet also writes on different serious issues plaguing Nigeria and indeed the whole of Africa. He condemns the new African elites who use the opportunity afforded by their positions in government to devastate the resources of their countries. In 'Praise Song of the New Notable', he writes:

> I, Odozi Obodo, watchman of communal granaries –
> I stole the grain and blamed the rats
> I feast alone, throw meat to dogs and pelt with
> laughter servant faces beggared
>   by storms I
> start
> It is I, man of deeds
> I, eater of taxes
> I, graft millionaire
> I, swindle tycoon
> I, Lord of Uhuru (Energy Crisis, p. 46)

The tragedy is that the people hail this new notable, heaping praises on him. Chinweizu makes the poem satiric through the adoption of the language of Igbo praise poetry. Igbo praise poetry is used for celebrating positive contributions or substantiating magnificence but in this poem he uses it negatively in order to illustrate the extent of the tragic tergiversations of the new notable. He therefore expands the use of personifications to denote not only the choice of words but also to connote the economic devastations of the new notable.

Chinweizu also effectively exploits the limits of the epigrammatic style. On the colonial legacy, he puts it succinctly by writing of Chief Lobengula, who welcomed Cecil Rhodes, thus:

> With open arms
> He welcomed a smiling tiger into his home;
> With open jaws
> The tiger welcomed him into its belly

After all, smiled the beast
One good welcome deserves another (Energy Crisis, p. 34)

The essence of this style is that the cryptic statements eliminate wilful
obscurities of language. The images are clear, fresh and original. He
makes words, ordinary words, pulsate with new life. This is not surprising
since Chinweizu is an advocate of accessible diction, a feature that has
been missing in most of the poems emanating from Nigeria.

On the other hand, in Frank Aig-Imoukhuede's *Pidgin Stew and Suffer-*
head[11] we meet intricate experimental poetry. His jocular treatment of
polygamy, 'One Man, One Wife', has appeared in numerous anthologies.
One significant aspect of his poetry is the use of pidgin English. Bernard
Mafeni notes the primacy of pidgin when he observes that 'pidgin seems
to be today a very widely spoken lingua franca, many town and city
dwellers being at least bilingual, in pidgin and an indigenous language'.[12]
Aig-Imoukheude's pidgin poetry may thus be termed poetry for the
ordinary man. However, *Pidgin Stew and Sufferhead* is divided into two
sections of poems written in conventional English and pidgin, respectively.
The intrinsic quality of the poems in pidgin is illustrated in the poem
'Pidgin Stew':

So cook stew of pidgin
Give tyranny chop.
He go chop so-tay, lick
Finger dey laugh as
Dem dey rub 'im blockuss
For public place (*Pidgin Stew*, p. 3)

The idea is that, when criticism is presented in a humorous manner, the
person concerned will not realize its potency. This is an effective method
because it enables Aig-Imoukhuede to discuss very serious issues with
humour. The predominant style in this poetry is the gradual development
of an idea or theme until the denouement when it is unravelled through
an ironic twist of the words or phrases. The poem 'Flood done Come', for
instance, begins with the image of a flood that symbolizes the exploitation
of rulers and it ends with the injunction:

Rape na rape
Whether na gun or strong prick (*Pidgin Stew*, p. 1)

In the poem 'The Wrestling Match', where one wrestler unintentionally
causes the death of his opponent by throwing him heavily on the ground,
the poet comments: 'And for sake of common wrestle/Idode go five years
for manslaughter' (*Pidgin Stew*, p. 25). Imoukhuede's poetry is indeed a
radical departure from the poetry of most African poets and he adds the
subtlety of irony, sarcasm and pun to the lyrical patterns of pidgin
language.

In the poem 'Take Me Go for Corner-place', the poet captures the wit
of pidgin thus:

> Me cat wey him back no dey touch ground,
> Look wetin common woman go do for me
>   Let me go for corner-place
>   Make, I wit shame, hide my face
> Now I no fit talk, I no fit walk,
> I no fit tanda my own, bot people dey laugh,
> I no fit go bar, no fit look woman for face;
> Dem all dey sing shame song wit' my name.
>   God, find me some corner-place
>   Far place wey I go hide my face (*Pidgin Stew*, p. 31)

The humour here notwithstanding, the poet successfully uses sarcasm and irony to comment on human nature to the effect that excessive pride is dangerous as the man discovers when a woman knocks him down. The words are musical and the structure of the poem has a strong rhythmical cadence with the effective refrain at the end of each stanza.

Aig-Imoukhuede is not a bitter poet even when he prays God to bend the neck of his enemy, pull his eyes out and make the tongue too long to inhabit the mouth, in the poem 'Cosmetic Surgery: A Wish', because he ends the poem with the injunction that it should be done in the enemy's dream. This tendency for mildness in the condemnation of injustices may be a hangover from Imoukhuede's university days when he ridiculed Negritude. In 'Negritude (The Poor Black Muse)', which is ill-advisedly incorporated in this collection, Imoukhuede ends up exposing his lack of understanding of the fundamental issues of Negritude.

Nevertheless, this innovative poet explores the usefulness of pidgin through a metaphoric manipulation of words in order to achieve not only an ordinary but also an intellectual meaning. Moreover, Aig-Imoukhuede questions the very foundation of injustice, but this is done with a tone of confusion. The poet is worried but it does not seem as if he possesses an answer to human problems as he asks in exasperation in 'The Durbar':

> Who will halt the charge?
> And the scything searing run? (*Pidgin Stew*, p. 14)

The solution the poet envisages is not definite in the sense that he does not portray the type of individual who would solve all the problems. Nevertheless, his departure from convention has shown that Aig-Imoukhuede is a poet who has enlarged the frontiers of the poetic form through an adherence to contemporary issues and popular language.

With the poetry of Niyi Osundare, we turn to a poet who mastered the technique of fusing oral traditions and modern poetic trends quite early in his career. In *Village Voices*,[13] Osundare explores both the elasticity of poetic language and the intricate web of life in his society with a penetration unmatched by even the most notable poets. The personae in the poetry are varied and the thematic concerns multiple. If Chinweizu is the poet for the ordinary man, Osundare is the poet for the suffering man. His poetry confirms James Reeves's observation that 'what poetry does to the mass of ordinary experience is to make permanent and memorable whatever in it is vital and significant'.[14] There are the parallelisms, adept use of vivid allusions, stark imagery and pointillism of committed poetry. The 'rising voice' sets the scene:

> My words will climb the tree of wisdom
> Feed multitude with fruits of thought
> and plant the earth with potent seeds (*Village Voices*, p. 1)

With this mission Osundare commences a poetic exploration of the Nigerian social climate. The vision is that of a sensitive artist reluctant to allow his voice to become muzzled by rampant injustice. The division of the collection of poems illustrates the poet's sense of organization.

Metaphor is the idiom of this poetry. It is a technique that enables the poet to adopt abundant materials such as witty aphorisms and phrases from the Yoruba oral traditions. In addition, his poetry is highly political and social. It is not an attempt to beat the newspaper headline news of the day but a matter of effective generation of ideas related to stark realities. 'A Dialogue of the Drums' cautions reason as two drummers engage in dialogue to discover the effectiveness of their practice. Osundare uses dramatic language in this poem to capture humanity's weakness and predilection for sycophancy. The poet notes:

> Whatever song you raise
> Is what the world sings after you. (*Village Voices*, p. 6)

The voices who raise the songs are numerous. They include the street fighters, caricatured members of the ruling classes, farmers, politicians and market-women. Osundare matches language with characters and this technique necessitates the creation of appropriate patterns of linguistic behaviour. In 'Not in My Season of Songs' the language is that of a mature adult, in 'Eating with All the Fingers' it is that of a troubled elder and in 'Feigning a Rebel' it is the language of a poor villager. Language is made a component part of his poetic art and illustrates his ability to mould the chosen character to suit the artistic creation.

In the highly lyrical poem 'Akintunde Come Home', the poet creates a persona whose language indicates that he is a father. The frequency of proverbs and witty aphorisms are the marks of a wise father and Osundare exploits these linguistic devices in this poem, which appeals to Akintunde to return home from the land where money is god, since all men cannot be Irokos, and stresses that, though the home may be full of meatless meals, it could still harbour amiable souls. The poet aptly concludes:

> Akintunde, come home
> For though a man's penis is small
> he will not borrow a bigger one
> to fill up his wife's nagging mouth. (*Village Voices*, p. 23)

The reference to the size of a man's penis is not an attempt at vulgarization because it is derived from Yoruba oral tradition. The poet obviously manipulates not only English words but also Yoruba thought-patterns as he further teases symbols out of their normative order through a complex use of images and personae.

The poems 'The Prisoner's Song', 'A Reunion', 'Month of Falling Leaves' and 'To a Passing Year' exhibit symbolic connotations. They are used to comment on the society through selected incidents that portray the aberration of social disjunctions. The use of parables also effectively encapsulates the poet's sensitive concern for his fellow men. 'A Reunion', for instance, describes the failure of the persona's primary-school colleague to continue his education due to penury. This poem is used as a parable for an indifferent society. It is this parabolic concern which exhibits the ideological creed of Osundare and makes him 'the public poet, the town-crier briefly glimpsed in Okigbo'.[15] He thus becomes an artist influenced by a tradition which he strives to fashion into a distinct personal poetic style.

The images are original and the twists of phrases happily refreshing. In the poem 'The Stars Sob', the poet attaches poetic significance to the stars and endows them with tears. This personification of the stars emphasizes through apt choice of words that the suffering of the toiling masses is becoming unbearable and it is moving even inanimate stars to tears.

The same concern for the toiling masses is shown in the poem 'Cradling Hands'. However, in this poem the poet advocates that all hard-working people should earn their due reward. The message incorporated in the image of the hands of the farmer is to illustrate the extent of the suffering and pain that has gone into the production of a harvest which is often denied the farmer.

The section labelled 'Voices of Anger and Indictment' is explicit. Here Osundare condemns politicians and the local exploiters who parasitize the poor farmers. The politician's peculiar penchant for deceit is highlighted in the poem 'The Politician's Two Mouths'. The poet caricatures a politician and fashions him with two mouths to portray the extent of his untrustworthiness. The effects of the politician's dishonesty are further presented through the poem 'A Farmer on Seeing Cocoa House, Ibadan'. Cocoa House was built through the wealth derived from the sweat of the farmers but it is for the enjoyment of the politicians. Osundare comments on this social anomaly by proverbializing his language to echo the reflections of an apparently ignorant villager.

Village Voices incorporates many instances of language experimentation. The poetry moves with a vigour which links medium and content artistically. There is also an interesting lyrical control that is uncommon even in the poetry of Soyinka, who is informed by the same oral tradition. Soyinka, for instance, writes in the poem 'Dawn':

> Breaking earth upon
> A spring-haired elbow, lone
> A palm beyond head-grains, spikes
> A guard of prim fronds, piercing
> High hairs of the wind.[16]

The alluring lyricism absent in that stanza is abundant in Niyi Osundare's poetry. There is also carefulness in the choice of words, attention to syntactical structures and use of internal rhythm. It is both form and substance that elevate Osundare's poetry above the ordinary run of literary expression.

It is obvious that the three Nigerian poets analysed exhibit distinct uses of language that satisfy the experimental spirit which 'implies that one keeps giving variety to the readership rather than capitalize on one successful form'.[17] They have imbued recent Nigerian poetry with verbal rhythms and rich imagery. Their choice of words, pidginization, syntactic structures and thematic concerns have expanded the poetic forms available. Their effective use of language justifies the view that 'poetry is one great source of the maintenance and renewal of language'.[18] The poetry of these Nigerian poets gives lovers of poetry joy: poetry is not ossifying in Nigeria, as Awoonor fears. Moreover, they also justify Lamborn's view that 'the greatest poet is he who has felt the most of all things that move the hearts of men and felt them most deeply and can touch the most hearts with sympathy'.[19] Chinweizu, Aig-Imoukhuede and Osundare can touch most hearts because they make us react to their experiences. Their poetry excites, titillates, arouses serious thoughts and also nudges slumbering minds into wakefulness.

NOTES

1. Foreword in Critical Perspectives on Nigerian Literatures, ed. Bernth Lindfors, London, Heinemann, 1979, p. vii.
2. 'The poem, the poet, the human condition: some aspects of recent West African poetry', Asemka, no. 5, September 1979, p. 7.
3. T.S. Eliot, 'The social functions of poetry', On Poetry and Poets, London, Faber and Faber, 1957, p. 18.
4. Towards the Decolonization of African Literature, Enugu, Fourth Dimension, 1980, p. 165.
5. D.I. Nwoga, 'Modern African poetry: the domestication of a tradition', African Literature Today, no. 10, 1979, p. 53.
6. Archibald A. Hill, 'What is language?,' in Languages into Literature, ed. James D. Barry and William U. MacDonald, Jr, Chicago, Science Research Associates,
7. Chinweizu, Energy Crisis and Other Poems, New York, London and Lagos, Nok Publishers, 1978. All page references are indicated in the essay.
8. Obi Maduakor, 'Review of Energy Crisis and other poems', Okike, no. 21, July 1982, p. 102.
9. Don L. Lee, 'Two poems: from Sketches from a Black-Nappy-Headed Poet', Black Pride, Detroit, Broadside Press, 1968, p. 13.
10. Christopher Okigbo, Labyrinths, London, Heinemann, 1971, and Ibadan, Mbari Publications, p. 6.
11. Frank Aig-Imoukhuede, Pidgin Stew and Sufferhead, Ibadan, Heinemann, 1982. All references are incorporated in the essay.

12. Bernard Mafeni, 'Nigerian Pidgin', in *The English Language in West Africa*, ed. John Spencer, London, Longman, 1971, p. 98.
13. Niyi Osundare, *Village Voices*, Ibadan, Evans Brothers, 1984. All page references are indicated in the essay.
14. James Reeves, *Teaching Poetry*, London, Heinemann, 1958, p. 88.
15. Funso Aiyejina, 'Recent Nigerian poetry in English: an alternative tradition, *Guardian*, 11 April 1985, p. 9.
16. Wole Soyinka, *Idanre and Other Poems*, London, Eyre Methuen, 1967, p. 9.
17. Jared Othieno-Angira, 'Experimental writing', in *Writers in East Africa*, ed. Andrew Gurr and Angus Calder, Nairobi, East Africa Publishing Bureau, 1974, p. 73.
18. Elizabeth Drew, *Poetry: A Modern Guide to its Understanding and Enjoyment*, New York, Dell Publishing Company, 1959, p. 69.
19. Greening Lamborn, *The Rudiments of Criticism*, Oxford, Oxford University Press, 1921, p. 11.

The Language of Post-war Nigerian Poetry of English Expression

J.O.J Nwachukwu-Agbada

The texture of post-war Nigerian poetry of English expression has been mediated by both the events of the Nigerian civil war (1967-70) and the alienating linguistic structures of pre-war Nigerian poetry. D.I. Nwoga once remarked that 'in defining the generations the crisis has been recognised as creating a new urgency in Nigerian poetry' (p. 44). The urgency is in the direction of expressiveness necessitated by the horrors of the holocaust. According to Aiyejina,

> In such 'season of anomy' the poets could no longer afford to speak in inaccessible riddles and occultic tongues. New and strident voices were needed for the immediate and unambiguous expression of our tortured and fragmented psyche . . . In addition, the pervading aura of death, especially in Biafra, made directness and 'immediate delivery' the *sine qua non* of the poetry of this period. ('Recent Nigerian Poetry', p. 9)

However, it is known that before the civil war there had started the debate on whether or not the foreign metropolitan languages of Europe should continue to be linguistic models for African creative writers. Obiajunwa Wali, Chinua Achebe, Gerald Moore, Ezekiel Mphahlele and Edward Ukwu, to mention just a few, have each made their views known on this matter. Ali Mazrui's 'Abstract Verse and African Tradition', directed at the mind-boggling linguistic configuration of Christopher Okigbo's early poems, contests the cryptic linguistic convolutions displayed in much of first-generation African poetry and insists that abstract poetry is 'as alien to Africa as is *laissez faire* liberalism or egotistical Protestantism'. Rather than abandon the English language he advocates that it be transformed 'into an African poetic medium' (p. 48), a suggestion very close to Achebe's.

It is also true that certain African poets had let it be known that they cared little for their audience because they would not like to be impeded in their poetic visioneering on account of the accessibility of their linguistic formulations. In 1962, and at different interviews with Lewis Nkosi, both Christopher Okigbo and Wole Soyinka showed by their utterances that they gave little place to audience consideration in their writings. Okigbo is known to have said: 'Somehow I believe I am writing for other poets all over the world to read and see whether they can share in my experience . . . Nowadays everything is done for the study and on few occasions it steals out, I think it is to please, but not a large public' (*African Writers Talking*, p. 135). Soyinka said a very similar thing then: 'I don't think I need bother my head . . . at all about the audience, whether Nigerian or the European' (p. 177). It is interesting to note that these views were never sustained by these two writers, as evidenced in the twist in Okigbo's poetic career with the publication of his *Path of Thunder* poems a little before his death in 1967 and the perceptibility of Soyinka's verse of post-war vintage.

The whole business of the Chinweizu trio (Chinweizu, Jemie and Madubuike), for which they had either been vilified or commended, has been to call attention to the 'addiction to archaisms' by those they refer to as the 'Ibadan–Nsukka poets'. Chinweizu and his collaborators accuse the poets of writing poems that are 'craggy, lumpy, full of obstructions, unnecessarily and artificially difficult' ('Decolonization', p. 29). Much as their assessment of pre-war Nigerian poetry is harsh and prescriptive, there is no doubt that their diatribe brought to a peak all the grumblings nurtured against this poetic trend by the local audience of Nigerian poetry. The post-war poets set out with the desire to write verses which would be accessible to the average readership. How successful they are so far is yet to be investigated. However, it is important to note that there is a noticeable hiatus between the language of the pre-war poet and that used by his post-war compatriot. Even where a poet has written during the two periods, there has been a considerable softening of the oracular tradition of Nigerian poetry before the civil war. Jeyifo has noted the effort on the part of the younger poets to demystify the language of poetry, 'for while the older poets generally deployed a diction and metaphoric, highly allusive universe calculated to exclude all but a small coterie of specialists, the new poets have taken the language to the market-place' (p. 13). In other words, the poet's 'puny ego' (Chinweizu et al., p. 56) or his 'preoccupation with personal reflection and alienation' (Maduakor, p. 55) is very much avoided in the new poetry; instead an effort is made to cultivate a public language, to utilize a civic medium founded on the alembic of the people's linguistic essence.

In order to realize the desire to be understood by a majority of the Nigerian verse readership, the post-war poet has had to return to the local speech pattern so that, whether the poet is Hausa, Igbo, Yoruba, Urhobo or Nupe, there are linguistic models in his poetic afflation which every member of a Nigerian, if not an African, audience can relate to. Although the language is still English as in pre-war poetry, English in the recent Nigerian poetic articulation is stretched in such a way as to approach the linguistic mediation of the poet's mother tongue, which at any rate shares some affinity with the flavour of the other local languages. Banjo's comment to the effect that 'the presence of locally-derived metaphors does not necessarily guarantee accessibility to an African audience' (p. 33) is an important one, yet an African audience is more likely to be receptive to and appreciative of African linguistic structures than foreign-based linguistic and mythical models which have little or no relationship with the African tradition.

Osundare, Udechukwu, Aiyejina, Garuba, Acholonu, Ofeimun, Enekwe, Ojaide, Ezenwa-Ohaeto, Osofisan, Ogundipe-Leslie, etc. make extensive use of modes of linguistic articulation rooted in communal traditions. Osundare's protagonist in 'The Prisoner's Song', for instance, copiously employs the tradition of exchanging verbal insults in the African cultural setting. Here the poet's use of sustained lyricism and dramatic tone, achieved mostly through repetition, as in most of his poems, points to its oral source:

The warder's wife never bears a proper baby
The warder's wife never does
If she doesn't give birth to a truncheon
She delivers a lunatic (*Voices*, p. 24)

The subsequent name-calling and personalization of the issue at stake remind one of the face-to-face altercations during quarrels in a village: 'We know you, son of Tanimola,/we know every branch of your family tree . . .' (pp. 24-5). In another of his poems, 'The Bride's Song ', the local emotion attached to manliness, reminiscent of the Negritudist strand of African poetry, is evoked in the bride's preference for the 'solid man who pins you down/with a penis stronger than an iron bar' (*Voices*, p. 42). The 'singing' bride further gives us her vision of a married life:

Children playing in the moonlight
Are the dream of a maiden's womb
Child is honour, child is gold
The bouncing seed of tomorrow's harvest (*Voices*, p. 42)

The oral stylistic approach is easily observable in some of the poems by Ofeimun and Enekwe, especially in their fervent utilization of the town-crier model, popularized by Christopher Okigbo. Prominent in their poetry is the interchangeable and interdependent use of 'I' and 'we'. In her foreword to Enekwe's collection, Edith Iheakweazu observes that the poet 'tends to say "we", thereby making himself the speaker for a group, instead of a lone individual' (p. iii). In his 'Whatever Happened to the Memorial Drums', the poet moves from the use of 'we' in the initial lines of the poem to the one single deployment of 'I' in the middle of the poem, before finally returning to the use of 'we' once more. The 'we' seems to refer to the collective historical experience of the community while 'I' is the artist's questioning pronominal model as in 'I wonder why we're sick of heroes and monuments/and lie defeated in every victory' (*Broken Pots*, p. 10). In 'Broken Pots', the title-poem of his poetry volume, not only does Enekwe make an interdependent use of 'I' and 'we', but he also employs the folkloric mode, thus calling to mind the Igbo gnomic tale sub-genre, in which spirits and goblins play tricks on human elements straying into spirit-land. In the poem, innocence and experience are brought together with ironic subtlety, and the poem obtains its effect from the poet's desire to leave the confrontation unresolved as is reminiscent of the Igbo story-proverbs meant for the informal education of the traditional youth.

Ofeimun employs a similar model of the use of 'I' and 'we' in his poems such as 'Pray on Friday' (*Poet Lied*, p. 23) and 'Flood and Fire' (p. 31). In each case the use of 'I' rather than 'we' could still have retained the essential meaning of the poems, but it seems that the poets make an obvious effort to avoid the idiosyncrasy of the early-generation Nigerian poets who would rather stick to the 'I' model even when themes are of public import.

The verbal pattern in African language use is noticeable in the employment of two subjects in a short utterance, which in the written linguistic model would be strange. In Ojaide's 'Map of Time', the pronominal 'he' stands next to the noun it represents:

A river-god he gets reverence
He gets reverence because of nativity (*Iroke*, p. 1)

Acholonu employs the same model in 'The Dissidents':

... and the daughter of my father
she spoke to them again
from the top of the hill (*Nigeria*, p. 39)

In Aiyejina's 'After the Last Shot', the oral medium is its forte, bringing thesis and antithesis together in one stroke, a juxtapositon that is common in the proverbial form:

the child who over-turns his noon meal
because it is not big enough
it will merely taste hunger
before the chickens come home to roost ...
(*A Letter*, p. 18)

There is a mix-up in the use of the pronouns 'he' and 'it' for the subject, 'the child', occasioned perhaps by the native impulse to use 'he' for a baby boy and the acquired foreign linguistic insistence on 'it' for the infant. However, the poet might have consciously used these conflicting pronouns as a way of heightening the use of thesis and antithesis to which we have called attention. He returns to the same traditional speech mode in

the masquerade who strays out for too long
he will surely return home with exposed toes
crabs that sleep carelessly
they will become the doomed companions of the flood ... (p. 19)

The proverbial form is popular among the post-war poets. Of all the pre-war Nigerian poets, it was Christopher Okigbo who embraced the aphoristic mode in his later poems. Being an essential accoutrement of the oral medium, the post-war poet in his love for accessibility may have found it very expedient to employ. In addition, the proverb, being a rhetorical genre, may have interested the recent Nigerian poets because of the capacity of this form to drive home populist expressions known to be the common forte of the younger poets. In Aiyejina's 'If a Star', a pattern of contrasts is set with a series of proverbs in the conditional mode:

> If a star sets while the moon rises
> it asks to be ignored
> if the sun continues to raise new dawns
> we have no need for a moon
> that hides behind frail clouds . . .
> if those who are of the land
> learn to swim long enough
> they will make it into depths deeper than sea beds
>   (*A Letter*, p. 15)

Here the poet creates a series of contrasts and employs the conditional in a bid to establish 'rhetorical proofs' and by so doing convince his listener of the deliberative tone of what he seeks to say. Ojaide's 'Message of Lust' achieves a similar effect through the antithetical juxtaposition of statements:

> The fowl is guzzling corn
> It knows not how much it's bought;
> The woman is frying eggs
> She doesn't feel the labour of the hen's anus
>   (*Iroko*, p. 3)

In the poem proverbs are deployed for satiric ends as sayings of pristine and mundane values are inverted to become questions, an element which enhances their rhetorical impact:

> Tigers own the homes, where
> Shall goats sleep, where shall
> The travelling virgins sleep in a town of lust? (*Iroko*, p. 2)

Two post-war poets whose poetry relies much on the proverbial model are Obiora Udechukwu and Ezenwa-Ohaeto. Udechukwu's love for proverbs as literary signposts is exemplified by the following poem of his, published in *Omabe* (Nsukka), vol. 28, April 1978:

> How many baskets of water can mould a block?
> How many he-goats can guard a yam barn?
>   And we talk of yam-masters
>   But their sons eat *alibo*
>
> Fish that lives in the ocean
> That same fish washes with spittle.
>   And you talk of hell
>   Does it need death to survive?
>
> The question looms in the evening cloud
> It hangs so it's now part of the sky
> The question that questions their stools (p. 6)

There is no doubt that Ezenwa-Ohaeto must have been fascinated by this artistic use of proverbs in poems as almost all the poems in his *Songs of a Traveller* (1986) collection owe their effectiveness to the proverbial form. His admiration for Udechukwu's use of saws and aphorisms is demonstrated in 'Song of a Madman', a poem he dedicates to Udechukwu:

> If rain wipes away footprints
> Does it wipe away words?
> Rather than drown in a stream
> Let the water sweep away my cloth . . .
>
> The man outwitted by a snail
> should not be offered meat
> If you like funeral rams
> Why recover from sickness?
>
> If a shrew smells when it is alive
> What horrible odour will exude at its death? (p.16)

Another aspect of the use of language in post-war poetry has to do with the artistic recourse to humour evident in much of this poetic movement. The impact of a humorous remark, even in ordinary speech, is a factor of precision in the use of language. Ordinarily humour can rob an utterance – literary or not – of the veneer of seriousness, yet, in post-war Nigerian poetry, it goes to show the amount of confidence with which the creators of this vintage of Nigerian poetry set to work. Chinweizu often attains his humour in the undercutting, sometimes irreverent, use of incidents such as love encounters, religious truisms or sexual titillations. In 'Energy Crisis', the title poem of his first poetry volume, euphemistic, slangy symbols of sex are deployed to humorous effect. Categories of women with whom the male protagonist of the long poem associate include, 'Chevys, pickups, VWs,/Banged-up Volvos, sleek Cadillacs' (p. 29). The term 'energy crisis' is a parody of the American fuel problems of the sixties during which policies were initiated to conserve the energy resources of the country. However, in the poem the term stands for a period of sexual inactivity, a period of shrivelled libido, of 'rationing time' when it is hard to 'make a dry hole gush'. The male protagonist presumably is a petrol pump attendant while the female persona with 'her thirsty engine snorting' asks the former 'to fill her up', insisting that to 'drive on heating oil' is to 'burn my engines out' (p. 30).

Chinweizu's archetypal poem, 'The Saviour', is an echo of the fate of Christ in the hands of the Jews. In this poem, the Christ-like figure literally begs to die for the sins of the people in whose midst he finds himself, but is cast off, unaccepted by those he had come to 'save'. The humour here, somewhat maverick and Bohemian, is lodged in the people's rejection of this display of selfless love for one's hosts:

> He arrived and went straight to the city fathers and declared:
> 'I've come to die for your sins.'
> The surprised fathers looked at him and said:
> 'We have no sins!'
> 'How can that be?' he answered them. 'Don't you
> drink or smoke or cuss? Don't you rob?'

'We do that everyday; what else is there to do?'
'Well then I've come to die for your sins.'
'Very well', said the elders. 'But first sit
among us and eat and drink with us.' (*Energy Crisis*, p. 35)

However, as this bizarre fellow would not identify himself with his hosts,
he is helped to his death, thus literally satisfying the request he makes on
the one hand, and on the other ridding themselves of an enigma.

Fatoba's poems are also replete with artistic humour; every line of his
poem is charged with an underlying laughter-evoking twist of comment,
a ventriloquist vivaciousness yet to be rivalled in Nigerian poetry. In
'Signs and Times', a soldier stops the protagonist and accuses him of
'carrying a dangerous weapon' only to discover to his astonishment that
'all I had on me was/A pen' (*Petals*, p. 11). In his other poem, 'Christmas
Message to My Relations', the supposedly affluent persona virtually
abandons his flat to his numerous younger relations who had come to
spend the Christmas holiday with him. He leaves a 'note' behind for the
benefit of the visitors, who are bound to behold the 'unfilled fridge' and
the 'thick webs/over the soup pots':

Am gone searching for an occasional job
Because in January the renewal is due
On the insurance policy
And the vehicle licence
Of that car you all love
To ride in. (p. 55)

In 'Jesus Saves', a poem which so far has only been published in the first
issue of the Ife-based journal, *The River Prawn*, Fatoba deploys humour
to great effect:

From funeral mass and wedding banns
In slums and well planned states
From hymns and sermons
In the very lean month of lent
Jesus saves . . . (p. 21)

He is here satirizing the church, which has gradually replaced its pious
and evangelical missions with the search for material and substance like
any other commercially oriented organization:

From the saint and the sinner
From the robber and the robbed
From the pauper and the rich
From the fanatic and the atheist
Jesus saves at Barclays Bank (p. 21)

In Fatoba's poetry, humour is accomplished through the use of irony, the
subtle impersonal linguistic model often mischievous, often terse and
laconic; effect is heightened by a clinical detachment, an understatement

of image. Certainly he must have been influenced in his stylistic approach by his training as a theatre man. Harry Garuba has put it succinctly:

> Perhaps being a teacher of mime, he [Fatoba] has acquired that economy of movement which is the mark of mime ... Instead of the 'grand', explicit linguistic gesture he uses the 'dwarfed' one, precise and laden with a seething series of implied meanings. ('Ofeimun and Fatoba', p. 21)

Morphological inventiveness is an element of post-civil war poetic afflation. Until this period, the Nigerian poet had never been keen to twist and hammer words and expressions in order to subject them to newer meanings and connotations. The post-war poets have shown an adventurous inventiveness in this form of wordsmithery and thus enhanced the effectiveness of their poetry. C.K. Stead has said that the richness of a poem is heightened in 'the poet's use of those words where choice and chance are exactly coincident' (p. 327). However, the post-war poet does more than just insert the appropriate word for the appropriate emotion; where no appropriate words seem suited to bear the weight of his sensibility, he selects a word or two from his verbal stock and strikes them until he makes new linguistic items or stretches the meaning of existing words. Again, a lot of meaning resides in these nonce words and expressions, probably used as a way of inviting attention to an idea, an impression, a truth or a not-too-obvious fact.

Most of the post-civil war poets who play with words employ catechresis, which Egudu defines as the liberation of language 'from the bondage of conventionality, of re-locating, even re-registering a word from one collocational habitat to another' (Ndu's Poetry', p. 9). Pol Ndu was one such poet. Little wonder, then, that Echeruo remarked in his introduction to Songs for Seers (1974) that the poet remained 'the most verbally exciting' (p. ii) since Okigbo. This is neither an exaggerated observation nor a contrived epithet meant to please the poet. The truth is that words for Ndu are like wet clay, very malleable and kneadable into new linguistic figures of speech. In 'Homesick', for instance, he dislocates the use of 'graft' and makes the word serve a new function, though in a relevant context: 'when they graft me/to a new master'. He is here referring to the compulsive rejection by the African of his own culture owing to the arm-twisting constraints put in his way by the colonial master. In the second section of the poem, man is satirized as an inhuman, beastly creature; the poet characterizes man's descent from a human to an animal plane in this manner: 'Manking, mankind, apeking, apebrand'. Apart from 'mankind', the other words in that line are the poet's neologisms in the same way that 'mis-makes' – a pun on 'mistakes' – is. Instead of 'lazy drone' in reference to the irritating, droning sound of a distant jet bomber, Ndu prefers dirty drone' and 'dirty croon', and by so doing invests a sound with an adjective usually reserved for concrete, physical objects. In 'Peace-Songs' – a hypogram on 'Peace Talks' – he satirizes officials at peace conferences as 'addressing diplomatic corpses', an obvious reference to 'diplomatic corps'. The impact of this stylistic device seems to have been brought to a head in his 'Reflections'. In the poem paradoxes, punning, catechreses, hypograms and paragrams are freely employed. In the following lines the poet does a paragrammatic redeployment of words in a bid to carve new coinages:

> ... what blot is blacker than my *ibory*
> hall-marked imitation jewelry
> hard-cast thick-set ivory
> out-cast in-caste *jewry*

In the above passage, Ndu reflects on the fate of his (Ibo) race which he calls 'ibory' – metamorphosed from 'ivory', an 'imitation jewelry'. He characterizes the race as an 'out-cast' ethnic group, fated to be so because of their 'jewry' – derived from 'Jew'.

Fatoba, Aiyejina, Garuba, Osundare and Ofeimun employ morphological inventiveness as part of their artistic form. In each case there is an underlying epiphanic glint as new meanings are conferred on hitherto known terms or neologisms are deployed to bear specific significatory connotations. Fatoba talks of 'monuments/raised to *syphilisation*' ('Guided Tours'). This is a pun on 'civilization'. Chinweizu's 'siphilized' (*Invocations*, p. 26) leaves one with the same sour taste for modern life as Fatoba's. Fatoba's use of 'Napatitis' (from NEPA, National Electric Power Authority) is derived from either 'meningitis' or 'hepatitis' while 'Mercedezzzzzzzzzz' is an effort to joke with the blissful sound of the prestigious Mercedes Benz car ('A View from the Flyover'). Aiyejina refers to Nigeria as 'our Kingdom of Chance' (*A Letter* pp. 12 and 23) while the money-guzzling new Nigerian capital at Abuja is described as 'our Project Oliver Twist' ('Flowers of Hatred'). He regards the 'waterless fountain at our memorial squares' as a signal of 'the death of the *in* of our independence . . .' ('Let Us Remember'). Osundare prefers 'kolatera' to 'collateral' (*Voices*, p. 50), thus playing on 'kola', the Nigerian euphemism for 'bribe', just as he spells 'executives' as 'executhieves' (*The Eye*, p. 46), which is a way of drawing attention to the level of corruption among the country's elites in positions of leadership. In his *Songs of the Marketplace* as much as in *A Nib in the Pond*, Osundare uses these coinages quite copiously. He describes malnourished infants as 'Kwashiorkored children' and uses 'kinsvice' for a vice connected with another vice (*Marketplace*, pp. 3, 21 and 33). In *A Nib* he juggles with words as in the following: 'mercedesed Pharaohs' (p. 15), 'the beggared/of our just and egalitarian country' (p. 15), 'Before you lark into the libertine sky/of another day' (p. 16), 'Comrades or comeraids/trail-blazers or blaze-trailers' (p. 21), 'from democracy to demoncrazy/from conscience to con-science' (p. 21), 'allies or all lies/adultery or adult tree/message or mess age' (p. 21), 'suffrage or suffer age' (p. 22), 'Of statesmen or statemen' (p. 22). Odia Ofeimun in his *The Poet Lied* collection talks of 'many-petalled lust' (p. 4), 'hawk-beak of assault' (p. 6), 'Their harvest reports/manure the earth/with hawking questionmarks'(p. 8), 'the Judas-eye of his camera' (p. 27), 'sweat-loads of harvests' (p. 44), 'Lagosed to a fault, they waited' (p. 51), 'man's hike to Jehovahood' (p. 57). In both *The Poet Lied* and *A Handle for the Flutist* (1986) – another collection by Ofeimun – the coinage 'tricknology' appears as a play on the word 'technology' in the same way that Garuba refers to 'politicians' as 'poli-trick-cians' in his *Shadow and Dream* (1982) volume.

The obvious conclusion to be drawn from these linguistic features of recent Nigerian poetry is that there is a hiatus between what was practised as poetry in Nigeria before the civil war and what is now regarded as poetic articulation. This is in addition to the differentiation in thematic structures existing in the two Nigerian verse vintages, which we have not considered in this essay because of our chosen direction as dictated by its title. There are no large linguistic or thematic gestures in post-war Nigerian poetry, but certainly its texture is an indication of a new direction, a new tradition of writing which has hitherto been non-existent. It is an artistic utterance aimed at revisionism, provoked by the occult legacy of pre-war poetry. Fortunately a majority of post-war poetry practitioners are highly educated, and cannot be said to be ignorant of Western poetic touchstones. However, the highbrow achievement of these 'touchstones' seems to be what they have set out to avoid, and in some cases denounce by their use of a simple and bare linguistic flavour.

WORKS CITED

Acholonu, Catherine, *Nigeria in the Year 1999*, Owerri, Totan Publishers, 1985.

African Writers Talking, ed. D. Duerden and C. Pieterse, London, Heinemann, 1972.

Aiyejina, Funso, *A Letter to Lynda and Other Poems*, Ife, Ife Monographs Series, 1984.

———, 'Recent Nigerian poetry in English: an alter-native tradition', *Guardian* (Lagos), 27 April 1985.

Banjo, Ayo, 'The linguistic factor in African literature', *Ibadan Journal of Humanistic Studies*, vol. 3, October 1983.

Chinweizu, *Energy Crisis and Other Poems*, New York, Nok Publishers, 1977.

Chinweizu, *Invocations and Admonitions*, Lagos, Pero Press, 1986.

Chinweizu, Onwuchekwa Jemie and Ihechukwu Madubuike, eds, 'Towards the decolonization of African literature', *Transition*, vol. 48, 1975.

Egudu, R.N., 'Transformation and Dislocation as Features of the Language of Pol Ndu's Poetry', paper presented at the 5th Conference of the Literary Society of Nigeria, University of Port Harcourt, 26 February – 1 March 1986 (unpublished).

Enekwe, Ossie, *Broken Pots*, Nsukka, Afa Press, 1986; first published 1977.

Ezenwa-Ohaeto, *Songs of a Traveller*, Awka, Towncrier Publications, 1986.

Fatoba, Femi, *Petals of Thought*, London, New Beacon Books, 1984.

Garuba, Harry, 'The poetry of Odia Ofeimun and Femi Fatoba', *Guardian* (Lagos) 7 June 1986.

———, *Shadow and Dream*, 1982.

Jeyifo, Abiodun, 'The Poetry of Niyi Osundare', *Guardian* (Lagos), 10 May 1986.

Maduakor, Obi, 'Violence as poetic focus: Nigerian poetry and the Biafran experience', *Nsukka Studies in African Literature*, (Nsukka) vol. 4, January 1986.

Mazrui, Ali A., 'Abstract verse and African tradition', *Zuka*, vol. 1, September 1967.

Ndu, Pol, *Songs for Seers*, New York, Nok Publishers, 1974.

Nwoga, D.I., 'Modern African poetry: the domestication of a tradition', *African Literature Today*, vol. 10, 1979.

Ofeimun, Odia, *The Poet Lied*, London, Longman, 1980.

——, *A Handle for the Flutist*, (1986).

Ojaide, Tanure, *Children of Iroko*, New York, Greenfield Review Press, 1973.

Osundare, Niyi, *The Eye of the Earth*, Ibadan, Heinemann, 1986.

——, *A Nib in the Pond*, Ife, Ife Monographs Series, 1986.

——, *Village Voices*, Ibadan, Evans (Nigeria), 1984.

——, *Songs of the Marketplace*, Ibadan, New Horn Press, 1983.

River Prawn, The, Ibadan, no. 1.

Stead, C.K., 'Poetry and the criticism of poetry', *Critical Quarterly*, vol. 8, no. 4, winter 1966.

Udechukwu, Obiara, in *Omabe* (Nsukka) vol. 28, April 1978.

Index

Achebe, Chinua, 15-23, 32, 52, 54, 57, 58, 155, 156, 165; *Arrow of God*, 2; compared with Armah, 2; and English, viii; and Igbo culture, 115; *No Longer At Ease*, 4, 6, 15; pidgin, use of, 54; *Things Fall Apart*, 4, 15, 23; epic nature of, 15; names in, 15-16
Acholonu, Catherine, 123, 131-40, 167; 'Dissidents, The', 168
African-language literature, 44, 45-6, 48; *see also under* Khaketla, Kunene, Ngugi, Poetry, Ubessie
African National Congress, ANC., 40
Afrikaans, 48
Aidoo, Ama Ata, 2; language, 53; narrative technique, 53, 57; style, 2
Aig-Imoukhuede, 156, 159-60; 'Cosmetic Surgery: A Wish', 160; 'Durbar, The', 160; 'Flood done Come', 159; humour, 159, 160; irony, 159, 160; and negritude, 160, 163; 'Negritude (The Poor Black Muse)', 160; 'One Man One Wife', 159; 'Pidgin Stew and Sufferhead', 159; pidgin, use of, 159, 160; pun, 159; style, 159; 'Take Me Go For Corner-place', 159; wit, 159-60; 'Wrestling Match, The', 159
Aiyejina, 165, 167, 173; 'After the last Shot', 168; 'Flowers of Hatred', 173; 'If a Star', 169; 'Letter, A', 173
Aluko, 155
Amadi, 155
ambiguity, 110
Aniebo, 54
anomy, 71
Anozie, Sunday, 61, 136, 137
apartheid, 57, 58
Appollinaire, Guillaume, 109, 120
Armah, Ayi Kwei, 1-12; *Beautyful Ones Are Not Yet Born, The*, 1; chieftaincy, 10; compared with Achebe, 2; compared with European novelists, 4-5; consequences of, 10; devices, 7; Frag-ments, 1, 5; knowledge of Africa, 4; narrative, 3, 5ff; and negritude, 12; and oral tradition, 1; style, viii, 1-13; *Two Thousand Seasons*, viii, 1-13; characters in, 6, 8; epic nature of, 2, 5, 11
Awoonor, Kofi, 146, 155, 163

ballad, 110
Balogun, F. Odun, 51-6
Banjo, 166
Bart, Andre Schwartz, *Le Dernier de justes*, 1
Barthes, R., 66, 122-3
Baudelaire, 131
Beckett, S., and Oyono-Mbia, 98-9
Biafra, 32, 33
Biko, Steve, 38, 41
bilingualism, 98-9, 100, 105; *see also under* Language
Black Consciousness Movement, 41, 47
Black People's Convention, BPC., 42
Boer, 39-40
Bradford, Ernest, 148
Brecht, 82, 83
bride price, *see* culture
Broyard, Anatole, 51
Burnett, Hallie, 51
Bush College, 41, 49

Caluza, Reuben, 45
Cameroon, 98, 99; culture, 98, 107n
catechresis, 172, 173
Catford, 17
Chapman, Michael, 42, 43
characterization/characters, 36, 62, 71, 83, 86, 91-3; and language, 92-6, 113, 161; *see also under* individual authors
Charley, Dele, 91, 94, 95; *Adopted Pikin*, 95; characters in, 95; registers, Krio & English, 95; *Titi Shain-Shain*, 94
Chase, 142
Chinweizu, 156-9, 160, 163, 166, 170,

173; *Energy Crisis*, 156; 'Energy Crisis', 157, 190; 'Faithful Mary Lou', 157; humour, 157-8; imagery, 157, 158, 159; irony, 157; 'King Fisher, The', 157; language, 156-9; and oral poetry, 158; 'Originality', 156; 'Praise Song of the New Notable', 158; satire, 157; style, 158
Christianity, 148-9, 150
Chukwukere, B.I., 24
Clark, J.P., 141-52, 155; and Christianity, 148-9, 150; and colonialism, 141, 143, 144; 145-52; culture, foreign & indigenous compared, 141, 142, 143; imagery, 142-3, 145, 147-8, 149; *Ivbie*, 141-52; audience of, 150; structure of, 141, 152; themes of, 141; indigenous culture, 141-5, 147, 150, 152; European colonialism, 145-50; polemics of his own inadequacies, 150-3; and myth, 142 143; rhetoric, 141-52; satire, 146, 147; types of, 141
Coleridge, 140
colonialism, 158, 172; *see also under* Clark
Creolised Languages, viii
criticism, 69; linguistic, 62; *see also* Modernism, Structuralism etc.
culture, 66, 67, 100, 115, 141; African, 138, 143-4, 157; bride price, 100, 103; foreign and indigenous compared, 142, 143; Idoto, 124, 131, 138, 140; Igbo, 15, 132, 138, 158, 167; and language, 98, ogbanje, 123-4, 125; Oyin, 142, 147; religion, 138, 140, 148-9, 150; white man's, 20
Curtis, 56

Damas, Leon, 115
Dangor, Achmat, 48
Decker, Thomas, 91
deconstruction, 109
Deressa, 56
Derrida, Jacques, 109, 123
dialogue, 71, 132-3
Dickinson, 111
Diop, David, 146
drama, 131, 133, 137; in Krio, 91-6; Sierra Leone, 91; translation of, 98; West African in English, 91; *see also* individual playwrights.
Drum Magazine, 43-4
Dube, John L., 41
Dunton, Chris, 8
Durban, Workers' Strike, 41

Easmon, 52, 53
Echeruo, M.J.C., 152, 172
Edebiri, Unionmwan, 98-107
Egudu, R.N., 36, 146, 152, 172
Ekwensi, Cyprian, 24-30, 56; *Beautiful Feathers*, 26; characterization & characters, 24ff.; *Iska*, 26; *Jagua Nana*, 24ff.; language, 24ff., 51; *People of the City*, 24ff.; and pidgin, viii, 24-30, 54, 56
Elimimian, Isaac I., 141-53
Eliot, T.S., 55, 112, 150
Emecheta, 155
Emenyonu, Ernest, 24, 31
Enekwe, 167; 'Broken Pots', 167; style, 167; 'Whatever Happened to the Memorial Drums', 167
English, *see* language
epic, 1, 2, 5ff., 11-12, 15, 52, 152
Essop, 53
Esu, 68
Ezenwa-Ohaeto, 155-163, 166, 169; 'Song of a Madman', 170; *Song of a Traveller*, 170

Fagunwa, D.O., viii
Fatoba, 171, 173; 'Christmas Message to my Relations', 171; irony, 171; 'Jesus Saves', 171; satire, 171; 'Signs and Times', 171; style, 171-2; 'View from the Flyover, A', 173
Finlay, Ian, 109
flashback, 71, 84, 95
Fletcher, John, 71
folklore, 56, 58, 123
Fraser, Robert, *Novels of Ayi Kwei Armah, The*, 4, 12n; on *Two Thousand Seasons*, 1, 4
free verse, *see* poetry
Frye, Northrop, *Anatomy of Criticism*, 5, 6, 12, 13n
Fugard, Athol, *Sizwe Bansi is Dead*, 43

Garuba, H., 167, 172, 173; *Shadow and Dream*, 174
George, Raymond de Souza, *Bohboh Lef*, 94
Gikandi, Simon, 61
Gordimer, Nadine, 37, 54, 56
grammar, 106; *see also under* Okigbo
graphology, *see under* Okigbo
griot, 4, 5, 11, 39, 44
Gun War, 39
Gurnah, 53, 54, 56, 57
Gwala, 53

Hassan-Deen, Eric, 91
Head, 54, 56
Herbert, George, 109, 110
Heyns, 53, 54, 57
Heywood, Annemarie, 115
Hopkins, Gerard M., 110, 152
Hove, Chenjerai, and English, viii
How Long, 43
humour, 81, 157, 159, 170-1; *see also* comedy

Ibadan-Nsukka Poets, 166
ideology, see under Soyinka
Ifa, 69, 143, 144
Igbo, 32, 83, 173; culture, 15, 33, 34, 35;
    language, 27, 29, 31, 33, 36; market
    days in, 16; names in, 15-16, 21;
    novel, 36
Iheakweazu, Edith, 167
Ike, 155
imagery, 79, 163; see also under
    individual authors
Inyama, N.F., 24-30
Irele, Abiola, 145
irony, 51, 57-8, 77, 79, 154, 159, 171
Isevbaye, Dan, 61-2, 115, 152

Jacobson, 62
Jagua Nana, see Ekwensi
John, Janheinz, 138
Jemie, 156, 166
Jeyifo, 166
Johnson, Alex, 91

Kargbo, Kolosa John, 91, 94; For Sayka
    Uman, 92, 93, 94; characters in, 92-3;
    English, use of, 92-3; Krio, use of,
    92-3; registers, Krio & English; 92-3;
    Poyotong Wahala, 92; characters in,
    93
Katema, 56
Kenyatta, 56
Khaketla, N.M., 45, 46
Khumalo, 56
Kibera, 54; imagery, 54-5, 57
Komey, 53
Krio, 91-6; drama, 91-6; and English
    switching of, 93-6; registers, Krio &
    English, 92-3, 95
Kunene, Daniel, 37-49

La Guma, Alex, 48, 58; imagery, 54
Lamborn, 163
language, 62-5, 71-9; bilingualism,
    98-100, 107, 159; borrowed, use of,
    vii, viii, 37-8, 42-4, 45-6, 47, 48, 53,
    58, 92-4, 145, 165, 166; and charac-
    ter, 92-6; colloquialism, 53, 157;
    English, African inlfuences on, 166-7,
    168; French, use in African writing,
    viii, 98-107; as ideology, 66-9; idio-
    matic English, 82, 83, 85; indigenous,
    use of, vii, 159; lexis, 108, 111, 113;
    linguistic representation, 108; of
    Nigerian poetry, 155-63, 165-74;
    parables, 162; pidgins & creoles, viii,
    25ff., 53, 83, 91-6; Krio & English
    switching of, 93-6, 159, 160, 163; see
    also under individual authors; plu-
    ralism, 91-6, see also translation;
    poetic, 55, 58, 62, 156-7, 163; pro-
    verbs, 53, 161, 168, 169-70; punctua-

tion, see under Okigbo; registers,
    French & English, 100; registers, Krio
    & English, 92-3, 95; in Sierra Leone
    theatre, 92; in South Africa, 37-49;
    and speech, 66, 68, 108, 109, 123; and
    writing, 109, 122, 123
Layne, African Child, The, 4
Lee, Don, 157
Lefevere, 98
Leshoai, 56
Leslie, Omolara, (Ogundipe), 112, 166
lexis, see under Okigbo
Lindfors, Bernth, 155; 'Armah's
    Histories', 12n; on Ekwensi, 24
linguistics, see under language
Liswaniso, 56
Lukacs, 4, 12

Maama, 39
Maddy, Yulisa, 91
Maduakor, Obi, 71, 156, 166
Madubuike, 156, 166
Mafeni, Bernard, 159
magic, see occultism
Mallarmé, 131
Manganyi, Noel Chabani, 43
Marechera, 56, 57
Marxism, 5, 11, 75
Matshoba, Mtutuzeli, 51, 56
Matthews, 54
Mazrui, Ali, 165
Mbiti, 138
McFarlane, James, 71
McIntosh, Angus, 108-9
meaning, 98, 141, 160, 172, 173; see also
    under Okigbo and Soyinka
Melamu, 53, 58
Mensah, A.N., 1-12
metaphor, 79, 85, 89, 161; see also
    imagery
Mocoancoeng, Jac, 46
modernism, 57-8, 71
Mofokeng, S.M., 46
Mofolo, Thomas, 41
Moore, Gerald, 165
Motjuwadi, 53
Motsisi, Casey, 57
Mphahlele, Ezekiel, 43, 44, 53, 165
Mqhayi, S.E.K., 41
Mubitana, 54
Munonye, 155
Musi, 53, 57
music, see Okigbo
Mvungi, Martha, 56
myth, 34, 109, 117, 123, 142, 143; Ijaw,
    142, 143; Urhobo, 143; see also under
    individual authors
Mzamane, 53, 54

narrator, 3, 5ff., 38-9, 52, 81, 86, 87
Ndawo, Henry Masila, 41

Ndu, Pol, 155, 172; 'Homesick', 172; hypograms, 173; paradox, 172; paragrams, 173; 'Peace Songs', 172; pun, 172; 'Reflections', 172; satire, 176; style, 172

negritude, 159, 167

Ngara, Emmanuel, Stylistic Criticism and the African Novel, 3, 12n; on Two Thousand Seasons, 1

Niane, Sundiata, 5

Nicol, 52

Nichols, 109

Nida, Eugene A., 98

Nietzsche, 131, 135-6

Nigerian Civil War, 31, 32, 35, 36, 57, 71, 165, 166, 172

Nigerian poetry, language of, 155-63, 165, 174; post-war, nature of, 174

Nigerian writers, and African literature, 155

Nkosi, Lewis, 75, 165

Nwachukwu-Agbada, J.O.J., 165-174

Nwana, Pita, Omenuko, 36

Nwanodi, 152

Nwapa, 155

Nwoga, Donatus I., 152, 156, 165

Obumselu, Ben, 111

occultism, see Okigbo

Ofeimun, 167, 168, 173; 'Flood and Fire', 168; Handle for the Flutist, A, 173; Poet Lied, The, 173; 'Pray on Friday', 168; style, 168, 173-4

Ogot, use of imagery, 54

Ogundipe, see Leslie

Ojaide, 167, 'Map of Time', 168; 'Message of Lust', 168

Okai, Atukwei, 111

Okara, style, 2, 155

Okigbo, Christopher, 131-40, 155, 158, 162, 165-6, 167, 168, 192; comments on public events, 115-6; and culture, 115-7, 132; 'Dance of the Painted Maidens', 116, 124; 'Distances', 111, 112, 118-22, 124, 139; and drama, 131, 132-3, 140; dramatic lyric, 133-7; 'Elegy for Alto', 117; and folklore, 123; 'Four Canzones', 111, 112, 113, 118, 134, 152; 'Fragments out of the Deluge', 116, 137; grammar, 108, 111, 113, 114, 120, 127; graphology, 108-27, 135; 'Heavensgate', 123, 124, 131, 132; idoto, 129, 131, 138; imagery, 115, 116, 121, 123, 133, 137, 139; influences, 112, 122-3; Labyrinths, 115, 118, 122, 126, 131-40; 'Lament of the Drums', 139; 'Lament of the Flutes', 113; 'Lament of the Lavender Mist', 113-5, 117, 118, 124, 127; 'Lament of the Masks', 115; 'Lament of the Silent Sisters', 124, 137,

138; 'Limits', 115, 116, 118, 126; lineation, 110, 111, 118-9, 120; meaning, 108, 110, 115, 118; and music, 121, 131, 133-40; myth, 117; 'Newcomer', 133; obscurity, 108, 111, 118, 122; and Obumselu, 111; as ogbanje, 123-4, 125; and oral poetry, 122; orthography, 122; 'Passage, The', 123, 124; Path of Thunder, 111, 115, 116, 117, 118, 122, 125, 126, 127, 140, 165; punctuation, 111, 112-5, 117; rhetoric, 134, 135, 139, 140; and ritual, 115-6, 138, 140; 'Silences', 118, 123, 137, 138; 'Siren Limits', 136; 'Song of the Forest', 112, 126; syntax, 108, 110, 112, 113, 114, 117; style, viii, 108-27; versions of, 122, 127; and Virgil, 112; and Wordsworth, 123

Okike, 156

Olaogun, Modupe, 108-127

Omotoso, Kole, 7, 13n, 56

oral narrative, 3, 5ff., 38, 43, 44, 47, 48-9

orthography, 108, 122

Osofisan, Femi, 81-9, 166; abstraction, 88; Chattering and the Song, The, 88-9; disjunction, 81, 84, 85, 86, 87, 88, 89; form in, 81-9; Kolera Kolej, 81-2, 88, 89; comic invention, 81; humour, 81; narrative, voice, 81; plot, 81; satire, 81; technique, 82; Morountodun, 81, 82-5, 86; characters in, 82-5; flashback, 84; idiomatic English, 82, 83; pidgin, 83; play within play, 82-5, 86; plot, 83; satirized burlesque, 84; songs in, 82, 83, 84; style, 82; Once Upon Four Robbers, 81, 85-8, 89; characters in, 85-7; idiomatic English, 85; metaphor, 85, 89; satire, 86; songs, in, 86; varied writing, 86; weakness of, 85; and pidgin, viii; songs, use of, 82, 83, 84, 86, 87, 88; style, 81-4, 85, 86, 88-9; technical brilliance, 89

Osundare, 156, 160, 166, 167, 173; 'Akintunde Come Home', 161; 'Bride's Song, The', 167; Cradling Hands, 162; 'Dialogue of the Drums, A', 161; 'Eating with All the Fingers', 161; 'Farmer on Seeing Cocoa House, Ibadan, A', 162; 'Feigning a Rebel', 161; imagery, 161, 162; language, 160-3; and character, 161; 'Month of Falling Leaves', 162; Nib in the Pond, A, 173; 'Not in my Season of Songs', 161; and oral poetry, 160, 161-2, 167; parables, 162; 'Politician's Two Months, The', 162; 'Prisoner's Song, The', 162, 167; proverbs, use of, 161; 'Reunion, A', 162; Songs of the Marketplace, 173; 'Stars Sob, The', 162; style,

160-1, 167, 173; 'To a Passing Year', 162; 'Village Voices', 160
Ouologuem, *Bound to Violence*, 1
Ousmane, Sembene, *God's Bits of Wood*, 2
Oyeleye, A. Lekan, 15-23
Oyono-Mbia, Guillaume, 98-107; and Beckett, 98-9; bilingualism, 98-100, 105; comedy, 107; discrepancies in, 100-4; errors & mistranslations, 106; *His Excellency's Special Train*, *(Le Train spécial de son Excellence)*, 99, 102, characters in, 102-6; *Notre fille ne se mariera pas*, 99; stage directions, 103; style, 98-107; translation, 98-100; *Trois prétendants . . . un mari, (Three suitors . . . one husband)*, 99, 102, characters in, 100-3; *Until Further Notice*, *(Jusqu'a nouvel avis)*, 99, 103, 105, characters in, 102-6

Paton, Alan, 52, 55
People of the City, see Ekwensi
phonology, 108, 109, 110
pidgins, see language
play within play, 82-5, 86
plot, 37, 71, 81, 83, 86
Poe, Edgar Alan, 51
poetry, 35-6, 133, 134; audience of, 165-6; Basotho, 39-40; compared with short story, 55; imagery, 115, 156, 157, 162, see also individual poets; lineation, see Okigbo; lyric, 132; Nigerian, 155-63, 165-74, see also individual poets; oral 122, 156, 158, 160, 167, 168; rhyme, 110; Sesotho, 45, 46; in South Africa, 41, 42, 45; Xhosa, 40; Zulu, 40, 48; see also under Okigbo
post-modernism, 57-8
Pound, Ezra, 112, 122
pun, 159, 172

race, 37-8
Reeves, James, 160
rhetoric, 168; see Clark, Okigbo
Rimbaud, 131, 137
ritual, 138, 140
Rodney, Walter, 38
Rowe, Juliana, (née John), 91
Rukuni, 54

Sackey, Appiah, 'Two Thousand Seasons & Petals of Blood as modern epics', 12n
Said, Edward, 109
Saidi, 53, 56
satire, 33, 74, 77, 79, 81, 84, 86, 91, 146, 147, 157, 171, 172
Searle, 19
Sepamla, Sipho, 42, 43, 46
Serote, Mongane, 42, 43, 53; *No Baby*

Must Weep, 43
Sétouke, Bereng, 51, 56
short story, African, 51-8; characteristics, 52, 54; compared with oral poetry, 55, 58: figures of speech, 54; and folk tales, 56, 58; irony, 51, 57-8; narrative tempo, 52, 53; realism, 56-7; songs, use of, 54; southern, 53; style, 53; symbolism, 54-5
Sizwe Bansi is Dead, 43
songs, 54, 82, 83, 84, 86, 87, 88
sonnet, 110
South Africa, language & literature in, 37-49; liberation struggle, 37, 42, 43, 44, 46, 48; prose fiction, 45; students organisation, 141, 147; see also poetry
South African Native National Congress, (ANC), 40;
Soweto, 38
Soyinka, Wole, vii, viii, 9, 10, 61-9; 71-9, 110, 155, 162, 165-6; on Armah's style, 9; and civil war, 72; *Dance of the Forests, A*, 72, 74; and English, viii; and Fagunwa, vii; *Idanre and Other Poems*, 71; *Jero Plays*, 73; *Kongi's Harvest*, 71, 73; 'Luo Plains', 110; *Madmen and Specialists*, viii, 71-9; As, philosophy of, 72-8; biblical language, 79; cannibalism in, 74; characters in, 71-9; dialogue, 71; expressionistic technique, 71; flashback, 71; imagery, 79; irony in, 77, 79; language, 75; meaning, 76-7; metaphor, 79; modernism, 71; plot, 71; poetry, 75-6; satire, 74, 77, 79; theme, 71, 72; word play, 75-8; Marxist criticism of, 75; October poems, 71; *Road, The*, 61-9, 71, 75; characters in, 63-9; conflicts in, 67-8; as ideology, 66, 67; language, 62-5; language difficulty, 61; meaning, 62-3; 64-6, 69; Word, The, 62, 63, 65, 66, 68; *Season of Anomy*, 72, 73; characters in, 72-3; *Strong Breed, The*, 73
Spencer, Julius, 91-6
Staffrider, 44
stage directions, 103-4
Stead, C.K., 172
structuralism, 61
style, viii, 43, 158, 159; in African short story, 53-8; Africanized English, 2; narrative, 3, 37; see also individual authors & language
Sundiata, 5
symbolism, see imagery
syntax, 156, 163; see under Okigbo

Taban lo Liyong, 56; style, and modernism, 57-8
technique, see individual authors

text, 109, 110
theme, 71, 72
Things Fall Apart, see Achebe
Thomas, Dylan, 109, 110, 112
tragedy, 136
Transition, 111
translation, 48, 53, 56, 98–107, 107n, 112
Trek, Great, 39
Tutuola, Amos, vii; style, 2
Two Thousand Seasons, see Armah

Ubessie, Uchenna, 31–6; anecdotes, use of, 31, 32–3, 34; characterization, 31, 35; characters in, 32–5; humour, 31, 33; Igbo, use of, 31, 33; irony, 31, 33, 34, 36; *Isi Akwa Dara N'ala*, 32, 33; *Juo Obinna*, 31, 32–3, 34; language, 31, 33, 36; satire, 33; subjects, 36; technique, 32, 33, 35; *Ukpana Okpoko Buru*, 33; *Ukwa Ruo Oge Ya O Das*, 33; works, 31

Udechukwu, O., 167, 169, 170
Uka, Kalu, 155
Ukwu, Edward, 165

Valéry, Paul, 131
Virgil, 112

Wali, Obiajunwa, 165
Webb, Hugh, 'The African historical novel and the way forward', 12n
Weinrich, Uriel, 98
Williams, Emmett, 109
word play, 75–8
Wordsworth, W., 123
Wright, Randy I., *How For Do*, 94

Yankowitz, Susan, 61, 71
Yoruba, Ifa, 69, 143, 144; myth, vii; oral tradition, 161–2

Zeleza, Paul, 52, 57